# The MOMENTS
## That Define One's Life

Rise to Your Destiny with Purpose

LLOYD N. MOFFATT

The Moments That Define One's Life
Copyright © 2022 by Lloyd N. Moffatt

All rights reserved. No part of this publication may be reproduced, distributed, or transmitted in any form or by any means, including photocopying, recording, or other electronic or mechanical methods, without the prior written permission of the author, except in the case of brief quotations embodied in critical reviews and certain other non-commercial uses permitted by copyright law.

ISBN
978-1-957895-08-6 (Paperback)
978-1-957895-07-9 (eBook)

*Every stage in your life where you fall generates a stage of another rising moment that lines your destiny.*

**LLOYD N. MOFFATT**

# TABLE OF CONTENTS

Preface .................................................................................. vii

Acknowledgments ............................................................. ix

Chapter 1    My Moment, My Time, My Destiny ................. 1

Chapter 2    Nothing Is Impossible.................................... 26

Chapter 3    Divine Connections....................................... 58

Chapter 4    Life Is a Game of Inches ................................ 86

Chapter 5    I Can Only Be Me ....................................... 109

Chapter 6    Absolute Power .......................................... 124

Chapter 7    The Ultimate Reward ................................. 146

Chapter 8    Never Say Never ........................................ 168

Chapter 9    A Leap of Faith ..........................................197

Chapter 10   The Battle for Recovery .............................216

# PREFACE

Each moment plays a significant role that defines the next stage or the rest of a person's life. This book is written from the perspective that each moment in an individual's life was created in this world for a reason. That reason, for all purposes, creates an impact that will shape his or her life for many years to come. Look at the time line for every heroic human figure, and you will notice from the inception of his or her birth, he or she was destined to leave a mark in this world because a moment in time was carved out in history with his or her name on it.

These people have lived and maximized every moment in their lives to create an impact that this world has never seen. Whether it is to become president of a country or to utilize their talents to become a singer, doctor, actor, writer, or humanitarian, these people clearly have an intention to be who they are in the moment to change other people's lives for the better.

Incredibly, no matter how a moment emerges, everyone's time to capture that moment is not the same as the next person. I believe that I am blessed with not only a talent to write but also a purpose to display that talent by impacting the lives of others. Obviously, I knew it existed, but it was always internalized. The challenge that I had was I could never use it to my full potential, where it was backed by a purpose that will transform my life for the better.

For me, it had to take the experiences, obstacles, and situations in life that occurred in a series of challenging moments that somehow slowly released this hidden talent. I believe when much time had passed and enough of this talent was released, all I needed was one defining moment that would cause it to rise to a point where when it emerged, it would gain all the momentum necessary for it to never lose ground.

I believe that is what this book will do for you. It will ignite every passion to utilize the talents you have in your life and reinforce it with a purpose to achieve greater and defining results in your future. Truly, it is a moment that one can only call for it to happen. It can only happen if it is your time and moment for it to happen. I believe there is no greater time than now to allow that time and moment to emerge in your life.

# ACKNOWLEDGMENTS

I would like to, first of all, thank my Lord and Savior Jesus Christ for the life and talents that he has given me. I don't believe any of it will be used and utilized to the fullest capacity without him. Second, I would like to express my sincere appreciation and love for my wife, Chinwe Okeke-Moffatt. She has provided endless support and encouragement in allowing me to press on in making my purpose and goals in life become a reality. Moreover, I would also like to initiate a special thanks to my uncle Errol Shaw, who is also an author of several books of his own. I am inspired by his relentless work ethics and determination to push through and overcome all the obstacles in his path to bring all of his desired endeavors to the forefront.

Errol, I am amazed at what you can do. Writing five books in a year is an incredible goal and achievement for any writer. Furthermore, I would like to acknowledge my mother Dorothy Moffatt, who has used her endless efforts and time to market my first book. She stands behind all my endeavors and wants the very best for me. Finally, to friends and relatives that I did not mention, I appreciate the encouragement and all the support you have given me over the years to help me grow as a person. It is the support and faith that you have in me that allowed a special moment such as this to emerge and be captured in my life.

# MY MOMENT, MY TIME, MY DESTINY

## CHAPTER 1

More than twenty-five years ago, a special moment was carved in my life. It was not a moment that I could easily erase, but one that when the day and month arrived each year, it would remind me how that day significantly mattered and continued to matter when it emerged. I knew that it could not be taken away, nor could I wish that it could be another day because the day, moment, and time it happened was brought into existence for a reason—reasons, initially, for which I may never be able to have the answers to, but one that is certain to make me uniquely special from everyone else. Indeed, it would be that very day from which I was born that would give rise to my time in history and identity in this world. It will be from that moment on how I live my life with my friends, family, and people that will determine the impact the rest of my days spent in the world will have on the next generation. Through that time, they can celebrate, acknowledge, or honor me for every special moment that comes into my life; or they can ridicule, disown, or show their lack of appreciation for who I stand for as a person when each special moment in my time arises.

Thus, the moments that one can truly remember entail life, its achievements, failures, and every defining memory that is etched into the soul of one's life—even death. From the time line of one's very existence, it is evident from start to finish that one will either impact the world with one's gifts and talents, or one will exit it, having no impact to create a necessary moment or momentum to be remembered. Indeed, I knew how important each moment means to me and how much it also means to others. After all, everyone was born for a special moment in his or her life.

Once the moment is born, it gives birth to other moments. Once other moments come alive, each person's time and destiny start to take form in his or her life.

Surely, my life is no different from yours because each person, just like me, lives for a special moment to be remembered. When it comes to your life, how passionate are you to make each moment special? Are you ready to bring your moments to life, or are you ready to leave them in complete darkness? Apparently, no matter what you are feeling right now, the only way that part of your life will change is when you are passionate to create the necessary change it needs to awaken that burning desire that is locked inside of you.

Sure enough, when it comes to unlocking your desires, all the desires that become unlocked give rise to each moment that is resting in your heart. When it decides to wake and come out in full force, that is the time that your moment in life has emerged. Surely, your moment can never happen if your desires are at rest. Your desires must come alive so that each moment in your life can be ignited. Your desires must also remain alive so that every special moment in your life never dies. Each moment in your life will never create a spark if the desires of your heart are not strong enough to ignite it. If the desires of your heart are weak, someone else will come along with a stronger desire and make it his or her moment.

Thus, when it is your time, nothing can stop you from believing it belongs to anyone else but you. And when it is also your moment, it is almost impossible to think it should happen to anyone else but you. When it's your time, the moment will be just right. Every passion, effort, dream, and goal that you ever put forth in life will bring forth a moment that will reside solely in your presence.

The moment that you are in belongs to the time you are living in that moment. No person can be alive and not experience a significant moment in his or her lifetime. Knowing how strong a light can shine on a center stage, if you don't do anything in the spotlight, soon enough, that light will begin to lose its glare; and it will be projected toward someone else who desires to have his or her moment fulfilled. This is the same defining example of the heart. The decisions that you make to bring forth the desires of your heart gives rise to the actions that you need to take so that the desires of your heart are fulfilled. When the desires of your heart have been fulfilled, you have captured that moment of fulfillment. Now you can wait for other moments to come your way so that every special moment that has come alive can ignite other ones to emerge.

Obviously, no special moment can come alive without a decision to make that moment happen. Every moment that one has must be continuously maximized in order for one to experience the blessings one wants to see in one's future. No individual can accomplish winning a championship, attaining a degree, creating a successful business, and starting a family if he or she doesn't take the necessary steps to get there. In the same token, no business can flourish if the person decides not to build and market its product effectively. The moment will never happen if that individual decides to continue living in the same state of mind day in and day out. He or she must decide to build his or her skills, utilize the time to work hard, make the sacrifice, and believe that what he or she is doing is channeling a moment that will enable him or her to leave behind past failures and disappointments to move toward greater endeavors that can set forth a blazing trail of success.

**One Moment in Time**

Most people approach life as if they want the moment to belong to them. Unfortunately, every special moment just can't belong to everyone. In life, someone has to win, and someone also has to lose. Someone has to move forward, and another person has to be left behind. When it is your time, everything that has shaped your past will catch up with your present and break through whatever you have to accomplish to define and shape your future. All the efforts that you put forth now will create the momentum you need to experience greater moments in the future. If you want this to be your time, you have to own it by being ambitious and driven for the things you want to have in reality.

The definition of now is more important than the definition of never. Never creates moments that will never happen, while now creates a sense of urgency in the moment that now must happen. If you want now to happen, you must be willing to make sacrifices and plan your life in such a way that nothing will defeat or deter you from making the things that you desire the most to become real to you.

When you have the skills, hard work, sacrifice, belief, along with effective decision making, you will be a contender to any person who feels that the moment in life belongs to him or her. You will possess every right to claim it and make it belong to you. Each special moment in life can only belong to those who are hungry enough to believe there is no other time than now to get what they want. They, just like you, will do what it takes just to see their moment come alive because these people know that it is their time. When you realize it is your time, you own the moment that belongs in that time. No one else can claim it but you. Your moment will give birth to other moments that will define your true purpose in this world. When that moment is achieved—moments such as getting a dream job, graduating from school, winning a competition, getting married, bringing a child into the world, starting a successful business, or buying your first home—it will be the one that will shape and define the rest of your life for many years to come.

Decisions can be made momentarily or in the moment. But when some people are inspired to somehow make a decision because they feel that by committing to a particular moment will change their lives, their best results will come only when they don't waste any time in doing it. Once the moment comes and you are inspired, you must run with your inspiration and let the light that comes to you in the moment develop into one great ball of fire. You have to surrender to every special moment while you can because it will never be the same the next time around. It is never good to delay and wait when you are inspired and passionate about making a decision to get into school, start a family, change your career, or pursue a personal ambition.

When you delay and wait too long, there is a great possibility that the desires will burn away. The decision will become harder for you to make because you are shifted into an entirely different time period. Being in an entirely different period of time will shift you into a whole different moment with many different desires. When a moment emerges for you to make an important decision and indecision results, the moment, then, disappears without you being able to experience or live through what possibly could ultimately lead to something that changes your life and could generally line the course of your destiny.

For every person, there is that one moment that defines the time he or she is living in. The moment can be anything his or her heart desires. For some, it could be a career choice that will lead to greater financial rewards. For others, it could be getting married, having children, and buying a new home. For many people, it could also be a goal that they have been trying to reach for five to ten years where they could walk away from their jobs and start a business to become their own boss. Indeed, every person was born for a special moment in his or her life. Each moment can only be defined by the level of his or her desires of the heart to go after what matters the most to him or her in that moment.

**One Moment Defines Another Moment**

Each person has a defining moment that will make or break him or her in life. For every defining moment, there are questions that one must ask oneself to see if the decision that is placed before one is worth leaving behind or worth taking action. Either way, once a moment has given birth to your life, it should not be one that you should let slip away. It is one that you should take on with urgency. Why? It seems when one moment gives birth, another moment emerges, which adds value to our lives. For example, getting married is a defining moment in many people's lives.

The reason for this is because two people have to make a commitment to spend the rest of their lives with each other. Ultimately, it is a big decision where the commitment leads to each person being married to his or her spouse no matter what type of situation or opposing force arises between him and her. On a wedding day, a lot of things are memorable. Some of these memories include the moment the person says "I do" to his or her spouse, the vows that were made, and the pictures that were taken with everyone. We all know how special moments are such as being at a wedding and being part of our own wedding. However, just how many of us remember that moment that defined our lives? How many of us go on with life forgetting the vows we heard or even the vows that we made to our spouses? Apparently, what some people don't realize is that the wedding that you are invited to can later emerge and become your own wedding one day. The moments that come into other people's lives can one day become a moment that emerges in your own life. It is those same moments that emerge and define your life that will one day emerge and define your children's lives.

Personally, it seems all the weddings I have gone to and have been a part of have all consisted of a single decision that has changed the outcome of other decisions to follow. For example, for myself and for every person who has ever been married, the choices in life are no longer your own, as every decision that you make as far as financial concerns, having children, or finding a place to live has to be jointly made with your partner.

When the time comes and a critical decision needs to be made that will shape the future of your relationship with your family, you must approach that decision with the right attitude in the moment. If it involves change and a chance for progress, it should become something that should be discussed with your partner. There will oftentimes be something to stand in the way of your plans; however, do not let excuses create a hindrance in the moment to discuss future plans because when the moment calls for change, the time is just right for it to happen.

There is no reason to continue to give your mind excuses like "I will wait" or "I will consider talking about it later on" when, ultimately, the time to do anything and to get it done is right now. You must approach life as if there is no time to waste. It is important that you have a killer instinct when it comes to getting things done and setting an action plan for your future. What may work for you now may not necessarily work for you the next time around. Therefore, why not make it work now so that you can see the results you want to see immediately? Life is not set in such a way that it works the same all the time for everyone. For this reason, every significant moment that comes is regarded as unique and special in people's lives. None of them, when they emerge, has the same impact as the last one that rises; but one fact that makes them special is when they continue to emerge, each of them will always be unique and special from the rest.

I remembered hearing a story about a nineteen-year-old youngster named Karl who was raised by very strict parents. Throughout most of his life, Karl's parents were always overprotective of their son. As a result of their strict rules and regulations, Karl's parents would never want him to stay out late on the streets, and they would always make sure he was keeping up with his studies and projects in school. During the time he spent in high school, Karl was an average student in all his classes. He appeared to be an individual who was more into fitting in with his friends instead of achieving academic excellence.

He was always independent and never liked restraints from anyone.

Whenever he felt his freedom was limited or denied, he would find ways to rebel and turn things in the opposite direction. Eventually, he would find ways to improve his grades in school and graduate in his senior year. It would be six weeks after Karl graduated from high school when his friends invited him to a party that was a forty-plus-minute drive away from his home. He knew not to ask his father or mother about their approval for him to go to the party because he felt that they would deny his request. Instead, Karl figured out a plan where he would take one of his parents' cars to get to the party. For Karl, Sunday evening was just like any other Sunday at home. It was a normal day with the same usual routine where his family would attend church, visit relatives and return to spend the rest of the day at home. Despite the normal traditions his family held on Sundays, there was something inside Karl that wanted that day to be different. He would stay up late that night to carry out a plan where he would wait until both his parents had fallen asleep to put it into action.

Karl waited and stayed in his room until both his mother and father were asleep that night. An hour later, after they were sound asleep, he decided to take his father's car without his consent to go to a party his friends were having nearly thirty miles away from where he lived. Ultimately, it was a gamble that Karl was willing to take. He knew that if he came back before six in the morning, there was a good chance that his parents would never know that he was away.

Karl executed his plans that evening and drove to the party. It would be a few minutes past midnight that he would leave home and arrive at the party after one in the morning. When Karl arrived at the party, he noticed there were many people who were dancing, smoking, and drinking alcohol. He was quickly engaged in the event. In no time, he took a few drinks, socialized, and smoked a few cigarettes right through the duration of the gathering. Apparently, he stayed there until he felt it was time for him to leave. He would stay at the party for a few hours, where the constant drinking and activity quickly got him tired.

Not realizing how much time had elapsed, Karl's adrenaline took over when he saw the time was close to six in the morning. He clearly knew at that point, he lost track of time and had no choice but to get home quickly before his parents realized he was missing. Instantly, Karl's anxiety took over, and he rushed immediately to his car and drove as fast as he could to get back home. In the haste of him rushing to return home, he drove eighty miles per hour on the highway. Karl, still feeling the effects of the alcohol he consumed and lack of sleep, stayed as alert as he could en route to his destination. It seemed no matter how weary he became, he continued to push himself to stay alert to all of the traffic in his surroundings. Suddenly, after twenty-five minutes of driving on the highway, the car in front of him made a sudden stop. As a result of fatigue and not paying close attention to traffic, Karl immediately made a sharp turn away from the car that caused his vehicle to forcefully collide into two other cars on the highway.

Karl was immediately rushed to the hospital, where he was unconscious and in critical condition. The police and medical staff were able to get the information from his license, which was enough to contact Karl's parents. Karl's mother and father hurried to the hospital, where they found their son bleeding and unconscious, with multiple bruises on his body. The doctors informed Karl's father and mother that he had an injury to his spinal cord, which left the lower part of his body paralyzed. In disbelief, Karl's father and mother tried to come to terms with what they could have done to deserve this as parents. Karl, for the most part, was their first and only son.

None of them understood why their son took matters in his own hands without their consent. Karl's mother started to become overly concerned as she became more nervous that her son may not live to see another day. Her husband, who was also in distress regarding the tragedy, did as much as he could to console his wife. Karl's parents knew at that moment that it was not only a defining moment in their lives but also in the life of their son. They would visit the hospital day after day, believing and hoping that their son would progress from his injuries. After a few days of traveling back and forth to the hospital, the doctors informed Karl's parents that the results from their son's X-rays were positive. Shockingly, because of the news, there was a great possibility that their son may never be able to walk again because of the severe damage inflicted to his spinal cord caused by the accident.

Standing outside in the waiting room, unsure if his son would make a full recovery, Karl's father stared blankly at a wall and reminisced on all the times that he could have spent with his son but did not make any of those moments with him happen because of matters he consistently had to attend to pertaining to his job. In addition, Karl's mother also meditated in distress on not being there sometimes to speak and encourage her son regarding his future endeavors. It seemed when she was upset with him, she never had the heart at times to turn her emotions around. It appeared that at every angle Karl's parents examined their lives, it was one that was based on rules and regulations rather than moments and memories.

Both Karl's parents would leave the facility and would periodically visit their son in the hospital for the next two weeks. In the second week of their visit, Karl's parents would hear the news from the doctors that their son was now alert and conscious. Both of his parents went inside the room to see their son. As they opened the door, Karl opened his eyes and saw his parents for the first time since the accident. They offered compassion to him without any sign of criticism. While lying in bed, he turned his head slightly to his father and mother and shed tears through his emotions.

His mother and father, moved by the moment, held their son's hand and bitterly shared the pain with him. The visit would end, but the tragedy that day would forever remain in their hearts. Eventually, when the doctors felt Karl was making some form of progress responding to medications and to the treatment he was receiving, he was released from the hospital. After several months of being released from the care facility, Karl would take on a whole different mind-set toward life.

Karl realized that, as a result of the accident, he was paralyzed from the waist down and might never walk again. He would be at a stage where he would need to start his life all over by going to a rehabilitation center to be trained on how to move the muscles in his lower extremities. Though this was a tragic accident in Karl's life, it has been one that has brought him much closer to his parents and brought him a much greater sense of awareness to how one single mistake can lead to a tragic moment. Karl's accident and a near-death experience brought forth a defining moment in his life where he remembered all the things that mattered the most to him. All the decisions that he made in the past flashed before his very eyes, knowing that if he wants his life to change, the decisions that he made in the past can't be the same decisions that he will repeat in the future. Karl asked his parents for their forgiveness. They would ultimately forgive their son, but their lives would be permanently scarred from that tragic moment. It would be an experience that they would internalize for many years to come. It would be a moment in their lives that would define and alter the course of other moments in the way the rest of their lives would be spent.

## Live for the Moment and Ignite It with Every Chance You Get

Each moment is special to someone's life. Therefore, every chance you get should not only be a special moment for you, it should also be a special moment for someone else. After all, it is the heart that seeks out all the things that it desires. Every moment that is captured by it is a moment worth moving forward. Every moment that is not captured by it is a moment that has been left behind. Once you have found a way to seek and sustain the things that matter the most to the heart, it can effectively be used to maximize any moment that emerges such that its power can transcend to other moments.

The Bible stresses the fact that each person in this world has been created to have life and live it to the fullest. Similarly, each person is destined to have a moment, and each moment should also be maximized to its fullest capacity. No person wants to live a mediocre life and go to the grave not accomplishing what he or she desires. Everyone wants to achieve a level of success, even if it means paying the price to get it. In today's world, it has not been easy for many people to achieve success and live up to their defining moments because their hopes and chances have been dominated by one dominating factor, time. In order for anyone to get the most out of life, he or she must be able to find ways to manage his or her time and use it to his or her maximum advantage.

As long as he or she is able to successfully manage and get the most out of his or her time, it will be at that moment he or she will realize the greater possibilities that can arise from how it has been utilized. Personally, I used to believe each person has twenty-four hours in a day, until I realized it just isn't possible for anyone to be fully awake for twenty-four hours. Somehow, everyone has to go to sleep and wake up and start the day with only sixteen hours left. You, just like me, have had to learn the consequences that time has on a person's life once it fritters away.

Once you know the value of time, you will know how important it is that when it is gone, it is left behind forever. What you do now with the time you have will be important in impacting greater moments and memories you will have in the future. I believe if you ever want to maximize the time that has been given to you, it is vital to make every moment a memory and make every memory a moment. The words that you say to your spouse or children before you leave home may be the last words that are said. The moments that you turned down with your wife and children are the moments that just may never return. The time that you should see your mother and father who are getting older may be memories you just can't afford to let slip by. Cherish the times that you spend with your family because that is a gift that God has given to you to enjoy.

Create goals and actively work toward making them become a reality. Each time that you use to accomplish your goal, you are working toward making a special moment emerge in your life. In addition, use and utilize the time that you have to find ways to improve your life. You must also consistently find ways to improve your relationship with others and achieve everything that has challenged you in the past. Write down what you need to do to get better at serving the people around you and put your ideas into practice. There is a magic that happens when people serve other people in the world. Good things return to you. God's favor comes your way because your heart and mind are rewarded for your actions and your sacrifice.

The moment is like a dream that creates images in your mind of the memories you had and want to have. When you look at the pictures of your friends and family in the past, you can reflect and remember how memorable it was when you were there with them when that picture was taken. Now that picture becomes a memory to hold on to, and that memory becomes a moment that is cherished long after the years are gone. You can then take on new moments that will add to the previous ones that were once there. Thus, it is that moment in time that constantly ignites a memory that will last for a lifetime.

> *The moment is all you have. Once that moment disappears,*
> *you will not remember if it ever existed if you did not do all*
> *that you had to do to make it and other ones memorable.*

## Seize the Moment for What It's Worth

When it comes to decision making and getting the most out of life, every moment should be seized, and each opportunity that arises in that moment should not be wasted.

Some people argue they let so many special moments pass by because they could not find the time to be a part of them. Either they were too busy working or attending to their own personal matters, or they simply believed it was not going to hold too much significance. In my opinion, if these people had another chance to recapture the special moments that they missed in their lives, they would make their lives into a photo album. Every step of the way, they would take a picture and write about their son/daughter taking their first steps in the world, experiencing the birth of their first child or grandchild in the hospital, and sharing a special reunion with family. Knowing this, these people would also take pictures of the times they spent going out on dates with their spouse and the other people that made those dates memorable for them. To make it even more memorable, they would keep every letter and song that was written that made them fall in love. After all, every moment that brought people together is a moment that will help them remember when they were there for one another.

Many people have made a mistake by not allowing those moments to enter their lives. If the moments were honored, it would spark a tale of successful memories for greater ones to occur in the future. Though some moments are regarded as special in the lives of people, there are ones that I recalled in my life that are not worth holding on to. I remembered being eleven years old, where living with my mother and father presented a lot of challenges. Growing up with my parents was one of the toughest experiences I have had to go through in my childhood. I had gone through challenging situations with both of my parents.

Apparently, when my brother was born, he did not share the same challenges that I went through. I remembered at a young age I wanted the times I would spend with my family to be memorable but I could never cherish the times I would spend with them because they had such a deep disliking for each other that created an intense conflict and disharmony in the home.

I looked back and noticed that hardly any of the moments my parents had for one another were special; therefore, as a result, there were no moments that were special for me. I don't remember going out to eat dinner in a restaurant with my family. I don't recall my mother and father taking me out to church together. There were hardly any pictures as a family or motivating words in the presence of my parents. No one prayed, and whenever words were spoken, it would often always lead to an argument. It seemed that when I got older, I wanted to erase the memories I had with my family by creating a new family that I can build new memories and moments with.

I now know the value of what moments can bring to a child's life. All that is left from what he or she experienced in the past is a memory from what he or she had gone through. Whether good or bad, the memories are transferred right into a child's future. Knowing that the life that he or she spends with his or her family is short, each day should be lived as if it were the last.

> *The loss of each moment makes us remember what we missed, but maximizing the time we have now makes us relive greater moments in the future.*

## A Turn for the Better

Mistakes were never meant to be made twice. In order for anyone to ignite a special moment, he or she should not repeat the same mistakes that has failed him or her in the past. Anyone who repeats the same mistakes will almost always get the same result from the first time. If one fails a task the first time and makes an attempt the second time around, one must use an entirely different strategy so that it will lead to different results.

No person can fail something and apply the same strategies the next time around and expect his or her efforts to reap success. In order for that person to be successful, he or she must create a change in his or her plans that will lead to an entirely different outcome. People don't realize their actions are results of their consequence, and their consequences are results of their actions. When life goes wrong, they desperately search themselves for the answers to make it go right. They try to gather countless questions and get all the facts together. The questions are ongoing, but facts are what they need so that their answers can become decisive. The facts somehow come before you get the answers. The answers, however, are more important than the facts because once you find the answers, it will determine if the facts are meaningful or meaningless.

The questions you ask yourself to find your purpose are endless. They are endless as you try to find an answer to their meaning. Once you find an answer and get the answers, then you have marked your purpose. Once you've marked your purpose, you will come across the most important and rewarding tool in making a critical decision that will forever change your life.

For the most part, I was a young man who looked back at all the mistakes I made growing up. I knew I needed a change to make me forget about all the times I failed to start college right after high school and how I made a poor decision to settle for a job that was not taking my life anywhere. I struggled to find a breakthrough moment from living in a dysfunctional home with a mother and father who had no care for each other. I sat on the bus one day on my way home, and I reflected on my past. My heart was looking for a change in my life, and my mind was dissatisfied that it was taking too long for me to experience it. I soaked in all of my experiences, both positive and negative. It seemed I looked gloomed and frustrated by all the experiences I have gone through.

In that moment, I paid little attention to anyone around me. As I sat on the bus, it came to a bus stop and yielded at the bus sign to let people on board. Suddenly, I was taken out of that moment and acknowledged what was happening in real time. As some passengers got on the bus, a few of them got on to find any seat that was not taken. One of the passengers, a young man who walked down the aisle, sat down next to me and started a conversation. I would turn my head toward the window, and he looked in my direction and asked me, "What do you think about the weather we are having today?" I looked at him and responded, "The weather seems to be good." "Yeah, I think so too. You know, it doesn't get too hot in the summer like it did many years ago. I believe it may stay around seventy degrees for the rest of the month," he said. I nodded my head with no response toward his statement. "By any chance, are you in school?" he asked. "Yes, I am in school," I said.

"What school is it? Do you go to a school in Brooklyn?" he asked. "Yes, I go to Medgar Evers College," I said. "I see. Do you like it there?" "Yeah, it is not a bad school." "How do you pay for school? Do you work part-time and go to school?" "Exactly, I work part-time in a bank and go to school full-time." "That is great that you work and go to school. It shows that you are a responsible person. There are not many people like you who would want to take on that responsibility. What about church? Do you go to church?"

"No, I don't have a church that I go to. I have not really been to a church in years." "Really, the reason I ask is because I would like to invite you out to the church I go to on Sundays." "What church is this?" "I go to the New York Church of Christ." "Yeah, where is that located?" "Well, our services are held in the auditorium of a school building." "OK. What kind of church holds services in a school building?" "All right, let me explain that as far as services are concerned, God's church can be held any place, and his message can be spoken anywhere. It doesn't matter where the messages are spoken, but what is important is that the teachings are consistent with the standards of the Bible. Do you believe in God?" "Yes, I believe in God, but I just have not been to church in a long time." "Don't worry about it. You will come out, and it will be a lot of fun. What part of Brooklyn do you live in?" "I live in the Crown Heights section of Brooklyn." "OK. So you are not far from the church then. It is just a few train stops from you on the number 2 or 3 train to Atlantic Avenue," he said. The young man spoke to me for what seemed to be nearly ten minutes. It seemed that I was taken out of one moment of remembering my past and brought into another moment where my future was almost destined to change. He introduced himself to me as Ronnie and told me that he is a young deacon in the church. Time seemed to be standing still in the moment until it was time for him to depart from the bus. "Listen, my stop is coming up soon. Let's exchange phone numbers, and I will give you a call the day before the service to see if you are still coming."

As he gave me an invite card to his church to write my number down, I gathered my thoughts and began to see that I must have met this young man for a reason. I returned the card to him with my name and number on the back of the invite. I was skeptical after I got off the bus if I would ever see him again. Little did I know two days later on a Saturday morning, he called to tell me where he would meet with me to go to church the next day. I was surprised that he called me. We both arranged where we would meet before church.

It made me all reflect on that day and moment I met this person on the bus. I was a young man truly searching for my destiny, and I wondered at that moment if God made our paths connect for a reason. It seemed I met him at a time I least expected to meet anyone, especially with what I was going through at the time with my family. I wondered from that day on how people can come in your life at a specific moment you least expect and change your direction in life forever.

After several months of coming out to the church, studying the Bible, building friends, and getting the help I needed with the problems I experienced with my family, I felt a sense of relief that I never felt before. I was around many people who genuinely cared for one another. I noticed that they had a genuine love for the God they served, and they cared a lot about other people. They were different from anyone I have been around, and it was clear that after many of them were baptized, their lives had taken a one-hundred-eighty degree turn where it changed for the better.

Many of them were happy to be part of something that defined a greater meaning and purpose for their lives. As a result of being around the body of members in the church and my own personal convictions to take my life in a new direction, I became a Christian who accepted the Lord Jesus Christ as my savior. This was the beginning and a defining moment in my life. It was a turning point for future decisions and moments that will surely change every decision I would make going forward.

> *Young children need guidance; but young adults,*
> *however, need good advice.*

## One Moment at a Time

For someone to make the decision to become a doctor because his or her spouse is already one, that would mean that this individual plays a critical part in his or her decision making and his or her faith to get into a field that he or she may not know if it was tailored for him or her. You may see how blessed your spouse is with the money and success that he or she has with his or her job that you may have a tendency to feel you can also attain the same level of success if you were to get in the same field and accomplish what he or she has already achieved. However, you must realize that in life, what was designed for you was not necessarily designed for the next person. Thus, the challenge that life brings and calls you to do is to find an identity that will make you excel in what endeavors you decide to take on.

That is why I believe it is so critical to find your niche because once you have found it, you have found yourself and what matters the most to you. After all, the decisions you make in your life create a moment that no one else could create for you. I remembered how I would have many dreams and desires in life, and how I would get tired of people telling me my dreams will never happen, no matter how big they were. Other people will look down on me and never believe I have what it takes to achieve the goals and visions I embarked on. To them, such a moment in my life will never happen for me because it never happened for them.

I regarded their negative opinions as nonsense because sometimes people who place their doubts in you make you feel you are just an ordinary person that can never become extraordinary in this world. I have to keep in mind I am an individual who is capable of doing and becoming anything and everything extraordinary once I put my heart and mind into anything I intend to take on. Words are powerful. They are even more powerful when it is spoken through you and from you for who you want to become and not anyone else who is telling you what he or she wants you to become. Critical words can travel so far until they fall to the ground, but your words and your mind are one element. This element is power! The power that comes through you, by you, and from you can change anyone's words on the outside because this is a power that lies within you.

You don't need to hear it from others who don't believe in you because it is already in you. It is something that you have to exhibit without internalizing. You must fight to release this power over and over again. Sometimes we need time for ourselves to discover ourselves. But once you have found what you are looking for, there is no need to search for what was missing anymore. One man's passion can't be another man's destiny. Each moment is a stage you must pass through to make another moment happen. The hardest feeling in life for someone to overcome is failure. You have heard when one door closes, another one will open. Maybe it wasn't meant to be. God has something better planned. Obviously, quite often, this life can be a game. You can play to win or play to lose, but the choices and the cards are all in your hands. Everyone wants the best possible life he or she can live. To live a great life is the key to success for many people.

A person with high self-esteem will always find a way to overcome failure. When it comes to making a moment happen, nothing matters more than capturing it to create a momentum for other great moments to follow. Even if it means driving a thousand miles to get it, he or she will get into a car and drive or even walk on foot all the way to reach his or her destination.

Thus, decisions are ideas that not only shape our lives; they are the choices by how our lives will be shaped. Your destiny is marked by God! Whatever it is that you are supposed to become, you will eventually become it. In time, it will all be revealed to you through him. Even if it means making the wrong decisions to make the right ones, your future in this universe is designed by trial and error. The good part about your decisions and finding what you were meant to do and who you were meant to be in this world is that you know you have found something good when it not only brings you happiness but it also brings you joy. Happiness is a state of mind. Without it, there is misery. Joy is a state of condition. Without it, there is no life. Happiness is temporary, while joy tends to last longer than happiness. Happiness comes in the moment, while joy keeps crossing over into many changing moments. Either way, you choose how you want each day to start and how you want it to end. Whatever moment in time you are in will give rise to the condition you want your mind at that moment to embark on.

## Define Who You Really Are

I was often told my time has not come yet when I failed at something. I tried, and when I gave it my best shot, my best was not good enough. Time and time again, I desire to succeed and chase after success; but every time I chased after success, it eluded me over and over again. Many times, the door seemed to close; but just as one door closed, I had to believe another one would open. I had to believe despite my difficulties, as long as my heart continued to search for the answers, I would continue to make the right decisions, and as long as my mind continued to search for a vision, God would give me the eyes to see what I failed to see on my own.

Obviously, at a young age, I never knew what I wanted to become in my life. I had to search my heart and mind to find out what mattered the most to me. When I would search and dig deep enough to find out the answers, I realized that in order for me to find fulfillment, I had to make some critical yet necessary decisions that would define my true purpose and identity in this world. There would seem to be something that I just could not find or come to terms with. It became important for me to find what that missing void was that followed me everywhere I would go. Surely, one necessary asset that I may have had was the gifts of being a scholar in college by graduating with honors. I enjoyed doing well in school, where I was one of the top students in my class. It was rewarding to work hard and get good grades. It is even more fulfilling to invest in something through working hard and get a return from what was invested. However, ask any A student, and he or she will tell you that it is not easy to get good grades.

I went to Baruch College and graduated from a challenging university. After graduating from there, I was able to go on many interviews after I received my bachelor's degree. When many of the top firms saw Baruch College listed on my resume, I was immediately called in for an interview. I was confident that I made the right decision to get an associate degree from Medgar Evers College and transfer to a college such as Baruch that was well known for business. Many companies were calling me for interviews before and after I graduated from Baruch during my senior year. I felt optimistic with what some of the companies had to offer. In my mind, I knew that getting my degree was important to me, but a piece of paper did not mean anything if I could not display my capabilities and abilities to my employer.

Graduation came, and a few weeks after the event, I was going on job interviews. I prepared for every interview and I researched each company I had an interview with. During the times I was called in for an interview, I would ask challenging questions that only someone who researched the company would ask. There was one interview I remembered, when it ended, I was confident I made a lasting impression on the person who conducted the five to ten minute session.

Apparently, a few days after the interview, the moment arrived where I would get a letter from the interviewer who would let me know if I was qualified to work for the company. Eventually, disappointment would set in as I would read a letter of rejection that stated why I was not good enough to get the job. At that point, I was not able to tell what was wrong and what kept going wrong. I had a bachelor's degree in Computer

Information Systems. I went to a top business school. I asked myself consistently, *What is wrong? Why is it taking so many weeks and months to land a job?* I started to get frustrated and made the decision that I knew I could not let my talents go to waste. Ultimately, I evaluated my talents, and I believed in myself and my abilities. I never had to employ too much effort because I believed that anything I was capable of doing with the least amount of effort would maximize the talents I had. Truly, you don't have to work too hard at something that comes naturally to you if it is in you. You can't be what another person already has become unless you truly also want to become it. All you can be is yourself and become what God has intended for you to become.

Because of this, how do you know then if something is meant for you when you strive and work your very best to attain it? And most importantly, how do you also know that you will succeed at what you start whereby you can maintain it to generate other avenues of success? Surely, the bottom line is when something is meant for you, not only will you be successful at it, the level of your success will be so extraordinary that you will keep building on it until it generates the momentum you need to bring additional avenues of success and satisfaction to your life. It projects itself as something that gives you so much satisfaction and pleasure that when you see it, you are not fazed by the challenges it brings. It can be something that can absorb so much of your time, but you go at it with so much belief, confidence, and enthusiasm that no matter what gets in the way, nothing will stop you from meeting and exceeding your end goal. With enough belief backed by action and prayer, there is no telling where you will take yourself and where God will take you when he desires to create a special moment for you. Ultimately, the sky is the limit, but to God, he has no limit with whom he wants to bless when the time has come for him or her to be blessed.

*People make timeless choices without making their choices in the right time.*

## Rebuild What Has Been Destroyed

There is not one person that I know who has not had a bad experience in his or her life where he or she had to start over and rebuild in some way. There is not one individual in this world that is not building on something because even if he or she is not building on anything then that is exactly what he or she is building on—nothing. There are positive and negative circumstances that shape the human behavior, and the more you have of each, the more others around you can see how much of what has been built is inside of you. People can build positive attitudes, or they can build on negative ones. It is not just everything that is good that people would make an effort to build on because people can actually build on negative thoughts and attitudes that they have internalized through their experiences with others.

It is incredible how your words, actions, and thoughts can be used as tools for construction or weapons for destruction. In just a matter of seconds, what can take you months and years to build can be destroyed in less than a minute. It is without a doubt that your destiny can be shaped by what you continue to build on. A house can never survive on straws and sand alone because when the winds come, it will take the house with it. However, when you build a house, it must be laid down with a strong foundation that is built to last and built to survive the greatest storms. The house that is well cemented and layered with strong support will take an army to tear it down. Too many times, people use love, joy, and encouragement to build a relationship then it is torn down by arguments, anger, and hatred toward the next person. Too many times you have also seen people go to school, and before they can get their degree, they exit the school because they lose the passion and desire that they once had when they entered.

It is amazing how some dreams come alive, and when they come alive, they also die if you don't pursue them. There are many other situations where people are content being in the same position at their jobs but don't build on their character, their resume, and their skills to advance into other positions. They remain in the same position with no hope but to live their lives each day just building hours and input on a job without any set goals or dreams in mind. Whatever it is in life, you must realize that if you don't build on the time you have, then time will build on you with what you have or have not given to it.

It is exampled by the fact that when you were born, you were only a small child, but when the cells kept multiplying, your bones got bigger until the point where you became an adult. Time has built you in some way, so now how do you build on the time that was given to you? The only way you will be able to do that is to earnestly look at the situation you are in and ask yourself how far do I want to go in my relationship, how much farther can I advance with this job, and where would I like to be in the next five to ten years? It has not been easy for dreams to come true, but it has been very easy for dreams to fall apart in people's lives when the time given to them is not maximized to its fullest capacity.

Most people need time to recover from their losses, and they need time to recuperate and regenerate themselves to something new and different. Nothing can be more painful than a person who has expended so much time trying to reach his or her goals only to come up short in doing so. Once he or she is given enough time to reflect and remember on what has happened, it can hopefully give them the surge that they need to pull themselves forward. Sometimes you can work extremely hard, but it is not your fault that the result turns out the way you least expect it to turn out. Though this has happened, it doesn't mean that you need to be defeated by the outcome. It just means that you need to take it for what it brings and be challenged by to change the outcome. Once you see the results as a challenge, you must do everything in your power to accept, overcome, and change it for the better.

Personally, it will be difficult for me to get anywhere in life if I don't find a way to conquer my emotions and face my challenges when they emerge. If my emotions and challenges get the best of me, I will be more inclined into making emotional decisions that can't answer the challenges I face once they are mounted. I have to build and believe that I can rebuild when a new moment to start over has emerged in my life. I realize once I make a decision that is quickly backed by desire and action, I can start building on my goals and dreams that will help me optimize a greater meaning and a regenerated growth in life.

Face your challenges and overcome your deficits in life.

*Overcome your challenges, or your*
*challenges will overcome you.*

## Drive Your Desires to Completion

I believe what people fail to realize is that whatever you do in this life requires you to start something and eventually finish what you started. However, that is not generally the case for some people because they develop a tendency to start something but don't have enough fire power to finish what they started. Success then to them is too time-consuming and strenuous for them to take on. Hence, one fact that is certain through it all is that success doesn't come without you paying a price for it. If success was easy, everybody will do something and be successful at it.

Unfortunately, success doesn't come without a challenge, and challenges surely do not come without you experiencing hardship from them. Whatever it is that you want to do you and will do, you will face obstacles along the way. Whatever it is that you need to build on and whatever you are planning to accomplish, you must expect something to go wrong en route toward it. However, when things go wrong, does that mean that you stop building on what you are building on? Does that mean you quit? No! Quitting is not the answer. What you must realize is that a house is not built in one day. A car is not built in forty-eight hours. An airplane can't fly without wings, and neither can it land without wheels. You can be anything you want to be, but whatever you become, you will have to make a sacrifice for it by taking the time out of your life to become it. Everything you desire to do will be a process. Once the process is complete, then the progress can begin. It's not over when you lose, but it is only over when you decide to quit.

You will never ever be a winner if you have always been a quitter. You can be all that you want to be, but you will never reach where you want to reach when you decide that you no longer have the fight and the desire to continue and finish what you started. Some people enjoy challenges because they know once they overcome them it makes them better individuals. After all, what is an accomplishment if it is just handed to you? Dreams and goals are better when you can work hard for them and overcome the obstacles you will have to face in making them become a reality. In life, you will appreciate it more when it is something that you have earned rather than something that is handed down to you from someone else. I believe people must first lose before they know how it is to win. Even for the ones who have already won, they must experience some kind of failure in their lifetime that will allow them to see that they can't take what they have achieved for granted.

*Every conscious decision that you have made to rebuild is a building block toward the next process to complete.*

## Setting the Mark

If you want it to be your moment, you will have to work hard to make it happen so that when it comes, you seize it and don't take it for granted. Obviously, the ride you take toward it is more important than its arrival. What you do now determines the impact that it will have on your future. What you will gain in your future determines the impact that it will have on the next generation.

Knowing this, no matter what time I am in, each time a special moment was brought forth, it calls for me to elevate my capabilities and abilities to answer them.

Knowing how I could rise toward my goals and fall in life to every setback, all that I needed to prove was as many times I would fall is as many times I would stand against the falls I have taken to rise again in this world. In life, when two people are fighting to claim a prize, there can only be one champion when that prize is won. One has to walk away a winner, while the other has to walk away a loser. On the other hand, when you have won consistently and fail to lose, you set an example for others who aspire to walk your path.

Even as much as other people create a moment for themselves to start a new record, there are people in this world who will create a moment for themselves to break the records that others have started. Because of this, these people know how special it is to leave a mark in this world that other people can remember. Indeed, it shows the importance of the measures people will go to in terms of having an identity and fulfilling their purpose in the world. Personally, my impact in the world is all incumbent on breaking through one significant moment that can create the momentum I need to achieve other special moments. Truly, the journey for me is just beginning. I am not designed by anyone else's plan, but by God's plan. The time to achieve all the things I ever desired to achieve is now. I can't let challenges and opposition break the dreams I aspire to attain. This is why

I believe when anyone can consistently achieve the impossible awards in that moment by overcoming adversity, challenges, and opposition in every changing moment, he or she can leave behind a memory and mark in this world that will never fade and one that is not easily forgotten.

# NOTHING IS IMPOSSIBLE

## CHAPTER 2

**Create the Change You Believe Will Bring Endless Possibilities**

Many decades ago, an enormous concrete barrier separated East Berlin from West Berlin. The barrier started out as an object that imposed its will on many people. It was built with an intimidating height and an unbreakable force. It would be a great wall that would stand for more than two decades. Its dimensions consisted of two million tons of concrete standing twelve feet tall, with a total length of 155 kilometers, which would be nearly equivalent to ninety-six miles that stretched through 192 streets. It was an enormous object that projected its force on many German citizens. Throughout its creation, it would leave many broken dreams and unfulfilled purposes. Apparently, lessons of pain and hardship would be learned from trying to overcome this immense object. Though many viewed the wall as a continuous obstacle in their path, there is an incredible history behind the causes that brought about its emergence. In 1949, an emergence of a Berlin wall would be forged into history when the great country of Germany would be split into two territories, an east territory and a west territory. All of the changes would be partly because of the Second World War, where the capital of Germany, Berlin, had fallen between its east and west borders. Life, indeed, in both territories was found to be in disharmony. It seemed people who lived on the west side experienced a democratic government, whereby those who lived on the east side dealt with a communist-type government. Overall, the split between the two cities created an ongoing conflict. As a result, 1.6 million people started to flee to the west side because many of them did not want to be part of a government that was communist and ruled by the Soviets. Many of them felt being under the rule of a communist-type system limited their freedom and rights as individuals. Thus, as a result of the way the government was run and the emotions individuals felt toward the system, many people rebelled against it by finding ways to flee to West Berlin so that they can escape the rules of what they believed was a corrupt system of control.

Obviously, something had to be done to control the influx of all the people going to West Berlin, so the East Germans built a wall in 1961 to prevent many of their citizens from traveling there. Apparently, constructing a wall would be the only way to prevent a massive transition by millions of East German citizens from heading to West Berlin. Interestingly, most people had their own point of view of why the wall was built. Some believed the construction of this wall could have been a symbol of the Cold War. Others claimed the wall was established as a means of parting off interference from the east and west sides of Berlin. After all, life for many in West Germany was far better than the people who lived in East Germany.

The reason for this was West Germany had a government that was for the people, whereas East Germany had a government where the State would plan and control the economy. Indeed, in the very moment the Berlin wall was constructed, its inception would all be incumbent on the events that took place after a historical world war. After the war, Berlin was said to be occupied by many Allied forces believed to be divided into four sectors: the United States, British, Soviet, and French. The west was said to be occupied by the United States, United Kingdom, and France, while the east was occupied primarily by the Soviet Union.

During this period, East Germany suffered many setbacks. They lost skilled workers, where the economy was vastly affected. People struggled to find work, and those who were employed had to settle for low-paying wages. Besides the economy, there were also political situations that began to arise, spreading toward other countries. As a consequence of declining conditions, this propelled many to take action against this wall. As a result of experiencing a downturn of economic and political conditions, this wall would put a curtain of impossibilities that would chiefly divide the two cities. Ultimately, it would lead to families being torn apart by this project—an act by the government that seemed incomprehensible to many. Citizens were blocked by a wall that divided an entire city into two. Many people grew angry and rebelled against this dominating construction. Their relentless attempts to overcome this obstacle led many of them to dig through tunnels, use hot-air balloons, swim in canal openings, and climb undefiant barriers to get over this incredible force.

As a result, many people failed and died at the expense of their efforts. Soldiers who stood guard would be instructed to shoot down anyone who made an attempt to climb over this wall. Tens and hundreds of people would die as many of them who attempted to climb the wall were imprisoned or shot down without warning. For over twenty-seven years, many people fought to bring this wall to an end. To no avail, this wall remained standing. Through its towering force, it continued to overpower and restrict the lives of many people who desired their freedom. Even though East Germany justified the wall as a work of peace, it kept many of them stuck in places where they lived and worked. It was a wall that hindered many people from seeing their families and loved ones who lived on the opposite side of Germany. In the minds of many people, their hope, justice, and freedom were destroyed. This built an uncontrollable rage within them that led to protests and riots across Germany. Again, citizens were relentless to find a way to get over this object. Sadly, so many grew angry; but as much as they all tried to combat its forces, they would still fail. There were stories of people who attempted daredevil acts of escape where one East German soldier stole an army tank and drove it straight in the wall. Though it did not fully penetrate the wall, army guards shot at the soldier relentlessly, where he recovered from multiple gunshot wounds at a nearby hospital. Another heroic tactic was a makeshift pulley that would allow someone to swing over the wall. This invention, although proven useful to some point, still disallowed anyone from achieving his or her purpose.

It seemed many people did not have an answer for their hopes. As much as every person made an effort to attempt to get over this object, the wall grew taller with even deadlier barbed, electrical fences and death strips that would injure or claim the lives of people who tried to tower over its intimidating height. Apparently, the wall that was built for more than two decades will never create the possibility of change that many people would like to experience. Unseeingly, East Germany built a communist system, but many people suffered under the hands from which it was built.

Time would advance to three decades since the construction of the wall, and the nature of this wall would continue to block the possibilities of citizen's hopes and freedom across Germany. In spite of a lot of people's efforts and heroic actions that placed their lives on the line to get to the other side, the wall still stood as a sound force that continued to block any hope or dream of a breakthrough. Still, many people kept fighting to develop new ways to get over this object. Despite their efforts, many of them died as a result of trying.

In 1989, a dawn of a new era would rise when Günter Schabowski, a member of the East German Politburo, announced a new law where he stated that a decision will be made soon to institute regulations that will permit any resident of East Germany to depart the country through any border crossing the German Democratic Republic. After many years of people being oppressed by this massive construction, it was time for a change. Members of the Politburo held a hearing to inquire how soon the regulation would be implemented. It would be at that time Günter would state a regulation must be immediately active, and the time for change is now.

Unfortunately, it was a law that was easier said than done. Many East Germans who heard the news was ecstatic that this impossible wall that stood before them for more than twenty-five years was finally coming to an end.

They fled to the border to see how possible it was to go through this wall without being blocked or shot down by security guards. Some knew if they dared to even make an attempt to cross over, they will risk a chance of being killed, imprisoned, or attacked by guard dogs. Apparently, when many people made an attempt to cross over, as according to the new law, there was an obvious error with the law that Schabowksi instituted. This law required that Germans first get a visa before they can pass through the border. Once they receive their visas, they would be stamped and would not be allowed to come back into East Germany. As a consequence, many people still felt betrayed. The implementation of the law was not enough. Even though people can now leave, there will be no way for them to return.

At this point, the law was not good enough. To many, it would be one that would be rendered useless. Tensions again grew worse. Tens and thousands of people revolted, and after decades of struggle, a strong action would be implemented as the gates to the border were finally opened. Large crowds gathered, and people crossed over the border to get to the other side. Even the law that restricted them from crossing over and returning became extinct. It was a moment in time for a change. The wall that stood for more than twenty-five years was suddenly in a state of dismantlement. People, who were tired of seeing this massive object that stood before them, started to take tools to knock down a wall that has limited their freedom for decades. Brick by brick and stone by stone, the wall that stood for nearly three decades had been completely dismantled, broken, and torn down never to rise again. Indeed, it was a moment a new history in the world was born, a history that would open the door to possibilities in the world that many never thought was possible. No longer can a wall limit the lives and freedom of many people. No longer can the element of control, imprisonment, and execution rule over the lives of citizens. The eradication of the Berlin wall marked a dawn of a new era, an era where people will exercise all their power into bringing what they desired for so long to become a reality. Once a new moment in history was born, it gave rise to future possibilities for people across the world (2011, February 24 Retrieved 17:17 *Berlin Wall, In Wikipedia, The Free Encyclopedia*).

During my time studying history, the story of the Berlin wall was one that sparked my beliefs into allowing me to feel that any obstacle is possible to overcome, no matter how long it takes to break it down. One fact that is apparent from the impact that this wall has had on people's lives is how evident a similar wall has been set in so many of our lives that have stayed there for years, never to be broken down. It seems that this wall has prevented many people from achieving the outcomes we so desperately desire. Not knowing if all of our efforts will ever amount to anything, some of us continue to work effortlessly toward our dream, not knowing that it could be blocked by a wall that is limiting us from achieving success.

So many times many of us have climbed over this wall that has limited us in life, only to be shot down by forces that make us aware that a significant moment in our lives will never arrive. Sometimes the barriers are all around us. It places a wall that makes us lose hope no matter how many times we try. The one vital aspect of climbing this wall is that climbing a wall is not enough to excel. One must be able to knock down this wall so that it can no longer be a hindrance in one's life. Imagine trying to pass a test that you have taken several times, you can feel defeated not knowing if you will one day pass it to get the job you want.

For others, some try year after year to lose weight, but their efforts continue to come up short, making them feel their efforts are in vain. How many times have these people encountered an object that is yet to be broken down in their lives? Even for athletes, imagine how many of them compete to win a championship only to experience roadblocks when a formidable opponent comes along and year after year snatches away their dream and possibilities of fulfilling a world title. In addition, even the very nature of relationships that has struggled to find ways for both people to progress can also engage in its own battles of achieving higher goals and dreams. It seems, turn by turn, the road carries people to a destination; but it reaches to the end of a road, where their possibilities become blocked by a dominating force. It appears that sometimes when one moment starts, it ends at that moment, not allowing you to transcend into another moment. That is the time for you to wake up and realize that something is blocking you from making it. Until you consistently believe in your abilities that will be the weapon you need and must continue to have that will enable you to keep attacking until you knock down this wall entirely. You are defeated when you stop trying, but as long as you continue to use action backed by belief, perseverance, and confidence, someday that wall has to come down. When it finally comes down, a new moment in your life will be born. It will be a moment where you will no longer live an impossible dream but achieve incredible outcomes.

> *Limitations live only in our minds. But if we use our imaginations, our possibilities become limitless.*
>
> —Jamie Paolinetti

## Take Action Now

When I was a youngster, I was never a firm believer of people and events that can change radically, but as a result of many historical life-changing situations that took place as I grew older, I became a strong believer that nothing is impossible to see change in this world. When blacks for many years were enslaved by whites, a decision was made to end slavery and segregation that brought about the necessary change to see both races as equal.

Many blacks who had to undergo discrimination stood against racial laws and took a stand for what they believed in, as a result of their actions, new laws, and the opportunity for change forged right into society. Women also faced challenges where they never got equal pay to men at jobs and were denied the rights to vote. When many of them spoke out against this, it altered the mind-set of other women who were not being paid fairly and equally to men. Now as a result, equal opportunity laws exist, and those who took a stand for what they believed in have changed the face of corporate America for women in the job market. Currently, in the world today, many women are now in powerful positions across the world. Change, thus, which at one point looked impossible, became a possible outcome that would reach to global proportions. In addition, in this era, many people across the world were able to witness the first black president of the United States.

If people like Barack Obama thought change was impossible, he would never run for presidency, win the election, and gain the respect of his constituents. If he thought that his time will be later, later may never arrive, and no one will ever see the results of his potential. He is a man that is a firm believer of the power of change, an action word that knocks down any impossible wall that dares stand before him.

He was able to persevere and overcome all the critics and doubters by putting his candidacy and life on the line to change a historical mark in the United States. Not once did a shadow of doubt step foot in his mind that his efforts would be wasted. He prayed to God continually, believed and trusted in him, even at the expense where his own life would be at risk. Now this man has led the country in the best possible way for all of its citizens to see changes that took long for past presidents to bring into action.

Personally, I thought of change in the past as an impossible task with the situations and circumstances I was placed in. It seemed that many of them required constant comebacks from every failed task I attempted. Now when I think and reflect on all the impossible situations that ever happened in the world, I no longer believe there is ever a possibility that change can occur. As time progressed, people were placed in unlikely situations that looked like it was going to last an eternity. However, through their persistent efforts, they made their way through those unlikely situations and turned them into outcomes that generated more positive possibilities. Suddenly, all the impossible situations that once ruled the world crossed into a moment where they can no longer be unstoppable.

They had reached their time of submission as well as their point of breakability where the stronghold that they took on for so long was weakened to the point where it shattered into a million pieces. When it crumbled, change was suddenly possible, and when it became possible, the moment in time for everyone changed. A new moment in life had given birth. No longer will change be deemed a word of impossibility but a definition of breakthrough and conquer.

Change would no longer be something that is feared, but now it becomes an action that people would want to embrace. Obviously, the time for change had to come. I was too comfortable with life. I wanted things to remain the same because I figured if my world started to change then many things around me would start to become complex. I never liked complexity, and because I often thought change would bring on a more complex life, I tried to avoid it at all possible cost. I thought of change as something that will create problems. I was used to my current lifestyle. To commit to change would be to alter what I was doing. Altering my lifestyle would only break me out of a rhythm I may not ever get myself back into. I was never a risk taker because risk takers dive in the water without knowing if it's hot or cold. My mind-set didn't make me take the plunge, and because I refused to take the plunge in several areas of my life, I never got to see the full impact of the possibilities that life could bring. Ultimately, my efforts in life were not only limited but also wasted. I can only go as far as my mind would take me. I had to see that stagnation was my wakeup call, and the time for my moment for change is now.

There is always a fine line between success and failure. The results became simple: whatever you do and want to do with your life, you will either fail or succeed at it. If applying the action and taking the plunge is too much for you, then you will forever be at one stage in your life without ever finding a desire or meaning to advance. For many, to reach the promise land, they have to find a way to pass through the unpromised ones. They should never have any doubts that will prevent them from achieving all they ever imagined to be possible. Unfortunately, to get to the promise land is not easy because success is not easy. If it was easy for everyone to become successful, then no one would encounter its roadblocks. Everyone would take risks associated with his or her ideas. People will take a plunge without checking the water. Everyone will be dancing with joy and lighting a great ball of fire to the promise land. However, just try passing through any barrier, and you will see that there are some forces and people who will stop at nothing to prevent you from getting there.

They will hate to see you achieve the impossible, especially when they have yet to overcome the same roadblocks in their own lives. Success is daring, but not too impossible for the unjust man. For the one who is strong-willed and knows what is best for himself or herself, he or she welcomes all the roadblocks that life brings because he or she knows what it takes to overcome them. Every setback that some individuals have experienced in life makes them reach one step closer to making their dreams a reality. All the circumstances and distractions that life brings only make them want to complete their journey until they reach the end. All that some people need is an opportunity so that they can turn their opportunities into possibilities and their possibilities into an outcome. Once that decision is reached and a chance is given, there is no turning back. You welcome all the possibilities that arise from the challenges you face ahead.

There is a vast difference, however, between possibilities and realities that derive from the possibilities you encounter. Possibilities are opportunities that are being worked on. Realities are possibilities that have been worked on, completed, and brought to life. Once the possibilities have been completed, the results from them will become a reality. Reality lets you know where you stand. However, having not worked on anything doesn't make anything real; it leaves you wondering what could be and what could have been the result if it was worked on.

The only way something will become real to you is if you put the work into it to make it real. In order for you to do the action, you must produce the deed so the action will result. Otherwise, whatever you try to do will always be a figment of your imagination unless you make it happen. Some people have worked rigorously to make their dreams become a reality; however, it is challenging to overcome the obstacles they are faced with. Individuals just can't think opportunities are what they need to pay attention to. It is the possibilities that can come from the opportunities that hold substance. If you are ever going to make anything possible, I believe it must start with an idea. Once an idea is generated, you must follow with a plan of action that will create opportunities that will make you follow through with that plan. Once the opportunities have been created, the possibilities from those opportunities also begin to generate.

*Losers become winners when they get tired of losing.*
*Winners become winners when they realize losing*
*is no longer an option.*

## Unleashing Continuous Power

In the past, I enjoyed the days of long ago much more than the days I am living now. I guess maybe because when I was young, I was surrounded by a lot more friends to do things I normally could not do today. The future, for the most part, is supposed to be better than the past; but the past creates your present, and your present creates your future. All in all, letting time slip through your hands is the killer. No one wants to be overtaken by time and the devastating results it could bring when it is wasted. As the years go by, the longer you wait, the harder it will be to accomplish the dreams you want to accomplish. Think about every wasted effort that never gets applied and every action that never amounts to anything and how much harder it gets when so much time passes by.

Think about children; the longer it takes for you to have them, the harder it will be to create and raise them when time moves on and moves you into a certain age bracket. Think about education; the longer it takes for you to excel academically and get into school, the harder it will be in the future to get in, pass exams, and graduate. Sure, everything becomes harder as you get older, but nothing is impossible no matter how old one gets. Sometimes it may seem you have left many years behind you, and you don't have that many more to go. I was at a point in my life where I didn't know where I was going and which way to turn. I needed some miracle to break through a trying moment in my life that once I have gotten through it, every other moment that I thought was impossible would become a possibility.

Each one of us has an incredible power from within. The problem is some of us find it very difficult to release this power and tap into it. Once you find a way to get from being ordinary to being extraordinary, you will identify with your abilities and capabilities and weigh them for what they are worth. They will be good enough only if your heart and mind are strong to sustain them. Look at the way life has been for many people. In the world today, there are many people who are losing what they worked hard for and encountering difficulties all at the same time. Houses are going into foreclosure; many people are out of work, out of relationships, and out of luck with everything they put their hearts and minds to. Their circumstances are all external, but all the power lies from within to break down and eradicate all of the circumstances that have limited their success. The power is there; it has been there since the very day you were born. It takes the mind and the heart to activate and release this power. Once your power is released and you practice what you do and become fearless at everything you go after, your skills and abilities take on anything that comes to you in the moment.

No more will your life be at a crossroad. No longer will you feel that you are incapable of getting any of your dreams and goals accomplished. You have inherited the power to excel. In order for the mind and the heart to release this power, one has to believe that it already exists inside of one. Nothing can ever be released if one feels that it doesn't exist. It must exist in order for it to be released. The mind has to make a decision to think and process thoughts differently than ever before, while the heart has to reinforce the mind's decision by consistently giving one the desire and passion to persevere and never quit in spite of all the obstacles it encounters. Now how can you release this power and achieve anything you ever wanted so that you can bring it to a reality in this world?

Answer? Every person has to believe he or she has what it takes to release that power; however, his or her power is futile if it is released in the moment, but it has no momentum to carry him or her through other moments in his or her life. People can have a sense of belief, but if their belief last for one day, one week, and one month, it has power, but it is not powerful enough to last and make a breakthrough in their lives.

For anyone to be on the path to his or her destiny where he or she can experience success in successions, he or she will have to practice the art of thinking much differently than the thoughts that have limited him or her in the past.

Once this person can find a way to release this powerful energy and tap into it consistently, he or she can see life-changing and dynamic results that was never seen or experienced in his or her past. All of us have a form of power by which the force it releases could either be positive or negative. Every thought and action was either meant to build your life or destroy it. If you have not successfully trained your thoughts to think positively, it will be easy for you to break down anything that is building in your life. It is no wonder that some relationships that go through intense arguments and counseling can never find a way to build back up again. When couples exercise their power by trying to work on their indifferences through communicating and ironing out their issues in counseling sessions, conflict will easily die down because many of them have released a power to start building on something new where they can alter their thought patterns. Consequently, as much power as any couple can release to bring their relationships back into balance, no power has meaning, and it is not intended to be powerful if it lasts for only a short time.

You may solve your problems for a little while, but in the walk of life, there is no road that anyone can travel on where his or her path is free from bumps, rocks, and obstacles. The power that the mind can release can hurdle over any obstacle, but if it is not released consistently, then it loses its momentum to channel its way through future obstacles. It is much similar to a car that runs out of gas as it tries to get to its destination. When all the gas is gone, all the force that could carry that car is also terminated. That person is left with no other choice but to get assistance from another driver to start moving again.

In all its glory, belief only works for those who believe they have the power to make it work. Therefore, what gives one the power one needs to believe? What gives one also the ability to ensure one's beliefs will still continue even when one faces distractions and difficulties in life? Answer? It is the power of perseverance. That is and will be the true test when someone can believe and continues to believe. It is the true passion of perseverance that comes by consistently putting your actions into practice every single day until you are able to break down all the negativity that you have built over the years. Belief, thus, is a word that is used interchangeably with faith. It is by far the most powerful and creative force in the universe. It is a power that when it is released can transform any outcome, condition, event, or circumstance into a desired miracle that many people would dream to be impossible.

It has all the power to change your perceptions about the world into one that is consciously purposeful and intentionally transforming. It starts with the power of a single thought that alters the thought pattern to store information in the subconscious mind. Once the information is stored, and it begins to accumulate, many of it spills over into the conscious mind to let one know one is capable of creating something that one wants. Once enough power is released and one goes after it consistently, one's actions and thoughts shift into the unconscious where one can carry out one's life without thinking about what one needs to do. These individuals' beliefs are so ingrained that their conscious does not have to tell them to think positively or to change their thought patterns for how they view the world. Their levels of beliefs are so strong that their daily unconscious thoughts in life are not wavered by any circumstance that intends to derail their focus.

Think about the Bible that requires for all Christians to change their past mind-set into a mind-set that belongs to Christ, where they have the mind like Christ and live the life like Christ lived. God knows that this is not easy for anyone that is why he encourages us to pray. Prayer changes your mind-set if you pray consistently and believe what you are praying about will come to pass. There is power in prayer. There is power when you can close your eyes and speak all the words and thoughts that come from your subconscious mind into your conscious thinking, which now awakens and gives you awareness as to what needs to be changed in your life.

Once you have prayed enough times on a consistent basis, I guarantee you that your thoughts and habits will begin to change. No more will you think in a negative way when you need to get something done. Once you keep praying and unleashing the power of prayer consistently, there is no situation or event you will feel that you can't overcome in life. You will have raised your power of belief to the point where it will become unstoppable. Only until you are fully aware of the power you have on the inside will your life become fully transformed on the outside. Don't think that impossible situations can't happen to the ones who don't believe. It is very rare that you see anyone happy with life that does not have strong beliefs in what he or she wants to do.

The strong believer fights daily to overcome his or her circumstance because he or she knows that there is a force in life that is against him or her that he or she just can't afford to mess around with. The people who find ways to succeed at anything they tackle are always on the attack mode in life. They know if they don't attack their situations, their circumstances will keep attacking them and will not give them any mercy or opportunity to revamp and alter the course of their direction in life. As great as it is for one to believe, belief is nothing if one does not transfer enough thoughts of faith into one's conscious mind so one can release its power not for one day, one week, or one year but for the rest of one's life.

**The Power of Belief**

The power of belief can only be meaningful and effective when it has dynamically transformed the inside and outside of one's life. You are where you supposed to be when the moment takes you there. In turn, you are where you belong when no new moment emerges in your life for change. Obviously, you have been through ups and downs in life only to get to a point where if you are able to overcome the obstacle that is placed in front of you, there is every possible chance that you will also be able to overcome other ones that come in your life later on. The question is what does it take for you to win and keep on winning? What does it take for you to taste victory just like everyone else who has tasted victory? Even to the point where you are trying so hard, practicing so much, and putting in so much effort, there has to come a point where you have to see the fruits from all your labor. After all, how can one surpass a challenging test that is the deciding factor of where one's future lies in this world if he or she does not plant the seed that will be sown later on from all their efforts?

A test, thus, is a lot like preparing for the most important moment in one's life. It can come when you least expect it, or it can come at a time when you have found ways to prepare for it. All that matters is that when it comes, you achieve what is necessary in that moment so that you have an opportunity to move closer to your desired goal. Only the power of belief through your actions can catapult you and bring you closer to it.

There are no challenges that are too daunting for the one who believes. The challenge that you have is only a challenge you can answer. No one can make a believer out of you. Only you can make a believer out of yourself. The mind has to be there, and the heart has to be right there with the mind to achieve a necessary purpose. In spite of all the factors that surround you, it's essential for your heart to remain positive until its desires are positively fulfilled. Incredibly, through belief, the mind and the heart can make everything at one time impossible become possible. The mind makes everything possible, but it is also the mind that can make the possible things become impossible if you let sin and negativity find and fight its way through. The only way to overcome sin is to have complete awareness of the damaging effects it can have on one's life if it is not dealt with accordingly. Here is a list of a few damaging effects that sin can have on one's life. Truly, the power of belief can't coexist with all of them if one wants to achieve a necessary vision in one's life. Unfortunately, if an individual consistently is defeated by his or her sin, he or she will not have the ability to overcome obstacles or the impossible forces that continues to emerge in his or her life.

## — PRIDE —
### The First Deadly Sin That Blocks Your Possibilities

At some point in one's life, one will have to let go of one's pride and overcome it to see substantial progress, or one can continue to hold on to it and see no necessary change evolve. Apparently, no matter the path to one's destination, until one is able to diffuse one's ego and take on a more humble approach, it will be at that time one can truly experience the possibilities that can extend beyond wanting to do things through the help of others rather than attempting to do it through one's own capacity. Pride, thus, is nothing new to any person that has a strong view to where he or she wants to take his or her life.

Every man and woman I believe that has had his or her own view points in the world has had to personally deal with his or her own pride of believing in his or her own ideas without wanting to receive the ideas of others. Apparently, if a person's ego gets the best of him or her, no amount of persuasion can shift his or her ideas to believing otherwise. Indeed, pride can surely lead to the downfall of one's success. If it is not dealt with accordingly, it can lead to one experiencing countless roadblocks beyond one's own motives in the world.

Incredibly, I could clearly recall how pride has been destructive in my life by allowing me to feel my needs are more important than the needs of others, and my quest for success in what I want to achieve can only be justified by my own actions and ambitions. I never realized until a much later time how devastating my pride was when I used so much time doing things for myself that it led to many of my friends walking away.

Maybe, it's my fault to believe that my pride made me feel that I should care about my own success rather than the success of others. Maybe, it's also my fault that I did not see how counterproductive my efforts became when I realized that I need other people in the world to be successful because I am nothing without them. Surely, it took some time for me to see, but when I became aware of it all, that is when I knew a breakthrough moment in my life occurred. It was then that I realized the time and moment has come to change my life for the better.

Therefore, in terms of your own pride, the questions I have for you are do you believe you are a winner? Do you have what it takes to make everything happen around you, or do you wait for things to get out of control before you start believing it's time for you to react and take control of the situation? In addition, can you be honest enough with yourself to get the help you need to make the changes that will help you move forward in life? Are you humble and teachable? Or is your pride so deeply rooted that you tell other people lies that you yourself can't define what the truth is anymore? The fact is, when your lies come to an end, it will give rise to the start of new possibilities.

Your life will be nothing but a mirage if you can't stop talking about what you want to do instead of start getting the things that you need to get done. You can tell people all the victory stories and throw all the victory parties you want from the stories you tell, and all it will be is a fairy tale until you find a way to bring your fairy tales to life. Listen to the voices that you hear in your mind. Those are the voices that tell you to tell your friends, family, and coworkers that you are approaching the next stage in your life. You tell them stories to make yourself feel comfortable that you are heading somewhere, but the truth of the matter is that your stories never amount to you going anywhere, unless you start acting and taking action on all of them.

You can tell them that you will get another degree in two years and other stories about how you will be buying a home and getting married soon, even the fact that you are getting ready to start a business that will bring you high income returns. Those are the stories that make you feel comfortable to tell people what they want to hear so that they could ease off of you in some way. The people who believe in you feel that you are going places in life. However, five years down the road or even ten, your life would have changed very little if you have not taken action toward many of the promising statements you made. It would seem that the stories you tell people are the same lies that you keep telling yourself time and time again until you hear so much of it that it begins to sound true. Obviously, they become lies when you don't act on them, and they become the truth when they lead to action. Some of us live in a fantasy world where we know how powerful our minds can be, but we use it in such an unwise way by telling lies to ourselves and to other people. We tell people the things that they want to hear instead of telling them what they need to hear. We lie to them and to ourselves without making any room for improvement. If we are not honest with what we do and where we are in life, we will never see the changes we desire to see. In order for you to ever accomplish anything in this world, you absolutely need to be real to yourself and be real with other people. The moment should never be enough to paralyze you from achieving greater moments. Put your pride to the side and let humility take its course.

You will never get the help you need or the possibilities that can come from that help if you continue to tell people make-believe stories of where your life is going that, through lack of action, never goes anywhere. Once you are honest with yourself, the life you are living becomes real to you. Every phony discussion that you had with people about the promises that you made to them or the things that supposed to be heading your way does not help you improve your life or achieve any of the dreams you set out to accomplish. Let's face it, people lie because they hate to have anyone look down on them. Their pride matters the most to them. Even though they may not be where they want to be in life, their satisfaction is to not let others know that they have not gotten there as yet. People will never act on something that will never happen.

People are more inclined to act on the truth than on a lie that will never work itself out. Stop creating stories and start living out the possibilities that can be endless when you are honest with yourself. If your marriage is facing a barrage of attacks, don't tell everyone you are doing fine. Get the help that you and your spouse need so that your marriage can be restored. If you do not like your job, and your performance has not been up to the expectations of others, get the help you need by improving your performance or find another job that will meet your expectations. Life is too short for you to settle for what it gives you. In addition, if you are sick, do not tell people you are feeling well when the person that you could be talking to may just be someone who could help. Be real and be honest with yourself. People will respect you for your honesty. Many of them will like you for who you are, not for what you pretend to become. Not being real to yourself is not being who you were born to be. Nothing can and will ever happen to a person who does not want to change anything but is holding on to so much pride that blocks any possibilities from finding and fighting its way through change.

> *Speaking powerfully without being powerful amounts to having no power.*

## — PROCRASTINATION —
## The Second Deadly Sin That Blocks Your Possibilities

Procrastination is considered one of the deadliest sins that deter people from making progress. Nothing can happen in the moment, and nothing can be achieved in another moment when procrastination takes over one's life. It makes you plan something that never gets completed. It makes you believe you can start a project and finish one. It makes you sleep longer and the days become shorter. Little by little, this sin starts chipping away at you. It starts telling you that there is enough time to get to work, arrive at an event, study for a test, finish your homework, and finish the papers that your boss left for you to complete. One more minute of sleep turns to two, two turns to five, five turns to ten, and ten turns into twenty. When the minute turns, the day turns, the weeks the same, the month follows, and then the year is finally over. Suddenly, you are right back where you started. You start your goals from the beginning, and procrastination is right there, waiting to attack you again.

It shows when you make a plan and are excited about it; you feel you are heading in the right direction because you set a time that it needs to be worked on and a day that it will come to an end. What some people don't see coming is that procrastination comes at a time you least expect it to arrive. It takes a unique and driven person to handle this deadly sin that has slammed people against the wall and delivered its many blows to make them surrender their goals and forget the purpose of why they were going for them in the first place. Procrastination is a true test to one's desire. It's a test to see if one can get pass this sin to see if one's dreams and goals can become actualized. It is a test to see how resilient a person can be when he or she has the fire and the drive going in the beginning to work on something to not be stopped no matter what the cost until it is done.

You are not the first or last person that has had to deal with procrastination. Procrastination has dug at the core of every man's heart and has left a place there that becomes evident when you walk through the door. At every encounter, people just know you have been hit by this deadly sin, and they are fully aware if you don't find a way to overcome it, your life will continue to be ruled by a commitment of empty promises, disbelief, failed projects, and lost hope. Through all of its attacks, procrastination blocks any hope of possibilities that could come your way. It stands there and tells possibilities to back off. It never feels bad. It always feels good. It makes you enjoy the extra sleep you deserve. It makes you turn to pleasure now and attend to your matters later. It makes you hang out with your friends all the time, leaving all your work behind. It makes you believe you have enough time when the time is never enough. It always leads to satisfaction first resulting in pain afterward.

You can hear the voice of procrastination when it comes. Some of the sounds are "I will do this tomorrow," "I have more time to get it done," "I will finish this later." Day in and day out, the voices never change; hence, your life remains by the words you hear and the actions you live by. Unfortunately, when tomorrow comes, it is the same story that goes on until the day runs out, the year runs out, and the time runs out on your life. It stuns and stumps you from reaching any of your dreams and blocks you from attaining any of your possibilities. The decision to live your life effectively can only work when the deadly force of procrastination and ineffectiveness is put to rest. You must live your life without a life of procrastination. Get the things that you desire to get done. Prioritize a list of all the goals you want to accomplish and get them accomplished.

Put the most important things before you that need to get done and get it done. Write it down on a calendar where you wake up to it every day and state why it is important for you to complete it. Keep yourself grounded by being active toward it even if you have to have someone else hold you accountable to it. Make your goals a part of your daily routine and tie it in your everyday schedule so it is practiced in rhythm. Place the pressure you need on yourself to get out of life's comfort zone. The time to do it is now. There is no greater time than now. There is no greater power than now, and there is no greater purpose to get it done than now. Now gives you urgency. No one knows the future and what it holds. Situations in life are unpredictable. It is evident you may walk today but may not be able to walk tomorrow. You may see today but you may not be able to see tomorrow. You may drive today but may not be able to drive tomorrow. You may live today but may not be able to live tomorrow. The faster you can get things out of your way, the quicker you can see the possibilities that lie ahead of them.

> *Most of the things worth doing in the world had been declared impossible before they were done.*
>
> —LOUIS D. BRANDEIS

## — EXCUSES —
### The Third Deadly Sin That Blocks Your Possibilities

How many times people like you and me have made excuses because we choose not to be a part of something? How many times have we regretted using a language that places us ideally in our own zone of comfort, but afterward, when it is used, we realize at a much later time how much it limits us to what we can do and what we can become for ourselves? How many enemies have we made because of the excuses that we project toward others?

Surely, there is not much to add to a person's character who oftentimes makes excuses when it comes to becoming someone better than who he or she could become in this world. There is nothing to boast about that person. It is either he or she wants to get an edge in life or shows no effort to seize advantage of the opportunities given to him or her in a moment to progress toward his or her dreams in the world. Thus, how can you compare the level of desire of one individual who oftentimes will do what it takes to go places with another that shortchanges his or her life by not having any place to go? How do you know the potential that someone possesses if you have not seen what he or she has accomplished with the time he or she has lived in the world? Answer? The person who wants to go places rarely makes excuses for all the places he or she wants to get to and the unexpected situations that emerge en route to his or her destination. He or she will be sidelined for only a short amount of time; however, his or her levels of ambition and focus are strong enough to steer him or her right back on track. No one can keep a go-getter down for too long because this person is resistant to making excuses for what he or she wants to achieve. Success means everything to this individual even if it means putting his or her life on the line to get what he or she is after.

Apparently, though having strong levels of focus and determination is a good quality and characteristic for many people to have, not everyone in this world is built or wired that way. Some people can't carry themselves past the finish line because there is always something that blocks them into feeling they can cross it successfully. There is often some problem, situation, or unexpected event that comes in their lives that makes them feel they are incapable of putting their best intentions to work. So, instead of having a chance to move forward, they struggle with the reality of their issues as an excuse to why they can't propel themselves onto a much higher level in their lives. Once their excuses have hindered or blocked them from attaining one goal, it is more than likely they will also be blocked from achieving the rest of them. So many times people create their own reality by the words they live by.

An individual can make promises for weeks; however, on the day those promises are to be fulfilled, something unnecessary comes out into the open to make him or her feel as if he or she can no longer uphold to his or her promises. Sadly, people live by the excuses they make; and it is no wonder when those excuses are made, they have no means of getting themselves out of stagnation. You can clearly tell a person who makes consistent excuses. It is the very words that are spoken from his or her experiences that have allowed him or her to develop a consistent language that has been geared toward living off of empty promises. The excuses can come after the moment has passed or shortly before a significant moment arrives. Either way, the cost of all the excuses made outweighs all the benefits and possibilities that could emerge afterward. How far can you take yourself into achieving any goal or attaining anything in life if you have not given yourself a chance to get beyond the risk associated with the challenges it brings? Only until you develop the confidence you need, it will be at that moment your possibilities in life can open the door to greater results.

## — THE BROKEN RECORD —
### The Fourth Deadly Sin That Blocks Your Possibilities

One of the most deadly oppositions people like you and me face at times is the ability to use a language that is consistent and refreshing to others. From the experiences I've had in dealing with certain people, I feel when I am asked questions regarding the status of my life, I would always say something that they want to hear instead of telling them what they need to hear. Maybe for me, because at some point, most of us have also been there, I would feel a sense of fear and shame if I disclose my life to others; and it is not where I or they would hope it to be. Truly, in most instances, that is how the world operates. It is bent mostly on other people measuring themselves and their lives to you. Though many of them will never be forthcoming about it, they will use your conversation with them as a measuring tool to see where you stand in the world. Even though that is the case, what is important is that you have to earnestly make sure you are progressing in your life where you are constantly sharing new and refreshing stories to others. After all, that is what life is based on—a language of progression. That is what makes people like you and me become more of what we want to become and what others expect our lives to become—a life that is based on choosing words of progression rather than words of stagnation. Thus, the words people live by are so important because they are used as a measuring stick by other people to let them know exactly where they stand in this world. Some people feel you have what it takes to be a winner when you are able to tackle situations successfully by applying action oriented principles reinforced by speaking positive words of affirmation. Hence, having the same words that you live by that repeats itself from what was said yesterday, today, and tomorrow can persist without having any impact on changing your life for the better. Obviously, people don't like to be labeled as broken records, but when the record has not changed its tune, it repeats itself with the same broken statement time and time again. These people then will leave you with no other choice but to think that your ideas can never be hopeful, and that your promises were always meant to be broken. You will know a broken record when you see one.

You will not only find some in the basement of a record store, on the shelf, or in a garage, but you will also find them in your home, in school, at work, and in people you converse with. Broken records can come in various forms, but the ones that are most common come through speech, lack of actions, and lifestyle of the individual. Quite a few people I have dealt with have come to me with their broken records and their broken stories through which they could never seem to seal the cracks in their tune. It's the same stories of what some people tell you they are working on, and when you see them months and years later, they will tell you they are still working on it.

When you look at their lives, it has changed very little for the better because the mind has operated on the statement that has been the signature record of their lives. How dissatisfying it is for one to make promises that never lack any substance or direction. These individuals who do this lack the reality with what is happening now because they always rely on the song that was played back in their past. To them, the past lyrics are more important than what they must do today to change what they need to, so tomorrow the story and the lyrics will be different. If some people can get in touch with what they need to accomplish now, tomorrow will take care of itself in the future. When you can feel life in the moment, then all that matters to you is now because tomorrow is not guaranteed.

I remembered a friend of mine named Santana who always had something to say when I would meet with him on occasion. Without question, you would be amazed to hear all the things that he aspired to become. It seemed that most of my conversations with him were about the big projects that would eventually catapult him to success. He spoke about his business that would help him retire, and that he would move out of New York and live in a beautiful five-bedroom house in the south with his wife and three children. Time would come around, and Santana would disappear for a long period of time without anyone hearing anything from him. One day, when he decided to break out of his shell and come out to church services, I would ask him how his life was going, and he would tell me the same story that he has been working on. It appeared, since I last spoke to him, nothing much has changed. He still had the same goals and the same dreams with the same tune. That, much to no surprise, has been the story and record of his life. Like Santana, we all fell victim to this deadly sin where we play the same broken record time and time again to others, never to change its tune. For many people struggling with this, it is only a lie until it becomes the truth. It is only the past until it takes hold of one's future.

The truth of the matter is when a record remains broken, the lives of the individuals remain shattered. Their lives do not change, and their statements don't create the changes they want to see in their lives.

It is just like the cracked record that goes round and round until it plays itself over and over again. When the crack is fixed, the record is fixed; the tune changes, and these people will be singing a different song. It won't be the same tune of excuses or promises that skips over and repeats itself all the time, but it is a tune that goes forward until the record plays itself without any breaks in between. Set yourself in such a way that you have a clean record with no cracks in your recordings. This way, when people see you and listen to the way you speak, it is always a new tune that is refreshing to their ears.

> ***Nothing will ever move forward if you make a decision to take things lying down.***

— INACTION —
**The Fifth Deadly Sin That Blocks Your Possibilities**

Once something happens, you don't remember when it happened or why it happened; all you know is that it happened. You will experience pain once you start working on something that you want to accomplish. There is no reward without the sacrifice. Each person must taste pain and defeat before he or she can realize what it is to taste success. The point is you must propel and push yourself to create your goals and accomplish your dreams. Lying there on your couch, watching television when the games and reality shows are on will never help you move further to attaining your goals. Everyone will experience pain working on a project. The point is so many projects start, but not all of them can be completed because people do not get themselves in a rhythm to complete what they started. Their inconsistencies in life have all but entangled them in a web, causing their routines to remain the same. Nothing has changed, even though they themselves know what needs to be changed. They place themselves in a circle of inactivity that oftentimes never leads to the changes they would like to see in their lives.

Don't be stuck in your comfort zone. People like you and me have all been there. When we get there, it is hard for anyone, even our own selves, to come out of it. When I reflect on certain aspects of my adulthood, I have been in places that have led to my life moving at a snail's pace. Why? I would get comfortable being in positions at jobs that would last for many years, never to advance to higher-paying ones. In addition, I have lived in the same neighborhood for years, not giving myself the opportunity to change my lifestyle and living conditions.

Inevitably, my life would go on without the prospect of it going in a different direction. Surely, on many levels, it took some time for me to realize that the only way my life was going to change was if I was disturbed about the way it was being lived. Indeed, for anyone to change and erupt out of their zone of comfort, he or she must be disturbed enough to make it happen. Obviously, your safe zone is your comfort zone. God will not move unless you move. God will not act unless you start acting. No setback can be a surprise when it can be a supplement for greater possibilities to happen. When it comes to being action oriented and making things happen, people have to see themselves for who they are and what they eventually can become.

When one thinks about possibilities, one must look beyond oneself to see if one's dreams, hopes, and aspirations that lie ahead can become possible. It has been said biblically, you have not because you ask not, and you have not because you act not on the things you want. The only way you have a possibility of attaining something is to bring it in prayer, believe you can get it, and act like you have already received it. You can't think the impossible and expect possible things to happen. You have to think the possible and expect possible things to happen even when at times they seem impossible. Sometimes you get what you ask for even when you don't ask for it. Other times, you don't get anything simply because you did not ask for it, or you just don't believe you will get it even if you tried. Thus, you may still take a shot to ask, but you don't get it because you asked for it with the wrong intentions. Despite this, you must take action with the right heart and the right motives to get anything accomplished to become someone in this world. Lack of action, along with the wrong motives, may block any possibilities from happening; however, the more action you take with the right motives can make anything you want to achieve in this world possible.

> *It is not how hard you try or how many times you try, but what matters is that you do try and get what you want by never surrendering until you reach your final destination when it's all said and done.*
>
> —Chinwe Okeke-Moffatt

— NEGATIVITY —
**The Sixth Deadly Sin That Blocks Your Possibilities**

It is apparent that so many of us have become victimized by the sin of negativity. The power of it can be so devastating that its very grip on one's life can stifle any possibilities for one having a successful future. Personally, people like you and me have battled to see an end to this sin, but oftentimes, it can be so dominating that there is no end in sight to it once it starts. Surely, one of its many aspects is conflict in a relationship. Apparently, it is not difficult for people to realize that as long as you are in a relationship with someone, there will be conflict; and when that conflict arises, so will thoughts of negativity toward that person.

Quite evident also, conflicts in relationships are not the only factors that cause negative thoughts to emerge, but one must also consider the fact that going through the difficulties of life itself can bring on an altering mind-set when you are constantly working to improve your own life, where you are constantly battling with the circumstances it brings. That is why I believe the less negativity I have in my life, the more I can allow positivity to be filtered right into my system. Clearly, it's easy for negative thoughts to infiltrate your mind. If you fill your mind with the right thoughts, there will be no room for the wrong ones. If you keep letting the negative thoughts enter, they will chase away the positive ones. If you let impossibilities enter your mind, you stifle the room for any possibilities that can enter your life. Truthfully, you can't stop the negative thoughts from coming, but you have to develop the power to do what it takes to have them go in the other direction. When those negative thoughts enter your mind and you are not able to combat them, you will not allow the positive thoughts from entering.

Our minds can be like a radio station. The station we listen to can trigger sounds of victory or voices of defeat, sounds of positivity or voices of negativity. We are what we tune into. When we listen to positive thoughts, it makes the journey more enjoyable; however, negativity does nothing for the mind. All it does is stifle you with all the wrong ideas that will never break down the impossible walls before you.

Minds that are positive and remain positive will see their way through impossible outcomes. It is so easy for someone to be negative and hard for him or her to be positive. Why? Life itself can throw so many curveballs at you that if you don't have the right bat to swing at it, you will always strike out. Even if the pitcher changes, the results still remain the same. You just can never hit the ball out of the park because every turn that you make in life, you feel a circumstance or someone has your number.

It doesn't need to be that way. You can handle it in such a way that no matter what ball is thrown, you will have the right bat for it. Circumstances have seemed to work their way into the lives of people, but just as they worked their way in, they can also work their way out. When some people feel that it is their time and their moment, distractions enter their path, and they amount themselves with endless excuses as to why they couldn't seem to make their dreams happen. It is sickening to see how some people can get thrown off by other negative people who are not going anywhere in life. These are the same people that pull other people down with them when their ship is sinking. If you surround yourself with those types of people who constantly weigh people down with their negative talk, you will never see the positive values that life has to offer.

Truly, these are the people who don't want to see you make it because they themselves don't have a future. Though they call themselves your friends, if they have not tasted success, there is no reason for you to taste it either. It is not difficult to detect a negative person from afar. They are shrewd human beings, but they carry with them a venom that could spew in all different directions. These are the same people that will turn against you and turn others against you so that you have nothing left to live for. Your downfall is their ultimate satisfaction. Your defeat is their victory. Your sorrow is their happiness, your love is their hate, and your happiness is also their shame. Your success, thus, is the greatest asset that you can have to combat all the impossible channels that are placed before you. That is the only way you can fight negativity. Change the mind of the unbelievers into ones that can start to believe in your abilities. Let them know that you are for real in this world, and nothing can stop you from making your dreams possible. Start speaking positive things in your life as if they will happen, even though others doubted you as if it will never happen.

**Create Your Passion and Channel Its Energy into Accomplishing Impossible Dreams**

You have to have the ability to convert your hopes into your dreams and your dreams into your passion. There is one thing to do something, but nothing is greater than when you can do it with passion. I have heard people sing the same songs, but the voice that sings with passion is heard louder and sung more beautifully than all the other singers who sing. There are so many players who can play basketball, but when you have a passionate player, he or she does not care about making the game winning shot; he or she just cares about winning and making the right plays to win the game. Greatness does not come naturally to everyone. Greatness is a skill that someone must acquire. When someone continues to succeed at everything he or she does, he or she is setting an example for others who follow the same path. Greatness will come, and greatness will go. Talents, no matter how great they are, don't last forever. I believe to be great, one must develop the art of putting their greatness into practice.

However, when someone is passionate about something, greatness is inevitable. He or she will not be told what to do because his or her mind and heart will guide him or her into making the right decisions to do great things. No longer can he or she be overtaken by the hardships in life, and no longer will this person hold his or her head down in defeat. These individuals know how to stand, and when they stand, they know how to stand corrected. One of the many people in this world who has had this type of energy that is channeled into being passionate about her dreams is British singer Susan Boyle.

Growing up, Susan Boyle was a woman who did not have too many special moments in her life. She was born when her mother was forty-seven years old. To many, Susan's birth would be considered miraculous. Her mother, at the tender age of forty-seven, was already at a high risk of being pregnant. Incredibly, at the time her mother conceived, Boyle was born with no known complications. Apparently, as she got older, any memory with the way she was raised as a child all encompassed her ability to battle through opposition. One of the oppositions she faced was in school, through which she battled through periods of obstacles where she experienced learning disabilities and was bullied as a child. The thought of being able to overcome her challenges may have been too overwhelming for her. It got to a point where even out of school, she would reflect on all her troubles of not being acceptable to many. Boyle wondered and kept wondering how she could find ways to overcome all of her childhood challenges. It seemed she encountered one roadblock after another. She would grow older and move onto a new life in college, a life she figured would take a turn for the better.

Indeed, as she grew older, the challenges in life she faced never came to an end. In her adult years, life was still equally challenging for Susan.

She worked as a cook at a university and had gone through training programs for the government. Whatever money she could make was what she settled for to make ends meet. Through it all, she knew deep in her heart and mind that she was a much better person in life than what many people projected her to be. She kept on striving and was determined to unveil her hidden talent, a talent that she wanted to come to terms and have an identity with. Thus, her talent became her own inspired dream. In her spare time, she would capitalize on her talent by singing for her church choir. It would be at that time she would take on singing lessons from a personalized coach, where she used her talents to audition at several choirs and karaoke events. Soon enough her talents were slowly but surely being recognized. Part of her began to feel some sigh of relief because now it was just the beginning of her exposing herself to others.

She knew at the expense of all her obstacles, she had a power within that will one day be unleashed onto the rest of the world. It was only a matter of time before her moment in life emerged. Once it emerged, all she needed was one shot at it, and the rest would be history. As her talents began to rise, she would attend local singing competitions where she would be the audience favorite and stand out a clear winner among all the other competitors. The local exposure was not enough for Boyle's mother who felt that her daughter's talents should be seen by a much wider audience. As to her mother's beliefs, she felt it would be best for her daughter to go on national television to showcase her talent where millions of people around the world could be witnesses to the event.

It would be then on April 11, 2009, when Boyle's moment of truth arrived when she was spurred on by her mother to appear as a contestant on *Britain's Got Talent* reality program. She thought such an action will be impossible. She felt many people will reject her because of her age. She was already approaching fifty years old, and she already believed she did not stand a chance to even achieve success after the audition. She would shy away from the event, believing that it was a hopeless case to win. She felt too old and lacked the belief she had what it takes to walk away a winner. In a two-year span, Boyle's mother passed away. She knew if there was anything that would make her mother happy was to make a decision to overcome her fears and perform in front of millions of people. After careful consideration, and a high altitude of faith, belief, and determination, she took the risk and appeared on the reality program, not having anything to lose. The vision that at one time looked impossible for her to win now became one that she set her sights on.

It would be the first time she sang before a public audience since her mother passed away. Not knowing what to expect, standing in front of thousands of people and millions of television viewers, she broke down any wall that was in front of her and took action in her performance. She channeled all of her energy into accomplishing an impossible but passionate dream. Boyle would ultimately perform, and it would be a performance that would impress the crowd with millions of viewers watching.

The final decision of the winner would be voiced by judges who compared Boyle and a set of other competitors who also won the praises from the audience. Unfortunately, as much as she tried to win, at the expense of her extraordinary performance, she lost the competition. Even though Boyle lost, her songs echoed through television broadcast, and millions of Internet viewers who watched her extraordinary performance applauded her efforts as a competitor. In one of the most memorable moments on *Britain's Got Talent*, she would honor her breathtaking performance to the passing of her mother. If there was any motivation driving her to overcome all odds, it will be the words, love, and presence of her mother who would have wanted the very best for her in life. If Boyle's mother was alive to hear and see her daughter sing, it would mean all the difference in the world to her.

A week and two days later after her audition, millions continued to access the Internet and watch her memorable performance repeatedly in awe. Incredibly, it was a performance that echoed through their minds that they could not resist watching over and over again. Even though she lost the competition, she instantly gained media as well as national attention. Boyle launched her first music album *I Dreamed a Dream* in November 2009, and it debuted as the number one best-selling album around the globe.

The album sold nine million copies, and Boyle was an instant success. As a result, she became the oldest person to reach number one in the United Kingdom, having been recognized by *Guinness World Records* as having the fastest-selling debut album by any female artist at that age. At last, Boyle's powerful moment carried the momentum in her life where her voice was now global. She now had a lasting impression on others where everyone wanted to interview, meet with her, and hear her sing. Many people applauded her efforts on stage (2011, March 10 Retrieved 23:00 *Susan Boyle, In Wikipedia, The Free Encyclopedia*).

Instantly, the success of her album made her become a world phenomenon. After constant auditioning and practice on stage, while doing what she loved the most, Boyle's moment would be one that did not come alive until she was in her late forties. Even though her moment was born at a later time in life, she dedicated most of her time and energy to her aging mother. Interestingly, Boyle always knew she had a talent for singing, but it was not revealed to her until she got older.

Many people, like you and me, also have the same hidden talents that have yet to be exposed in this world. I believe that once an individual decides to take that risk in life by putting his or her talents, resources, and gifts on the line, it will be at that time a moment in life will emerge for him or her. No longer will Boyle underestimate or place a limit on her abilities. No longer will she also believe that dreams at any age, as long as they are channeled with passion, are impossible to achieve in this world. Boyle is a prime example of how an impossible wall was placed before her, but she used the power of belief through her actions to knock down the wall that limited her from achieving and fulfilling her passion in a moment when it truly mattered the most.

*The only way a breakthrough is going to begin in your life is when you start breaking through the obstacles that have broken down your life.*

# DIVINE CONNECTIONS

## CHAPTER 3

**Step into Your Divine Destiny**
**Every connection you make in this world is**
**destined to be divine.**

Imagine dreaming of a fantasy and watching it play over and over again in your mind, never to experience it in reality. Envision dreaming of a possibility that makes you wonder if that dream you fantasized will ever play out so that one day it will no longer be a dream. Until it is brought into reality, all it will be is a fantasy. Until it also emerges in your waking moments, you fantasize of all the possibilities that can and could be if all of it was real. Knowing you have the power and will to make your fantasies come true, all you need to do is take the deed and produce the action that can bring that deed forth. To produce anything, you must already have a desire to create what is already not produced. All it takes is a single decision, a single fuel to light the fire that would take you one step closer to your dreams and channel your dreams to your destiny.

In every step you take, there is a time for everything. Everything doesn't happen to everyone at the same time, but when it happens, it happens at the right time. When a profound connection is made between two people, each person wants to be part of the other person's life. Unfortunately, not everyone has someone linked directly to his or her life. The destiny in someone's life is not as important as his or her destination. It is one's destination that leads to one's overall destiny. Therefore, there is no reason to force any relationship that was never designed to be a divine connection.

When a relationship is meant to be divine, it will go through a series of challenging moments and channel its way through all of them. It will always see the end, not the beginning. It will also face challenges, but it will always find a way to rise above them. For every relationship, there is a divine connection that people make in every stage of their lives. Some connections are life changing, while others are not life sustaining. They could come and leave in the moment, while there are others that could come and last forever. For the ones that come in the moment, they create memories that people could remember and ones that they could also forget. However, for the ones that come and never leave, they create memories that last a lifetime.

Those are the connections that are truly divine. Those are the connections most people wished their lives were based on, but such a connection in this world is a fantasy. Such a connection in this world is an imagination that is hard to come into realization. Some people can be lucky to have that kind of divine connection, while others have to wait their entire lives to experience that kind of bond that people could have with one another that can last for an eternity.

Let's face it, nothing good lasts forever. That only happens in a dream world. Somehow all good things must come to an end. No matter how hard you try to keep the fire in your relationship alive, if it does not have every intention to outlast the obstacles and hardships in the world, it will not last. It is seldom that two people can meet each other today and then remain friends for the next five, ten, or twenty years.

Maybe you will cross paths with someone; but when you cross paths with him or her, it is only for the moment, where he or she is here today but gone tomorrow. Maybe the encounter is not only for the moment, but would last through other moments that build something special over time. Such an encounter is not through human will but by God's will.

Only he has the power to make those kinds of connections. Only he can will his power into people's hearts to make their relationships last with one another. Through his will, he can make couple's pass through moments in their lives where they are tested with fire and never-ending obstacles that could tear them apart. It is through him that an everlasting connection can be made and a divine connection could last. There are individuals in this world who don't like to be tested, so they surrender when the test and challenges come. Their lack of power and unity in their relationships never allow them to see the rewards and blessings in the end. There are others, however, who have the ability to grind out what they truly desire in their relationship. Their strength and passion for one another allows them to rise above challenging and testy situations. Success to them is not being alone but being with a partner that complements their strengths and weaknesses. Through all means, it seems that on your own will, no matter how hard you fight for your relationship to last, if it was not meant to last, there is no reason for you to continue to hold on to it. Just let it go! Obstacles and opposition were meant to be placed in your relationship in a series of moments in your life to determine how strong two people's hearts are for one another. If one heart fails, but the other is strong, there is a 50 percent chance that relationship will fall apart. If both hearts fail in the midst of each passing trial, your relationship is bound to break and is destined for inevitable failure.

In life, you become united in peace, but you become separated through war. When you become separated, you never know who will cross your path. The next person may be better than the last person you met. There is no reason to ride all your hopes and prayers on one individual if you are pouring your heart and mind into that person, and you are not getting the same efforts in return. You can continue to wait until your relationship passes through another trying moment. If no change has commenced with the other person's efforts, there is a great chance that no moment can rescue what is destined to happen. Connections are made in this world where people come into your life for a reason, and just as they come into your life, they also leave for a reason. A man plans his steps, but it is God who determines his path.

You are not in control of people's hearts; neither are you in control of their minds or their destiny. You can't tell what another person is thinking, nor can you tell the next actions they will take. The only person you can control is yourself. When you look at the next person, you can see his or her face, but you can't see his or her heart. There is no telling where his or her life will turn or what the future holds for him or her. What you should be ultimately concerned with is what the future holds for you. When destiny takes its course, you will be in a divine relationship that lets you know no matter what circumstances arise, nothing can stop you from spending the rest of your life with that person. No obstacle, hardship, condition, or opposition can make you fall as you were intended by God's will to spend the rest of your life forever with that person. Don't ever miss the mark in your relationship where life becomes a routine. In each relationship, it is not about being loved but about being in love and feeling all the desires you supposed to feel.

Once you understand the meaning of love, you give without expecting anything in return. You forgive without bending your mind toward unforgiveness. You extend yourself higher without lowering yourself to retaliation. You don't ever need to be told to love because your heart displays it effortlessly. Love, in essence, has to be displayed continuously for it to last. Needless to say, the relationship my parents had with one another was not based on such or any of those conditions. Each day was about how each one of them would go his or her own separate ways. There was never any solid connection between them as the very words that they used against one another were more destructive than constructive in their lives.

It was apparent that the relationship my parents had with each other was one that was clearly not destined to last. They didn't have the love that created a strong bond and nucleus as compared with other people's relationships. Obviously, I had to learn from their mistakes so that I can be a better person in my relationships with people as I got older. I was determined to rewrite all the wrongs and history my parents had in their lives by routing my life in a direction that will produce entirely different results than they had. No longer would I be a father who did not want to speak to his child or be one that didn't know how to be compatible with his partner. I would not be one that would seek what I could get out of a relationship, but I would be one that will search my desires for what I can give to it to make it better. That is what I believe defines the love two people should have for one another.

It is a love that does not look for a reward because it infinitely aims to please. When love is united in a real relationship, it is a harmony that is sung harmoniously between two birds in a tree. It becomes a song that displays no intent to argue but uses every intention to resolve an argument. It is the pure focus for what you give in life that binds together a power that can never be broken or taken away. After all, love can only be produced with the right heart and the right motives. If someone has done you wrong, you must learn to let go of the wrongs and find ways to make the wrongs right. Happiness is not shattered through love, but it is one's anger that shatters happiness. What have you done to bring happiness and stability to your relationship? Anger does not solve anything! Having anger brings no form of benefit and satisfaction to one's life. It stifles any good that you want to do and any good that can happen for you. If your common disposition in life is the fruit of happiness, by design, it will overshadow, overcome, and conquer all the forces of evil.

You just have to believe that God has a plan for you, your relationship, and your destination in life. It is a plan that is meant to exceed any challenges that block your path from going in a direction that it's supposed to go in. It is a plan that gives a person hope and a future. Sometimes life makes you feel you are not going anywhere, but not every path you take leads to the same avenue. Each avenue lines you into an entirely different destination. Life takes a different turn when you reach the end of the block. Just when it appears your life is not going anywhere, God adds hope and value to your life to make sure it heads toward its proper destination. You just can't operate in life without a plan. Every plan that you make in your relationship can only go so far without God. Only he has the power to make your relationship last, and only he has a plan that allows you to see that life can only get better when you decide to align your dreams and destiny with him.

> *A real friend is one who walks in when
> the rest of the world walks out.*
>
> **WALTER WINCHELL**

**The Value People Have in Their Lives**

Some people value friendships and the relationships they have with their partners. Any relationship that you are involved in must go through periodic phases that will overall test its strength and endurance to outlast challenging moments. Once a relationship can stand the test of a challenging moment and make it through another challenging moment, it gives people a strong belief they have what it takes in their hearts to make their relationships with one another last. If destiny has it, your friend will continue to stay connected with you, and the person you marry will continue to stay with you for better or worse for many years to come. If all the cards fell in the right places and all the doors that open stayed open, then it will be evident that whatever started in people's lives will take its course and remain on a path that leads you to its rightful destination.

Personally, I have gone through many stages in my life. Though not all of them were promising, I found the ones that were fulfilling were ones that I lived to remember the most. I remembered the friends that made me laugh, made me cry, and also challenged me to be better than who I was as an individual. They found faults in me that I couldn't find on my own. When I felt my heart was closed to others and no one was there for me, God made sure at that moment to send the right person that I needed in my life to open my heart again. It seemed that only he knew what was best for me when I could not define the meaning for what was best for myself. It appeared as moments in my life progressed, different people began to come into my life. These people counseled and challenged me with changes I needed to make in my character. It was clear to me I wasn't living life the way it supposed to be lived.

I built friendships with people, but because I did not value what I was building, those relationships quickly fell apart. I didn't know what I had until I lost it. I just didn't believe I can apply the right mechanics and have the appropriate mind-set and heart into creating relationships I believe will last. Few people who became my friends were good friends of mine, but they were never my best friends. Although I was young, I still wanted to gain an understanding of what it was to build something successful and make it last, even if it had to be relationships I had with people. It became evident when people made me realize what I have been missing in my life, but it became factual when God made me realize that something in my life was missing. I knew if I wanted more out of life, I needed to add value to it. Value to the things I would buy and value to the relationships I had with others. When I altered my mind-set and started taking my relationships with people seriously, I would spend more time figuring out the changes I needed to make within myself so that I can add value to other people's lives without expecting them to add value to my own life. I saw the importance of sharing my strengths and weaknesses with others so that I can be more effective and connected in my relationships with people.

I learned what it is to be better for other people without being better for myself. When I filled the needs of others, my heart in turn was also filled by God. Throughout this process, I started to feel I have a connection that not many people have in this world. I started to see the importance of what value can have in a relationship. Value adds quality to a relationship that gets better with time. You can instantly have a connection, but if the connection does not hold value, it quickly deteriorates. Any relationship that is bound to dissolve has no value when it crosses over into another stage of someone's life. Once it quickly loses value, it depreciates the minute obstacles attack that individual. Sometimes it does not even have to be an obstacle. Sometimes it is the simple fact that people forget what they have so they can't value what they can't remember. One that is cognizant of what one values never forgets the importance it holds in one's heart. If you hold on to the first printed comic book, and it has been in immaculate condition, the value of that book gets higher every year you hold on to it. In addition, for people who catch a homerun in the stands that was hit by a famous baseball player, the longer that person holds on to that baseball, the higher it will be in value. People collect rare items because they know how hard those items are to find. Any rare item, thus, is treated with the highest regard. The better it is kept and taken care of, the greater will be the value for that item.

How easy it is, however, to lose focus on the same principles in maintaining healthy relationships with people. Once people lose value in their relationships, they stop taking interest in their partner. Their words don't have value. The cards they write don't hold value, and the gifts they buy for each other also don't hold value, and even the love they have for one another also loses value. It seems that instead of it getting better with time, it gets worse as time goes along. It is evident once you add value to what you have, you take care of it as if it's your prized possession. You will not allow anything to harm it because you will be willing to fight and protect it at all costs. You will keep it around and let it grow with you and make your life be magnified by it. I believe because some people do not place value in what they have in their relationships, it quickly plummets, stunting the possibilities of growth and fulfillment that they can have for one another.

Once you put value in anything you do and possess, you make a commitment to make it last. It is not something that you find on the street that you hold on to for one week, one year, and then toss it out. It can't possibly be a connection with someone who comes into your life today and leaves in a short amount of time. This is also not something that someone has worked hard and handed to you only for you to mismanage and damage it later on. It has to go back to the heart of the individual where he or she must be able to place value in the relationships he or she has with his or her partner. It shows that at every moment, God knows exactly what he was doing when he allowed certain people to come into my life at a particular moment in time, and when that moment in time was over, those people that walked into my life suddenly began to walk away.

I started to see my life take a dramatic turn. I didn't understand what was happening. I wasn't the type of person that liked to let go of things and let go of friends. I started to look at myself and tried to examine what I was doing wrong but couldn't figure out why the people I met were leaving. No matter how much I wanted my friends to last, I knew that it was virtually impossible to hold on to something that probably wasn't meant to last. The value I had in them was not the same value that they had in me. I know life changes, and times also change at different stages of a person's life.

Nothing will ever stay the same, especially when some of my friends began to cross into different stages and moments of their lives. It seemed that as the old stages began to disappear, new ones began to emerge. As the new ones emerged, new friends, moments and memories were also raised with it. After all, friends come in your life for a reason, yet some of them only remain for a season. Once that season ends, a new season takes form with new people and new beginnings.

It shows that you can't hold on to something that was not meant to last, especially if your values are not aligned with the other person's values. Sometimes some people have to leave, and by them leaving is the best thing that can happen to you. Your dreams and destiny are not tied to any of them walking away. God knows exactly what he is doing, and he is using your time in that seasonal moment to allow someone else to come into your life to make you stronger and more equipped in allowing you to advance through other challenging moments.

No person knows his or her destination. You can plan all the steps you want to take, but it is God who ultimately controls each step toward your destiny. I have passed through many stages in my life, and at every stage, the people in my life that were placed there were significantly there for a reason. When they walked away, I did not take a step back; I moved forward. God always opens new doors and can give you new friends that are more appropriate for a certain time in your life. When people walk out of your life, you must realize it is only meant for you to grow. When some of your friends walk away, and new people come into your life, God is giving you exactly what will allow you to be equipped for him in that moment.

After all, you want people in your life that are supposed to be there. When God brings people to you, it is a plan that he has destined for that person's life as well as your own to succeed. If they leave, and when they do decide to leave, it is also part of his plan. Don't try to hold on to someone who is not supposed to be there. Don't try to follow someone who does not want to be followed. Sometimes God will cause people to walk away because they stunt your growth when you are around them. Once you decide to step into a new level of where your destiny should belong, this season is no longer the results from last season.

God will always bring a new season into your life with the right people into your life. Apparently, if you don't let the wrong ones go, the right ones will never come along. A true friend lets you try to do things on your own. He or she will never oppose what you want to fulfill or add to your life if having value is part of it. That is why you do not need people in your life that disable you to function effectively. You need ones who will enable you to function. You can't rely on other people to carry you when you should be able to carry your own weight. You should know that God has put something inside of you that no one else can take away. Through prayer and reading his word, he conditions your heart to never surrender in times of duress. He channels through you a power to be driven to accomplish your dreams and purpose in life. Your destiny with him matters more than any destination you reach in this world.

He will never give you the desire without giving you the ability to accomplish that desire. This is your time. This is your moment. What you value in the moment with power makes it transcend into another moment with momentum. You may have some limitations and setbacks now, but your limits and setbacks will not last forever. If you lose sight of what is in front of you, you will miss what you intend to accomplish. If you let go of what took many years to build, you will lose value in the treasure you have stored in your heart. You don't need to go through anyone else to hear their voice when God's voice is all you need to hear. What is important now is not how you start but how you will finish. God adds value to your life by trying to take you to a new level that could make a difference in your life when all the other ones have failed to make a difference and add value to your life. He puts promises in each one of our hearts to let us know that nothing can happen before its time. He continues to add value to your relationship that many people can't add to their own lives.

*If you are not with me, but you are for me,*
*you should bring out the best in me.*

—UNKNOWN

**Attitude of Expectancy**

It's not over until God says it's over. You are only defeated if you let life change the face of who you are and the name that you have in this world. You only lose when you feel you have nothing left to live for. You can only continue when you believe you have everything to die for. You have come too far and have been through too much to stop now. You must continue. You cannot die, and you cannot surrender! When you feel like dying, you have to talk about living. God already has the right people lined up in your life, and he will not let you die until your destiny is fulfilled. It is all about having the right attitude that will steer you in the right direction. Don't ever forget what you came to accomplish and the reason you are still living to get it done. Remember, you have a purpose in this world. There is no way he will allow you to leave this planet until your promises and purposes come to pass. The seed that God puts in your heart is a seed that never dies. It is a seed that has a dream that must grow until it becomes actualized. It is a seed that rises in every season to bring justice and satisfaction to your life.

At times, you can't think about the fact that your time is coming; you have to think about the fact your time has already come, and the time to get anything and everything done is now. You have shed many tears in your lifetime, but the time is coming when all your tears will be wiped away. You have faced many disappointments, but the time is coming when all your shortcomings will be obliterated. There will come a time where you will reap in joy and breathe a sigh of relief when all the battles you face will one day come to an end. Only the believer who has the attitude and expects great things to happen will happen.

Your attitude can't be right all the time when some of them shift you in the wrong direction. You have to believe you can do great things so that those great things will happen. Before you leave this earth, you must have an attitude that each day you will be victorious—victorious not in the sense that there are no limitations that can overtake your life, but victorious in the sense that you can overtake your limitations. When you face an impossible situation, you must believe that a breakthrough can still happen. The reason dreams don't become possible is because you don't ask for them in prayer. In the Bible, it states, "You have not because you ask not."

So why not ask and let God work? How do you expect God to move mountains if you don't believe they can be moved? How do you expect your life to be bigger and better if you don't believe he can break through the impossible forces in your life? Sometimes obstacles look impossible, dreams look unattainable, your opponents look powerful, while the rest of your life seems to be spinning out of control. Though that happens, God doesn't put anything in your path if he doesn't believe you will overcome it. He can steer your life back on track when it becomes sidelined by circumstances. You will only get what you want to receive if it is requested with a good heart along with good intentions. If you think bigger, God will act bigger. But if your attitude of expectancy is small, God will not act, and you will settle for what life gives you.

You must release your faith in a big way that is similar to the release of a tidal wave because when the water is big enough, it moves and carries everything in its path. It has enough force to carry everything to shore. No matter how many barriers you place to stop the wave from coming, it will find its way to break down those barriers. You must go in a place where you can tackle your endeavors and make your dreams happen. When you are at the point where you are living a life where you are just getting by, that could only mean you have to change your environment so that your mind-set can change. You have to come to a point where your heart must be ignited so that you can change what has remained the same. You have to do something differently, something that gives you the passion to do something you have never done before.

A few years ago, I remembered hearing the story of a woman named Jennifer who was diagnosed with breast cancer. Having no history of breast cancer in her family, regular visits to the doctor happened to put her in a state of shock when the results came back positive. Two weeks after an annual mammogram checkup, Jennifer felt a lump under her breast, which resulted in her going to the doctor immediately for a checkup. Upon visiting her doctor, she was able to detect her breast cancer early so that she could get the proper treatment in dealing with it. Thinking her life would be hanging in the balance, Jennifer decided to go with proper nutrition and exercise and followed the doctor's advice regarding medication intake to fight off the disease. She clearly knew time was of the essence in dealing with something that was aggressive and invasive. Thinking positively was her only weapon.

Speaking positively to herself allowed her to believe her life was not over. She did not focus on death; she focused on life and living it again. The positive attitude that she had toward the disease gave her hope that she was not going to stop fighting until she was able to overcome its attacks. Suddenly, within weeks, she made a dramatic recovery with an incredible turnaround time. All the treatment, exercise, and dieting regimen proved to her advantage, but not as much as her incredible attitude toward the disease. Ultimately, it would be the result from it all that allowed Jennifer to make a full recovery. Just being positive alone allowed the healing process to generate quicker results than any of the regimen she was taking to treat the disease.

Even though Jennifer was fortunate to fight off the early stages of cancer, other women had battled with issues where they were not as fortunate as she was fighting off its attacks. Brenda was thirty-eight years old and realized her body was going through a stressful period. She worked long hours, had three children she needed to care for, and had classes that she needed to study for to get her degree. All of the responsibilities she took on had caused her to get sick often.

In spite of a decline in Brenda's immune system, she continued her normal everyday activities. After many weeks, all of that came to a crashing halt when one day she woke up and noticed that there was a lump on the side of her breast. She went to the doctor, and the doctor diagnosed it as a cyst. Brenda didn't think it was serious. After all, the doctor didn't believe it was cancer causing, so with time she felt that it was something that will eventually go away. Apparently, two months after her doctor's visit, to no avail, the cyst got larger. The outcome would lead to Brenda going to the doctor to get a second opinion. She went to another doctor where a biopsy and sonogram were done only to notice that she was in the final stages of breast cancer.

The result caused her to immediately have a mastectomy, which resulted in her also getting chemotherapy and radiation treatment. She lost a part of her body, which destroyed her confidence in how she used to see herself in the mirror. Her new self-image made her feel that her husband may look at her differently and may not be as attracted to her. She was ashamed, feeling physically and mentally destroyed by what the disease had done to her body. Aside from the mastectomy, Brenda suffered hair loss and other emotional symptoms from having done chemotherapy and radiation treatments. It seemed that Brenda's life was slowly collapsing. She had no formula to put it back together again. All the circumstances that resulted from the treatment she was getting made her emotionally drained. In a matter of weeks, she aged, worrying if she will be able to survive what the disease had done to her.

She had gone through many days crying, suffering, and feeling sorry for herself. No matter how hard Brenda tried, she was unable to change her mind-set for the better. Her vision in life could not take on a new perspective as she was defeated and hopeless by the hands of the disease. Her attitude of expectancy became so negative that she no longer had control of any of the circumstances around her. Brenda's husband, who stood by her side through it all, remained positive toward his wife's situation.

He never gave up on her. He continued to love and support his wife and told her to never stop believing in herself. After more than a month, Brenda would wake up one day to have a different light shine on her. This light allowed her to appreciate life more, knowing that she can be taken away from it at any minute or second. It became an important moment for her which allowed her to see that the time to live her life more than ever is now. She moved on from all the pain and regrets she had in the past. Knowing this, there was no reason to be sorry about something that she did not have any power to change. Once Brenda's attitude started to take a different turn, she saw a remarkable turnaround in the treatments she was getting. It took only a few days before she began to see her hair grow back. She got out of the house more and would spend quality time with her family. Ultimately, it all led to her no longer feeling sorry for herself.

She decided to be more in the company of others and to express all the pain that she had bottled inside her heart. All of a sudden, what almost looked to be a lost cause in the eyes of other people, where someone was buried by life, turned out to be someone who took on a powerful comeback attitude to allow herself to rise again. The disease and its treatment had taken a dramatic toll on Brenda as she felt the need to isolate herself from others by finding ways to cope and come to resolution with all the emotional pain she was going through. The decision, however, to come out of herself allowed her to be more active, which overall strengthened her confidence and attitude toward life.

Brenda began to see her life in a way she never experienced it before. She now believes that there is no possible condition that will attack her that is not going to make her feel she has nothing to live for. The instant change was like a switch that was flipped, never to be turned in the opposite direction. Brenda decided she is not only going to be a survivor in life, but she is also going to be the one who thrives through it. She wants to be one who will share her stories with other women of her ability to overcome challenging situations by having a powerful and positive mindset. All it takes is changing your mind-set by having a positive attitude toward expecting the best out of life, even when the worse things happen.

Surely, Brenda and Jennifer were ordinary women with powerful mindsets. They used their conditions in life to channel an energy that changed their circumstances for the better. Everything you desire to do in your own life is in the very state of your mind. It shows you have to have the ability to control what flows through your mind. So why not let your mental state flow and let your experience in your mental state and life transform? We get what we focus on. If we don't focus on change, nothing changes. If we focus on the negatives, we will never get the positives. Sometimes you can't change the quantity of your life, but the quality of your life is what will ultimately change. Life is not an outcome but a process that produces how the outcome will be generated.

We feel good for a moment. Once that moment comes to an end, you control how you will feel the following moment. Hence, feeling good is a state of mind and a state of emotion where happiness is in a state of mind and a state of what you think and how you think. Change the way you use your mind, and you can change the level of your happiness. No matter how impossible your reality may seem, nothing will ever happen if you are not breakthrough-minded. Only the ones who have unstoppable minds can break down and break through any situation that tries to overtake them. No moment becomes a challenge to them, and no feat becomes impossible to attain in that moment as they have equipped themselves with a mind-set of positive expectancy that produces possible outcomes.

*The inside is what you give to the world.*
*The outside is what the world gives back to you.*

**Moments Create Choices**

Every moment in your life was meant to create a choice for better or for worse. Remembering and capturing the moment helps you to recall groundbreaking experiences that have changed and impacted your life through a series of challenging times. Whether it is the day you decided to change your life forever by walking down the aisle in marriage, a significant and life-changing surgical procedure, funeral, traveling to a foreign country, or the birth of your first born child, each situation that gave rise to the moment you are in is intended to last through other moments or intended to later on be denied or to complicate your life as it progresses. All you can do is make a choice in the moment that will forever add meaning to your life.

All you can do is speak the words that will change your destiny and align it with what is meant to bring justice with other actions that was never meant to be denied. Words are good, only if they are used to change your situation for the better. Every word you speak is spoken in a moment. If moments are used to change your life, then you need to use the words to change the challenging moments that come into your life. There are moments that channel different types of emotion that make words come out in ways intended or unintended. What are the voices that you hear in your relationship? In a moment of anger and emotion, do you hear words that trigger peace and harmony, or do you hear voices that want to destroy anything that someone is trying to mend. What are the voices you hear that compete for your attention? Are they the voices that steer you in a positive direction, or are they ones that lead you astray? Can the voices you hear be the voices of good over evil or evil over good? No one knows exactly at times when a moment calls for him or her to create choices because sometimes the moment is so strong with an emotional person that choices never get created.

You have to be greater than the choices that you create. People can't rely on choices to fix their anger when they rely mostly on their ability to attack the other person to resolve their emotion. Some people fail to realize just how important their words are to others in a relationship. Words are so powerful that it allows you to call what you want to happen in your life, and they are the same ones you speak what you want to call out of your life. People should not call things that are not, unless they are spoken for what they should be.

Obviously, the same sun shines on everyone, but everyone receives its light differently than the next person. The same wind also blows on everyone, but everyone receives its wind differently than the next person. The desire is in us, but at times we don't know what we are seeking through that desire. The fire is inside of us, but at times we don't know how to ignite it and keep it burning. The switch is also inside of us, but many times we fail to flip the switch. When we focus on the right things, we move in the right direction. When we focus on things we don't need, we move in a direction that leads to nowhere. It is time to let go of the battle we face. Life is too short to carry things we don't need.

When you go around feeling guilty and condemned, you lose your passion and your power. Spend time thinking about what is not right so that you can make choices in the moment that will be right. You made a lot of wrong choices, but in turn you will make a lot of right ones. You have the power to turn your life around when it spins out of control. Don't live defeated and discouraged. Don't beg anyone for a second chance, when you have to believe you are already destined for a greater chance. Keep moving forward in life without condemning yourself when situations in life pull you backward. When you understand your position, you can change your condition. When you condemn your life, you condemn your future. The one who wins is the one who knows what to do when trouble comes. He or she always has an answer when at times it seems there are more questions than answers.

The desire is in us, but at times we don't know what we are seeking. What you send out in words is what you feel from within. All the moments in your life create choices in where you are now and how you desire your life to be lived. If none of the moments in your life mattered, you will not be imposed to make any choices that will change your life in other moments. If you didn't make choices to be in specific moments of your life, you will be a person lacking purpose and fulfillment. You have to assume the best to expect the best. You have to see the best in yourself when no one else sees the best in you. You can't be hard and self-critical because when you criticize yourself, you criticize God's creation. You have to challenge yourself until you get what you want. Satisfaction doesn't mean settling for little; it means settling for what you want.

You will experience timely downfalls, and you will also go through impossible situations in the moment, but the more circumstances you go through should make you continue to rise higher than you ever been raised. Be happy with where you are, but don't be satisfied until you get to where you need to be. People constantly fill themselves with doubts not knowing what the future holds. These are the very doubts that consist of marital endurance, household payments, debt freedom, career choices, weight loss, or self-fulfillment. It seems that for every doubt that one has in the moment, the only way to conquer and override the doubts that one has is to combat each of them with faith. Look at how children are in every moment of their lives. Children are always happy; they don't remember yesterday because each day is a new day to them. They are happy to be alive. They celebrate each day and know that every day is a gift from God. You choose the day that you desire to have ahead of you.

How you live your life is totally up to you. Not your circumstances, but the choices that you make to deal with your circumstances will determine your true element of character. After all, happiness is a state of condition. It will never fall on you. Happiness is a choice, while misery is also a choice.

When you wake up in the morning, it is up to you to decide what day you will have. People normally have what they need to be happy.

They have the income, relationships, awards, and praises from others, but when all of it is lost, just how happy can they be in life when all of it is gone. No matter how much money one has in one's relationship, it will not be the only tool someone needs to use to connect to the heart. The mind finds ways to make money, but then it is the heart that will determine how that money is spent. Money can't last forever, and just as much as it is breakable, so is the heart. The heart is not intended to outlast all the emotions in this world. There will come a time when love will fail and be put to a serious test to see if it was meant to last. When it comes to relationships, it doesn't matter who you love; what matters is how you love. When it comes to money, it doesn't matter how it is made; what matters is how it could be used to make a difference in the lives of others. Money may have a place in many people's mind, but it is love that should have a place in everyone's heart. When you can appreciate and accept the person for who he or she was intended to be, you will realize that you are no different from the next person, who has to be willing to accept that person for his or her strengths and weaknesses.

*Life is not an outcome but a process that produces how the outcome will be generated.*

## Know Thy Neighbor

It is very evident how people can live in the same neighborhood for months and years and not know who lives next to them. How many of us can actually say that once we move into a neighborhood, we familiarize ourselves with others and share our hearts with other people? How many of us can say we knock on other people's doors and introduce ourselves and open our lives to them?

The truth is not many of us are wired that way because I will be the first to tell you that I am guilty as charged for living in quite a few neighborhoods in my time without making a concerted effort to know my neighbors. It is amazing how people like you and me can live comfortably in a place where we know very little about others who don't also allow others to know too much about us. You, just like me, have had a habit of being barred from other people because as individuals, we feel safe being locked away and sealed in our own world.

When we leave our homes, it is easy for us to walk away and return on a daily basis, having no interaction and impact on the lives of others in our own community. We never have a voice because our voices have never been heard. We never make a difference because we don't believe we have that capability to turn someone else's life around. Apparently, if only you give yourself a chance to discover and meet the people who live next to you, it will amaze you to hear the backgrounds and stories some of these individuals will share. You will be impressed to see how your journey in life may be no different from theirs with the struggles many of them have had to go through.

Amazingly, I heard of a story of a couple who lived in their neighborhood for five years and did not realize there were three people who lived next to them and on opposite sides of the street who were battling with cancer and was dying of old age. It was not until this couple decided to come out of their shell when they started to share their testimony with others in their neighborhood of how God has changed their lives that they now used that missed opportunity to be more supportive and serving to those individuals.

Incredibly, as a result of giving more to the persons with cancer and the young lady who was in her late seventies, they received their own blessings from God. It's amazing sometimes how devastating news have to erupt before we know the people who actually lived next to us. The only time we even make an attempt to look out our window is a time that some dramatic event is taking place right before our very eyes. When a building is on fire, someone has gotten his or her house burglarized, or a person is shipped away in an ambulance, it seems no matter what news we hear, that is the only time we acknowledge who lives next to us. At that time, it would have already been too late; the person's life could have already been claimed, and you could have made a difference before any escalated tragedy occurred. How inspiring is the fact that you could make a difference in other people's lives, and you can also use that opportunity to help them make a difference in your own if you open your heart and mind to them.

I was no different from you when I moved in a neighborhood because I was an individual who oftentimes expected no one to share his or her life with me because everyone, in my opinion, has a reason for why he or she deems it appropriate or inappropriate to open his or her life with other people. Indeed, my mind-set and my heart changed toward others when I became a Christian. I now saw the importance of opening a life that has been closed to people for many years. One important fact that is essential is people in the world need relationships, and if their lives are to be based on the connection they can have with others, they need to step out of their doors and open their lives with other people.

## Moments of Calm

It is hard to imagine that I spent many years fighting for my marriage. When I look back, I can't believe all the years that have gone by went by so quickly. I knew that I could not be all that I wanted to be for my wife, and she could not be all that I wanted her to be for me. I fought for a relationship that has served its purpose of challenges in the world. For every challenge I faced, I fought for something that made me believe I had every intention to overcome it. It made me remember the commitment I made when my hands joined hers in marriage.

It will be a commitment that symbolized two people's undying unity and love for one another. It would become a unity that would outlast any unbearable condition that could tear it apart. It would also be a power that would become unbreakable in the world. I would see through the midst of it all, other people would go through the same trying moments that spiraled their relationship out of control. I knew in spite of what I saw, I had to have an inner peace that would always bring my relationship back into balance. I looked at other couples and wondered, *What exactly would make my relationship different from theirs?* All this time, people would tell me that I was right for her, not knowing how much she was also right for me.

All this time, I would be fighting, not knowing what I was fighting for. When the arguments would erupt, my mind was always bent on being right. When in actuality, it would be more focused on the negatives than the positives. I needed to gather my senses. When a war was taking place on the outside, I needed to find peace on the inside. It was a peace that seemed inconclusive at times, but it would have to be a peace that mended the pieces of a heart that had been shattered time and time again. Even when everything around me kept breaking, I still would have to find a way to overcome the impossible situations to make everything possible in my life.

Being in the front is never easy, but being in the middle to try to get to the front is more challenging. When circumstances arise, my heart leaned toward attacking that circumstance and shutting it down. I learned that you can never rush into anything. I have to have a method for my attacks. I have to have a plan for my emotion and a plan for my actions. I have to realize it is not about harm, but it is about harmony. It is not about happenings, but it is about being happy. In moments of disruption and disharmony, I must do whatever it takes to stay calm and not attack. It is so easy to retaliate when someone has done you wrong. Love is much harder to fix when someone keeps breaking the pieces that have brought it together. In my emotion, I retaliate without any means of resolution that does not bring about any unification or change. I attack because I feel I can no longer put up with being put down. However, I am brought down to more than anything else with my attacks because I let my emotions get the best of me.

After all, people only attack when they feel they want to make something right for what has gone wrong. However, if I continue to attack with full intent, I will get what I am aiming for. If my target is respect, I will keep hitting it every time until I get it. If my target is to fight for my marriage, I must be willing to do whatever it takes to make sure it could stand the test of time. I just have to see my emotions are not everything. I have to be able to overcome my emotions so it does not put me in a state of frenzy and war. There is always another way. If I know what is right, I will build what is right. When I build what is right, I will do what is right. I can't change anyone's heart because only God can change someone's heart. If my relationship was destined to last, it will not be judged by others, but it will be judged by God. If you want to go fast, you go alone, but if you want to go far, you go together. It takes humility to have great relationships, and it takes a lot of pride to also destroy what you created.

When nothing matters the only thing that should matter is what you want in your life. What you want in your life must be called in your life. What you want to last, you have to make the effort to make it last.

Having divine power is using everything that God has given you in life to transform your relationship for the better. Can you singlehandedly use that power to transform others around you? After all, a good man brings out all the good that is stored in him, while an evil man brings out all the evil that is locked in him. If people, like you and me, desire to see the best, we have to strive to bring out the best in ourselves.

There are relationships that people have been in that has taken so long for it to grow, making people like you and me feel paralyzed. Is it not time that we get well? Is it not time that we seek life over death? In order for us to grow, we need people in our lives, not circumstances. We need moments in our lives, not momentous breakdowns. We need to have the strength sometimes when all the power is gone. We need to have the vision at times when no one else is able to see. We need to have the dream sometimes when all the nightmares make us feel we no longer can dream. What used to be there is no longer in the same state you left it. Once someone pulls the trigger on a pistol, it fires with enough force to leave a mark on its intended target. It creates a moment of war that if only the trigger is held, it would create a moment of calm.

**Moments of Retribution**

What may be so easy for you could be so hard for other people. If you don't persist and go after your dreams, it will never happen for you. Your dreams will be lost, and it will be found by someone else. The cause of failure in people's lives is the reality they feel when they believe their dreams are defeated. If you don't pray, believe, and fight for what you want, your desires and dreams will never come true. Don't ever think defeat, or you will be defeated. Don't ever be in shock, or you will stop moving. You choose the battles you want to take on. Sometimes when you try hard, you die hard. And when you live fast, you die even faster. When you are too slow, you are left behind. You can get the rewards, but it makes no difference if your rewards can't impact someone else's life in the moment they are achieved. It goes to show each and every moment in your life counts as a memory.

The time you spend with your family and the words that you live by day to day must be maximized and used wisely to carry and propel you for the next day. You choose your own reality. In your emotion, you must know what is best. You must make your life count for something. If it counts for nothing, how will it ever amount to something later on? A while back, I read an article about a youngster in high school who dropped out of school never to graduate. In and out of school, Dalen had many emotional problems, which served his punishment for suspensions and run-ins with the law. He faced plenty of uphill battles with being a foster child since he was nine years old. His parents were drug addicts who often felt they would do everything in their power to feed their habits. They had no care in the world for their son. School officials and child welfare thought the best possible choice for Dalen was to be removed from his home, and the agency found a place for him with foster parents where he could grow to become a much more positive person in life. No more would Dalen worry about where his next meal would come from and if he was going to have a roof over his head. The action taken was a good move for the agency but one that proved to backfire as Dalen continued to struggle with neglect and emotions from his past.

Under the guidance of his new foster parents, Dalen could not sustain a proper behavior in school as he still got into many fights with other children, which led him to receive poor grades and additional counseling for his emotional outburst. Dalen was bothered. He had a troubled past that seemed to follow him everywhere. He couldn't shake off the past hurt of being subjected to neglect by the only parents that he had in the world. He could not face the world because his parents were not able to face him and be an example to him. He did not have a mentor or a friend to rely on that could guide him in all his troubles. It seemed with all the situations that Dalen had gone through made him reach a crossroad in his life that had him at the point of thinking suicide.

Dalen reached fourteen, and the problems he had ranged from gang violence, stealing, to vandalism of other people's property. It seemed that he was influenced by the wrong crowd. The people he thought were his friends only cared about what he could do for them. Dalen's constant trouble with the law made his foster parents question their ability to care for him. He constantly disrespected and battled with his parents to get whatever he wanted. His parents would give him what they could afford, but over time their efforts never proved to be enough. When Dalen reached fifteen years old, his parents made an effort to part ways with him.

They visited foster care services and decided that they could no longer emotionally care for their adopted son. He became too much for them to handle. The couple stated how desperately they tried to work with Dalen to turn his life around, but every time he made one step forward in the right direction, an incident with him and other people on the street would push him in the opposite direction. The foster care agency tried to persuade Dalen's parents to give him another chance. They will provide counseling and any help that would improve his behavior over time. Dalen's foster parents believed that he was unchangeable. He had way too many emotional issues to resolve and too much hurt from his past to overcome. However, after two weeks of letting him go, feeling sympathetic and hopeful for Dalen, the couple had a change of heart and decided to give him a second chance. All would go well with their decision. It seemed that Dalen took a step in a positive direction. After four months, Dalen's parents grew content with his results. However, in the sixth month of his turnaround, they would pay the price for their decision.

During that time, Dalen, who regained his parents trust, turned against them by stealing valuables from their home. Unable to deny his actions, Dalen had hit an emotional point in his life when he was caught stealing. He couldn't understand the motives for his behavior and what led him to having many timely downfalls. Unfortunately, his actions proved this time to be all that his parents could take, and he was now in the custody of a foster care agency that needed to find a place for him to stay. Dalen, at the age of seventeen, reflected on his past life, and all the times that he was given a second chance were repeatedly blown with no opportunity for advancement.

At seventeen, he dropped out of high school and found a full-time employment working off the books for a retail store. Dalen stayed at the job never to attend college but used whatever opportunities he received to prove that he can become someone successful in the world. He was punished many times for his wrongdoings in the past. Every moment that Dalen had was a moment of retribution instead of a moment of recovery. He could never seem to fight the battles that he could win. Whenever he fought, he used the wrong weapons and a mind-set that constantly rebelled against life. He was not compatible with anyone. He didn't have the antidote to overcome his lack of interpersonal skills nor did he have the medicine to rise above all of his defeats. When people tried to connect with him to give him the help and support he needed, he turned against them. In the next few years, Dalen would turn twenty-five years old, and his responsibilities placed him in a managerial position after working for several years in a sales and cashier position.

Life seemed to take a different turn for Dalen. He learned his job quickly and suddenly became someone who gained the respect of his fellow coworkers. This moment and reward that were given to him in that moment proved that it may very well be the turning point in his life that may rewrite all the failures and disappointments he faced in his past. He worked hard to get into a position that many people did not believe that he could achieve. The one important fact was how Dalen was going to maintain it by doing a good job as a manager. Only time would tell what will be the result of his job performance in that position.

After eight years of being with the company in a sales position and seven months of being a manager, Dalen took on the task that dealt with managing difficult employees, attending meetings that outlined the company's goal, and maintaining the standard of principles and projected vision the company set forth. All of this became too much for Dalen to handle, so much that he could not see himself working as a manager in the long run. He started to feel pressured and stressed with the workload he was getting as a manager. Slowly, but surely, his feelings of maintaining his integrity in the position began to chip away. It seemed his very desire of maintaining his status and functions of a manager burned away, and in his tenth month as a manager, Dalen started to sell many of the store items illegally to customers where the money he received from them was pocketed for his own benefit. Eventually, he got caught and was fired from his job. It proved that Dalen's biggest threat was himself.

Dalen reached a pinnacle in his life, and as quickly as he reached it, he was not mature enough to sustain it. He had an uncontrollable urge to steal and had no care in the world to create choices that would enable him to have a better future. It seemed that one moment of mistake created other moments of misery. His actions all but had a deleterious effect on him, which led to his timely demise. Instead of having moments of honor, he destroyed it to have moments of retribution, which all but stemmed from the pain and emotions he could not erase from his past. We, too, have been like Dalen in some way, stubborn to change, defiant to forgive, and unwavering to make a difference in our lives. When a voice cries out from within to make a decision, we shut it down with our pride and egotism. As a result, we never make solid connections with others because of the conflict that we are dealing with in our own hearts. We struggle to overcome because we can't find a way to battle through our own challenges in life.

Thus, we allow it to follow us, and instead of making a difference with our lives, every moment that we have to shine is a moment that creates a dark cloud upon us that shunts us from achieving anything possible that will give us light. The constant battle of the grudges and pain that we have as individuals has taken control over our lives to the point where it completely destroys our future. Thus, it is time to let go of all indifferences that you have had with your life so that you can make a difference with the one you are living now. No longer will you experience moments of retribution, when you have all the power and potential to create moments of recovery.

*People are never satisfied just climbing the mountain or just playing the game. Their satisfaction comes when they have won the game and have climbed on top of the mountain.*

**Love Never Disconnects**

Love has an important meaning in everyone's lives. Just as much as love is hard to find, some people will do whatever it takes to keep their love from falling apart. Even though some people will fight for their love and what it means to them, not everyone will win the battle of fighting for his or her love and keeping his or her love connected. Some will go the distance, while others will wait to see how their hearts progress throughout the hardship that their love brings. I realize that if you want your love to last, you have to fight to make it last. Nothing will ever last if you don't put the time, energy, and faith into making it last. In life, it is easy to start something, but maintaining what has been started so that it can cross the finish line is the toughest test that many people face.

After all, nothing stays the same in a relationship. The heart and mind constantly go through changes in a relationship where they absorb pleasure and pain and make decisions that matter the most to them. Keeping the mind and heart in place is never an easy task. Think about all the situations that a relationship must go through just to keep life running at a satisfactory pace between two people. It is a challenge to keep something special, but it is more rewarding when you keep it from falling apart. It is all about what you want, how bad you want it, and why you never will let it go. In the moment, no matter what trials you face, you will not allow anything to destroy what you have worked so hard to build.

Sometimes your relationship must be tested to see if it is real and if it is meant to last, even if it means you being separated from your partner so that time will heal all the pain and conflict you have gone through in your relationship to bring you and your partner back together again. For sure, tragedy creates separation. However, it also leaves us with a memory of what is lacking in our lives when the moment leaves us with special memories we can never seem to erase.

There are so many people who have separated only to realize they are not complete without their true partner in life. Tragedy often comes at a moment you least expect it. It comes at a time you are emotional, when you dare to take revenge from the pain you experienced in your relationship. It comes with you believing that you are better off with someone else when in reality you can never be strong on your own.

Once a strong foundation is built in any relationship, the love that it's built on can walk on breakable grounds, fall through the cracks, and find a way to rise and walk again. How many times have people separated only to find themselves falling in love again? Love does have a disconnection, but when two people remember that they have something missing from their lives, it finds a way to reconnect all over again. It may take on tragedy. It may experience conflict, obstacles, hardships, and grueling circumstances; but when it is defined, no other source or force can cut into it in making it fall apart. It fights through the duels and withstands all the tests from the testament it was built on.

There will always be something telling in life that will make it seem that two people's hearts for one another can't possibly be divine if it is separated through constant friction and emotion. However, God designed emotion, and it is through our emotions we feel things that are right or wrong for us all the time. Time heals everything that breaks. Sometimes it seems that two people can go their own separate ways, and as they travel on their paths, they find a way to connect to one another all over again. Destiny, then, works their path in life, not allowing any separation to take place but allowing a connection to be fueled by a desire that was intended by all true purposes to be divine.

# LIFE IS A GAME OF INCHES

## CHAPTER 4

**You are either one step away from failure or an inch toward success.**

Life taught me a valuable lesson one day, a lesson that made me learn that you can never accept things the way they are, but you should accept them for the way they should be. It is a lesson that made me see there is no use in changing something that is destined to become what it is intended to become. I should just let it be and let it take its course in life. Personally, I always felt I had to wait for my time to come; and when it finally arrived, everyone else had already gotten their turn. Each moment for someone else was on a late arrival for me. Each time I failed at something, I had to wait to receive a second chance all because my first attempt was not good enough. I had to make a decision at that time to give up or wait for another defining moment to reoccur in my life, not knowing the results it would bring. After my first failed attempt, it would be made clear to me if I should leave something the way it is or have the desire to continue to attack, change, and conquer it along the way.

As a result of it all, I learned that no matter how hard I tried and no matter how many times I kept on fighting, the actions from all my efforts would be separated by a mere set of inches that will be the deciding factor of whether I win or lose in the game of life. All of it would be incumbent on my thoughts and actions of the past, knowing that every one of them has played a key role in making a defining moment in my life special. All the efforts that I ever put forth in my lifetime will make a difference in whether I get to experience a breakthrough moment. If I fail, all I could do is look back and wait for the moment to come again. This time, when it comes, I know I have to be ready to capture it. However, if I should try again, I must ask myself, "Am I one step away from defeat or an inch closer to victory?"

If it means going the extra mile, I will do whatever it takes to fight for my accomplishments and gain the edge I need to gain in life. However, if I fail time and time again at the expense of trying, I will feel that I am in a situation that is already too complicated to fix, and the only way that it can ever be resolved is to leave it alone. It just may not be my moment or my time for my dreams to become actualized. In all my efforts, it would make me feel there is no sense in trying to start a fire if it can't catch a spark. Sometimes no matter how hard you try or how many times you try at something, if it was meant to be, it will allow you to go all the way with it and take you right there to the very top. It is similar to an individual who decides to take on the task of playing a game. When the time in the game is completed, there will be a clear difference between a winner and a loser. You can never win and lose at the same time.

The winner leaves the loser behind and takes on the next stage of his or her life, while the loser is forced to take on failure and learn the raw facts that life has handed to him or her. Each person is given a chance and an opportunity to win at some point in his or her life. Every opportunity and possibility that can arise as a chance for someone to be successful teaches a lesson in life that each individual should embrace. Everyone should be able to embrace life as it is even as graceful and devastating as it may come. Losing may not come easy for the person who tries hard, but for the person who does not try, losing is not painful. He or she is used to losing because winning for him or her is hard work. Individuals who lack ambition are not willing to work hard and go the extra mile, so what matters to them is living a life where they can get by each day with a minimal amount of effort to improve their existence. Consequently, it is painful for each person who tries hard and loses because he or she is desperately trying to find ways to win. Sometimes these individuals want to win so badly that losing in their lives is a direct blow to their talents and self-esteem. Losing to them is a hard and bitter pill to swallow.

After all, winners don't feel they deserve the right to lose because they put themselves in a position every day to win. They will constantly beat their bodies and make it become their slaves to succeed. Winners know in order for them to win, they realize that losing so much has made them stronger at knowing how to win when the moment in their lives decide to give them a second chance. Obviously, everyone wants to come out a winner, but two individuals are never created the same. When both of them go against one another, only one will seize the moment, while the other will let it slip away. Surely, there is no outcome in anyone's life that can always be positive. There will be setbacks as well as disappointments when you decide to go against an opponent. Losing, thus, will make you fail to reach your goals and accomplish a long-desired dream. There is no possibility of changing an outcome once it is inevitable. If you are destined to make it, you will. On the other hand, if you are destined to fail, you will not make it. It's that simple! It is in the moment that your destiny is known. If it is in the moment your dreams are supposed to come alive, it will happen without any force being able to stop it from being born. Sometimes success is a matter of luck, and winning or losing is just a matter of inches. You can be one step away from victory or one inch away from failure. Either way, to get to your dreams, you must put your best foot forward so you have a chance of crossing its line.

If attaining awards and achieving accomplishments by all means create the drive in you to work hard and make endless amount of sacrifices each day, then you have no other choice but to display that type of passion in order to get what you want. Being an achiever and one who could achieve anything in life is hard work; failure is even twice as difficult when you have to experience it time and time again. Searching for an answer, some people have to wonder why their time can't come the same as everyone else's.

Some of them wonder why they have to be the one who work and tries hard only to experience the agony of defeat, while others who supply the same gallant effort find a way to power their way to victory. Life, in turn, makes their efforts feel their labor was in vain because it is unreasonable to try so hard and fall short of accomplishing their dreams. It just shows in the game of life there is a distinctive ability that separates you from the next person when it comes to winning or losing. Winners and losers are separated by what is commonly known as the fine line of gift and talents. The more gifts and talent a person has, the greater his or her chances of winning the game.

If you are on a team and you have more talents and gifts than everyone else on that team, there is a great chance because of your abilities and capabilities, your teammates will be better than they were supposed to be. You will realize the greatness of your talent by the consistency of your statistics when you play against other opposing teams. Every game that is played, your statistics are higher and more consistent than the rest of your teammates. Even though that is the case because of the greatness of your skill, by playing on a team with average players, you will notice that your gift and talents will elevate the other players around you to increase your team chances of success. These players will feed off of your skills and desire to win. They will, ultimately, find themselves winning games they never thought they could win.

Even though your team will win games, just how far can they get without you when you can't pull the weight for too long? Soon enough, you will be faced with the most important game that you play to win only to fall short because no one else's talents are good enough to match yours on the team. As a result, when it comes time to play the game you want to win, you fall short because you were good, but your entire team just wasn't good enough to defeat their opponent. Falling short and experiencing defeat then will make the most important moment in your life slip away. Nothing can overtake the purpose at hand that comes with winning when the circumstances are already set in place. You have to be able to overcome the circumstances at hand so that the purpose is ultimately achieved.

It just seems in life when two people want something the other person has, they will fight till the very end to get what they worked and trained night and day to get. Unfortunately, as much as someone can want something to belong to them, nothing can easily be handed over to anyone. You have to scratch, crawl, and gnaw your way to victory, even if it means sacrificing your time and energy you left on the table to get it. Obviously, winning any task or achieving any dream or endeavor is not easy. You have to continue to push yourself and believe that you can cross the line that separates you from victory or defeat.

> ***Every record that has been made in history was meant to be broken in a specific moment.***

## Claim Victory over Defeat

Losing is not an option, especially for the person who is tired of being defeated. Soon enough, that person will figure out a way to win and keep on winning. After all, you can't keep losing forever, just like you can't keep winning forever. A loser's time will come where he or she will stop losing, and a winner's time will come where he or she will stop winning. In either case, you have to have a relentless heart to never surrender to the hands of defeat. When it comes to victory, there are times when people need a lot of skill and luck to carry them the rest of the way. There are many instances where people are lucky when it comes to being successful. To them, skills are essential because they are linked to performance, while success on the other hand is a matter of luck. At times, skill is good, but luck takes you on a much higher level when you least expect it, and in doing so, it calls for your talents to be elevated.

Luck is important. Sometimes this is what improves your chances in life. Sometimes you need to be lucky when you decide to go the extra mile. Sometimes you also need to be lucky to get a break from all the challenges you have gone through. Having luck almost always has a way to play in that person's favor when the results emerge. Indeed, it is what improves your skill and your chances to get ahead. It is the force that produces the result in moments where miracles are needed. What gives people luck in sports or any activity is practice. With enough practice, your skills will increase, and as your skills increase so does your luck in life to increase your chances of winning. Some people need a lot of skill, but sometimes what they also need to gain an edge in life is a little bit of luck. There are times you can try so hard and miss passing a test by a single point.

There are times when some athletes can also train hard and keep the game close, but when it comes down to the final shot to win the game, that person can likely miss the game-winning shot if luck is not on his or her side. In another scenario, you have to be lucky to be in the right place at the right time when incidents or situations in life happen. Sometimes there are people who just miss life by a bullet and are lucky to be alive.

How many times have you seen a situation on the news about a crazed gunman who decides to take the life of everyone around him? What are the chances that he goes on a killing spree and everyone who is threatened in that vicinity make it out alive? Think about the lives of the families that he will leave devastated by his actions. Even though he loses his mind in that moment, some lucky person can be in the same area and make it through that situation untouched. In other cases, when you are driving, how many times have you come across a tragic accident that has taken place on the highway?

You will see trucks turned over, cars that were impaled, and other drivers who lose their lives to others on the road who drive while intoxicated. You see these situations all the time. Just imagine if you were five minutes or ten minutes ahead of schedule to your destination, how you could be the one involved in those accidents and be tragically injured or have your life taken by someone else's ineptitude? Look at even a track meet where eight runners run the race and when the race starts, in a matter of seconds, all the runners are separated from one another.

When they reach the final lap, two of the best runners are running neck to neck with each other, only for one of them to cross the finish line a few inches more than the other person. It is obvious that both of the runners want to win; however, because of luck, there could only be one winner when the race is that close. Thus, a close race can separate you from a winning moment or a losing one. The difference of one point could also mean the difference between you going forward or being left behind.

Success or failure for many people in the world is all a matter of what is achieved in the closing seconds. Sometimes you feel that in this life you need capabilities to gain an edge for advancement, but what you really need is a lot of practice and luck to be on your side. People can try so hard but miss the mark, and others can try just as hard and make the mark to forge ahead. Your conscience sometimes is the best weapon you have because it lets you know how the game is supposed to be played. The conscience doesn't lie! If you are stuck and don't know how to respond to a situation, your conscience will let you know what is the answer.

After all, after you have failed in the past, your conscience even gets better in time to correct the mistakes you made in the past so you will not make them again in the future. You have worked hard enough for your conscience to give you a chance, and when you are granted the opportunity the next time around, your conscience will let you know you can't make the same mistakes again. I guess this is why great players, when it comes down to making a decision in the final seconds of a game, know exactly what to do to win the game because consistent practice gives their conscience the ability to make the right decisions. You could work hard, be smart, and go the extra mile, but sometimes it may just not be enough to close the deal on being successful.

You must see that if you are ever going to get anywhere, you need to have luck on your side. I am not saying to play the lotto on a daily basis, gamble at the race track, and place your bet on a sporting event. What I am saying is that for anyone to experience luck or become lucky at anything, that person must have consistent practice along with strong beliefs and work ethics with what they are doing. Luck is not only a miracle, but it is also a skill that increases your ability and chances of winning when it is predicated on consistent efforts taken in succession.

*If you had one shot at life, what will it be, who will you become, where will you go when that moment in time arrives?*

## Playing the Game to Win

It is so easy to quit when you are tired. When you have exhausted all the fuel you have and have nothing left in the tank, all that is left for you to do is surrender and wait for the next day to recharge and start all over again. Each person knows what quitting feels like. There is absolutely nothing you can do and can be done when you come to a conclusion that you have lost, and there is no way for you to win. It is very similar to playing a sporting event where the opposing team has dominated you in the game. When you realize that you are too far behind, you may feel you don't stand a chance to catch up and overcome the adversity that has been placed before you. When the clock stops, that is the deciding factor of who moves forward versus those who have to wait for the next game to begin so they can have another shot at trying to win.

Eventually, when the time is over in a game, you have to be either a victim to another person's success or a witness to their downfall. It is easy to be weary and lose heart when you are playing a game that you are losing even though you are doing everything you possibly can to tie and ultimately win it. After all, every game played is played to be won. When you enter into any game against an opponent, he or she has the same mind-set that you have, and that is to prevail and come out the winner. Either way, everyone has a game to play, and that is a game that has to be won when it comes to getting ahead in life. Life changes at you in every moment. There is the first half and second half of the game. Similarly, there is the first and second half of life. Sometimes no two halves can be the same. A team can have a great first half, but come out rugged in the second half of the game. In sports, it is a tale of two halves, one moment crossing into another moment. At times, players on a home team could only hope that their efforts will transcend from one moment to the next, where it goes from the first quarter to the final quarter; however, the visiting team is trying just as hard as the home team to redeem themselves from a moment that slipped away. Playing the game to win is believing that you can win, even though you are losing. Winners just have a comeback mentality that desires to not lose even when the obstacles have been mounted against them.

It just shows that as you play the game, people adjust to the moves and plays the other team is making because they have to continue to find a way to get ahead and keep scoring so that they have a chance to win before the clock runs out.

Think about all the players who play the game to win. You can't play a game well if you have not had sufficient practice before entering the game. That is where you will know and have to grapple with the idea of how useful you will become when the game is on the line, and your ability to make an important play that will win the game. When he or she starts a goal, the next step that he or she has to take is to go beyond it and find a way to finish what he or she has started. Too often, people run a race; but when the race is too long, they eventually get tired of running. Other times, people get into the ring to fight, but when enough punches are thrown and enough hits are taken, they eventually get tired of fighting. Some people even take on the task of completing an exam, but when the exam is too long and the brain has processed too much information, people eventually get tired of thinking, which, in turn, results in them making poor choices on the test. Even when it comes to entering a game, after you have defended your opponent well and have found a way to score if you have no way of sustaining your effort, your opponent will quickly take over because you became too confident in feeling you were winning the game in the beginning, but you could not seal the victory in the final seconds that mattered.

I often heard that the lessons of learning from one's mistakes is not the only thing that one should remember but the lessons of learning how to win and to keep on winning are the lessons that one should not forget. After all, it takes guts to win. It takes heart. It takes character, and most importantly it takes perseverance. If you are ever to see the results you want in life, you must go the extra mile every single day until it is time for you to win the game. That is how the game should be played. It should be played so well that even when you are not in it, as long as you are giving it your best shot on a daily basis, you have every chance to come out on top.

It is all about going the extra mile, practicing and working hard, and staying focused with what you want in life. When it comes time for you to play the game and take the test of a lifetime, you have every capability, ability, and ounce of desire in your blood to believe the driving force in you will not let you fail. You have given yourself enough times and chances to succeed. Sometimes you will even know whether you are capable of winning the game, especially when you have not played it yet. Just imagine what it will be if you never practice, or even if you do practice, you don't practice hard enough, and you have too many distractions steering you in the wrong direction all the time, you will definitely be able to play the game, but you will not possess the skill and talent that you need to win.

In order for you to win at the game of life, you have to approach it on a daily basis as if every single day is your last. You have something special to offer to the rest of the world. The only way it will be released is when you tap into your God-given talents and potential to display what has been given to you. No one likes to see a person who did not come to battle equipped with battle armor. People like to see that you are well suited for battle with the right weapons and weaponry for war. That is the only way you will be respected by your opponent. He or she will know by your levels of skill and talent how much and how hard you practice to take yourself to a point in life where it is not easy for you to lose. When you win, all your dreams count for something. When you lose, all the dreams that you fail to accomplish would have counted for nothing. A great player is one who understands the game, knows how it is played, knows how to take on the challenges in the game, and knows how to win at the game he or she is playing. He or she knows how to make the right plays, hit the winning shot, and use the clock to his or her advantage.

These individuals know what it is like to go the extra mile because they have been doing that consistently, so much that when it comes time to perform, they have enough skill and talent to produce dynamic results. Life, in essence, is played out similarly for many people who are not playing a real game but practicing and preparing for a moment that they have to win. Just imagine the obstacles in people's lives. Every day is a battle for them to make it. Some have to find a respectable-paying job, career, fight for their marriage, dreams, and a future. Life has become one challenge after another. However, in spite of all the challenges, there is a lesson that is taught once those challenges are won.

## Winning in the Clutch

You can't win at all the games you play. Sometimes a game could be played so tightly that it may or may not go your way. However, when the game starts, no matter how you play the game, you play it to achieve one purpose in mind. A person's life, then, is centered at times in winning in the clutch or losing in the closing seconds. In order for anyone to win in the clutch, he or she must be able to use the clock wisely.

Every second counts as he or she must take advantage of the time given to make the best plays to win the game. For example, in basketball, no one really is going to rush a shot that is against so many defenders, unless he or she feels members of his or her team has a chance to retrieve the ball and shoot it again. Think about how many times one has to live one's life by that design where one has to take repeated shots at what one missed the first time so that the next time around one will succeed. If many people see the importance that time has on the impact on their lives, they will take their days a lot more seriously than they normally would by using the clock more wisely.

After all, what matters is how much you push yourself and how much harder you keep trying to improve your abilities by working on your craft to sharpen your gifts and talents in the world. You can be yourself in the moment, but you can be more than who you are and what you want to become when you stretch and push yourself to go even further than what you expected. Sometimes the will to win makes you want to win so badly that your ego takes over and makes you forget about everyone else around you.

When your opponent and the obstacles you face against a team become overwhelming, it looks as if the cards are stacked against you to the point where you believe there is no way of winning. It is so easy to believe that a game is over especially when you are down by a large margin. However, in life and in any sport, you can never stop fighting until you find a way to win. In the midst of you fighting to win, your opponent will still do whatever it takes to not lose. You are a threat to that person just as much as he or she is a threat to you. Both of you are fighting to achieve one common goal. In a battle, when the game is close, someone has to take the final shot to win the game. If he or she misses the shot, he or she has to continue to practice and develop the self-confidence to keep taking it until he or she makes the shot that wins the game.

Isn't that what life is about? Isn't it designed for you to practice in such a way that you get better at what you want to do so that the next time you will not miss any of the shots you take? It is not designed for anyone to give up because it is up to you to persevere until you find a way to seal the deal for your victory. You have to dare to take the leap of faith sometimes and not let fear over rule your life. Fear paralyzes you and makes you believe that you can't win in the clutch. Being hesitant and doubtful makes you miss 90 percent of the shots you want to take. You have to develop the confidence so that you can conquer the fears you have in life.

If you are not confident, there is no sense in even trying. How else will you be able to go on a job interview and pass the interview? How else will you also be able to take an exam and pass one? All the people who have achieved some level of success in life have had to demonstrate a high level of self-confidence in themselves to believe they can achieve success. You can't be fearful and dare to try something if you don't back any of your efforts with strong beliefs. The end result is that you will try but not accomplish much because your level of beliefs did not support the efforts you had behind your actions. If that is the case, you might as well just surrender because it will defeat the purpose to try if you are fearful and faithless. Only the one who is fearless and backs their effort by strong beliefs will not show any ability to surrender and be defeated. They would have come to a conclusion that this life is a game, and sometimes you have to win it in the clutch to stand victorious among your opponents.

There are people who are rooting for you, but just as much as they are rooting for you, there are many of them who are also rooting against you. It is clear that most of the task that you take on in life require you to make clutch decisions and deliver a clutch performance in the moment. If you are unable to produce the type of results that can be delivered in the final moments when it really matters, your life will take on a dramatic turn. Look and examine all the clutch decisions that people have to make in their lives, which will overall determine their destiny and where they will lie in the future.

Why, then, is it so critical to win in the clutch? Answer? Time does not wait for anyone. What you do even in the last seconds before the day ends matters to the value you can add to your life when you wake up the following day. At least you can go to bed feeling that you did not close your eyes without giving it a fight. How important it is to keep doing, keep going, and keep believing in what you are doing to make every obstacle in your world possible. Never stopping because you feel tired but always trying to push in life for the next best thing because you were never designed to be less in order for you to win. You are designed to be more, and as your days on this earth increases and as you get older in age, so should you also become wiser in all that you do and want to accomplish.

Going the extra mile is important; however, hitting the game-winning shot to win it in the clutch matters more to everyone. You can take all the shots you want to take while you play the game, but the most important shot that people remember is the last shot to win the game. That is all the audience remembers. That is all they talk about—how the game was won. That is why you can't believe in the impossible, but you have to make everything in life possible because you must know exactly what it takes and what is required for you to win when your moment to win and keep on winning in life really matters.

*You can take all the shots you want to take while you play the game, but the most important shot that people remember is the one that wins the game.*

## The Art of Perfect Practice

I recall hearing the story of a man who was involved in a construction accident several years ago. The accident resulted in him losing both of his legs. Prior to the accident, Imran was an individual who would run in races against other competitors who would finish in third or fourth place. He would often run in city marathons where it required him to run against hundreds of other runners in the city. Imran was often motivated to keep himself in top physical form by exercising and taking daily jogs through the park. His motivation to qualify in the summer Olympics would be a challenging feat but one that he worked on consistently to achieve. It seemed Imran's life was propelling itself in a direction where he wanted it to lead him into a moment that was waiting for him to seize.

Unfortunately, one Friday, all of that changed on his construction job when he lost his balance standing on a high beam. He fell nearly thirty feet to the ground where he was immediately rushed to the nearest hospital. Upon his arrival, Imran lost a lot of blood and suffered multiple injuries to his legs, arms, neck, and shoulders from the fall. When X-rays of Imran's legs were taken, it projected a bone fracture and a dislodging of muscle tissue where his femur was broken in several places. The doctors had no other remedy to save Imran but to amputate both of his legs to stop the internal bleeding. That was the only solution to save his life. Family and friends aided their support for Imran by coming to the hospital where many stood in the waiting area to encourage and give him the support he needed. In spite of the operation, Imran continued to remain strong.

Most people believe it was his determination of wanting to hang on that made him believe that he would make it out of his situation alive. After more than three months in the hospital, Imran received discharge instructions on his medication intake and range of motion routine to get his arms strong again. Unfortunately, the doctors could not do anything else for his legs other than to provide pain relief through medications and to refer him to a prosthetic specialist to get prosthetic legs. Prosthetics will be just as if Imran has real legs. The muscle and nerve tissues in his body would have to control the movements of his legs where it would be Imran's only chance to walk again. Prosthetics, of course, is something that Imran could not get right away until his muscles and nerve tissue could make a full recovery from the accident. Imran had much more to work on before he had a chance of getting prosthetics.

First and foremost, Imran would need to make sure he has been fully healed, and that his body responds well to all the medications the doctor has prescribed for him. After four months of being on pain medications, and regularly visiting his doctor, Imran was successfully making a recovery. It would take almost a year of getting his strength back in his legs where after much of the pain subsided he now felt the need to not waste any time in getting prosthetic legs to aid his chances of walking again. In the following month, Imran scheduled doctor visits and rehabilitation training to get prosthetic legs installed. In no time, Imran attended a rehabilitation facility where he used it to build his muscles and nerve tissues to respond to the prosthetic legs that were placed on him after the accident. Incredibly, after weeks and many long months of consistent training, his leg muscles started to gain the strength to balance with the prosthetics. Imran was en route to a full recovery.

He took repeated steps where he kept practicing and building on his practices each day. The road to recovery was not an easy one for Imran as he struggled to make his mind and heart become connected with the prosthetic device. Emotions would run high as he kept reflecting on the devastating fall that has left both his legs amputated. It was a matter of will with Imran as he kept on trying effortlessly to walk again. After many weeks of therapy in and out of the rehab center, Imran made substantial progress. Surprisingly, the people who believed that Imran would never walk again now believed that not only one day he would walk but also fulfill his passion to run as well. There were so many days and nights that Imran could have given up and have called it quits. He stumbled many times while in training, but in spite of his falls, he never stopped trying. He practiced every day to gain the strength he needed for the damages in his muscle and nerve tissue. Each day, he was stronger than the day before. As a result, Imran's relentless passion to believe made him walk after several months of trying. As jagged as his steps were, he knew they can only get better with practice. Even though he made an effort to walk, he was still not satisfied because he believed there was so much more that he could do to improve his condition. As Imran's devoted exercise regimen continued to cross beyond greater horizons, he had no doubt in his mind that as he continued to habitually practice to keep his mind and body strong, he will one day run a race that no one expects for him to be in. After days and weeks of practicing walking, Imran's balance and gait steadily improved, enough for him to go on the treadmill. At first, the speed was a concern.

Imran went on a treadmill and set it to a medium speed, which quickly made him lose his balance. He then altered it to a lower speed level where that would be his set speed and practiced on it until he got comfortable with it.

Weeks would pass, and the speed levels on the treadmill would get higher. As a result, Imran, in turn, started to feel comfortable with adjusting the speeds on the treadmill. It was now proven that Imran's body was much stronger than it was before. Each day of practice and not giving up resulted in him running a marathon with prosthetic legs. When an accident nearly destroyed his life and took away his passion to run, he elevated his life through the art of perfect practice, which enabled him to rise again in an unthinkable moment. It took nearly four years of him gaining the necessary strength to regain the mobility he once had to finally run again. He used whatever training he received and participated in a marathon where he competed among a host of other runners. Ultimately, his efforts, strong belief, and arts of practice made him take part in a race many thought after his accident was a mere impossibility. Imran would ultimately compete in the marathon. He would finish the race, but it would be a race that he would not win. Despite the loss, he was able to compete and participate in an event that could have been rendered unattainable because of a tragic moment in his life that could have sealed his faith to make him believe he could never run a race again.

## Competitive Nature

When something happens out of the ordinary, it is almost impossible for it to happen again. There is a saying that lightning doesn't strike in the same place twice. If it strikes in one area, there is a less likelihood that it will strike again in the same area. It is similar to a record being broken in sports or someone capturing a historical moment in his or her life. There is just no guarantee that the same events will take place on the same day for everyone, especially when they are destined to happen one moment in time. There will always be an event that will take place on a different day at a different time with different results. It's obvious that two people can't be created the same, nor can one extraordinary moment belong to two people.

One has to have it, and the other has to leave it behind. Apparently, when it comes to a battle between two dominant forces that fight each other in the moment, where both teams and individuals are evenly matched, they stand as each other's opposition, fighting for a championship or a victory that means more to them than anything else in the world. That competitive nature within them takes over, and the only way to satisfy it is by overcoming all the odds to win. Unfortunately, it would be a task that would be easier said than done. When you have two individuals fighting for a prize and two teams playing for a championship so evenly matched with one another, winning every close game can be the difference in giving you the edge to get closer to your goal.

Obviously, because of the nature of the competition, the battles are so close that a victory can go either way. No person is guaranteed to win because a hard-fought battle gives that individual every reason to lose. Opposition often stares down the face of a competitor, but the competitor must be bold enough to not be intimidated by the weapons the opposition brings to the forefront. Being a competitor in life is all about not surrendering no matter what weapons are formed against you.

That is why each individual should carry that same mind-set and the values embedded in it when it comes to succeeding and not settling for mediocrity in life. As long as you have a competitive spirit, it will give you the edge you need to never quit even when the challenge and the task of overcoming have become too extreme and less likely for you to make it.

*All the talent you have is nothing if there is no depth to your talent. You can score if you have talent, but you will fail to keep scoring if you have not given your talent depth.*

## Chemistry Matters

You must have the mind-set to let some things happen instead of making some things happen. There is never a reason to force something that was never meant to happen. If something is going to happen naturally, it will happen without you trying to believe you have to do something out of the ordinary to get results. Instead, what you should do is let it flow and let the chemistry in it run its course. When you are part of a team that has the same drive and determination that you have, they take on an elevated mind-set when it comes to winning.

In the games of basketball, baseball, football, hockey, and even soccer, every member of that team knows how important it is to make shots in a game that they absolutely must make in order for them to win. Look at the teams that are surrounded by players who are disconnected from one another when it comes to achieving a common goal. How far do you think that team will go when their performance as a unit plays out poorly in the game? If a play is not properly executed, the team will fail to score, the ball will get tossed out of bounds, and players will not properly communicate with one another in the game. The coach can call the plays out of his or her playbook, but when the time comes to play the game, the coach expects what has been discussed in the huddle to take action on the court. A team with the right chemistry does everything that they supposed to do, whereas a team with no chemistry does something entirely different from what was talked about during a timeout. That is why it is important that every action that each member of the team partakes in is all about him or her making a connection with his or her teammates in the game. If there is no connection, there is a disconnection when it comes to winning.

A lack of connection means that a person trusts himself or herself more than he or she trusts others to win the game. Chemistry, thus, is never easy for a lot of individuals to develop. However, it is the key and necessary ingredient for every team to be successful and maintain their level of success. Sometimes it could take weeks, months, or years before the right chemistry develops. Once that chemistry is into place, every new member of that team plays right into the system that team has woven. Each player is interconnected to one another, knowing his or her strengths and weaknesses on the court. He or she knows the spots in the game that will help him or her function best.

Through this, it goes to show that it takes spending time playing alongside another teammate and playing against opponents, which, by doing so, ultimately enables you to learn from your mistakes so that you can become not only better as an individual but also united with who you partner with as a team. One person can have a strong goal to win a championship, but if every member of that team does not carry the same drive, passion, or mind-set of that individual, that team will not make it. I believe for every superstar that played any sport, none of his or her dreams of winning a championship will be actualized if he or she doesn't have the same dream and goals as a team.

Chemistry is thus a vital part of winning. When a team has it, no great player needs to worry about missing pieces on his or her team because when all the pieces fit together, it is just a matter of making all the pieces work and achieving maximum results with its performance. Most times when a team fails, it is a result of poor chemistry, but when they win and they win in special moments to achieve extraordinary results, it is a result of chemistry that has been practiced, perfected, and performed consistently in the game. Having great chemistry is not easy, but when it comes to winning in close games, it is extremely necessary. When a team has been established with the proper chemistry and mechanics in working on themselves and consistently getting better, anything can be possible to achieve for that team. When players on a team gel with one another, the trust is there, the rhythm is there, and the attitude to win is always there.

**Taking It One Step Further**

Each day, you do a little more than you did yesterday. Today, you can strive to make your life count for what you could not have made it count for the day before. All it takes is for you to take one step more than you did the previous day, not settling for what life gave you the day before but what you can do to make the changes your life needs to make now. I personally believe that each of us has a reset button that is programmed at the flip of a switch or the press of a button to reevaluate all of our efforts in the past week and the past year. The problem is not many of us decide to use it so when it is not pressed, we keep going through life not knowing what we need to change. It happens so often that we don't show any improvements in our future because we don't do anything with the present time we are in to change it. Pressing this button allows us to reset ourselves.

We start everything fresh, forgetting all the mistakes we made and all the disappointments that we had to go through in our lives that we have no way of changing. Once the button is turned on, we start off on a clean slate where we can recharge ourselves into restarting our goals for the week, month, and the rest of the year. We don't focus on yesterday, but we focus on what we can do today and the changes that we can make tomorrow. It goes to illustrate you have to elevate your ideas and take your mind and heart to another level. Sometimes when you don't have anyone to challenge you, you must find a way to challenge yourself. You have to push yourself when no one else is around to do it for you.

How many times in life have you seen people fall behind, and they have no way of catching up? They believe that the battle has already been lost before they start trying to fight back. Don't you realize in a war when one side loses a lot of casualties, that side could decide to keep fighting or surrender, but if they surrender, there is no chance that they will ever win. If those soldiers keep pushing themselves to go one step further, you never know how the battle will change. These soldiers can still win a battle they thought they were about to lose. The game you play and the battle you fight changes when you decide to push yourself a little further. You have to be relentless when it comes to doing more than what you did the previous time.

Do you know what it's like to do more than you did yesterday? When you create a project, the second one that you create should come out better than the first one. Similarly, when you write a book, you want to write one that will be better than the first one that was written. When you play a game, you want to keep getting better and better at the game you play. When you start a job, each day, you should be getting better at learning all the systems and functions that is linked directly to your performance. Some people may say the little things don't count, but it is the little things that actually go a long way. After all, life was designed for you to constantly get better.

At everything you do and whatever you aim for, the only difference that will make a difference is the effort you put into each day. You must make every effort to master your talent. If you are stronger and wiser than yesterday, today you will make the changes that will make you wiser and stronger for tomorrow. You have to take on the deeds and embark on all the actions that will make you push yourself to do more than you did the day before. You have to get yourself in a rhythm that can't easily be broken but one that will build momentum that will be geared directly toward the moment. Layer on top of layer and brick on top of brick, each piece begins to pile its way to the top until you build something that is unbreakable. It is similar to a tower that started at ground zero, but with constant focus of pushing yourself, it will create a project that will elevate to the sky. Make each day count, and you will see the results from the labor that you put into making it count.

Justin was one of my special students in class. He was a child who desired to always do right even when others never believed in him. He would make an effort to do the right thing even when other people chose to go down the wrong path. I could tell by the way he raised his hand for every question asked how studious and diligent he was in his school work. He, in my opinion, seemed to be better than the other students who were average. He consistently made an effort to help out during lunch time and received tutoring when he needed additional help on topics he had difficulty with. Everything appeared to be normal in Justin's life.

He did great on test and many of his projects, but as good as his greatness was, it only lasted for one marking period. Suddenly, a moment of change shifted all the momentum he had. As a result, Justin's test grades plummeted. For several weeks, Justin's focus was not the same. He seemed bothered when he would come to class. When the class would be engaged in a group project, he appeared indifferent and isolated through it all. It was apparent that something was wrong. I knew that something happened, but I could not pinpoint exactly what it was. In review of Justin's history, his records show that he did not live with his parents. Although he was in his grandparents' custody, I often wondered what his life was like before his grandparents took the responsibility of caring for him. Though I thought about Justin's situation at times, I felt one day he would overcome what he was struggling with mentally to achieve higher grades in class. Unfortunately, when the grades for the second marking period came around, I found out that he failed nearly all of his classes. It was inevitable that there was something that I needed to bring to the attention of his grandparents in hopes that they can help steer him back on track.

It was now the third marking period, and after a positive discussion with his grandparents, I wanted to see how Justin would react when it was time for him to get his projects in class completed. Two weeks into the marking period, no change resulted in Justin's performance. I could still tell there was something bothering him. When it comes to working on projects in class, he continued to be uninvolved and disinterested in learning. He was not participating as much, and it seems as if he lost interest in school and in life. No one could dig beneath Justin's surface to see what was bothering him. He could never get along well with other students in the class because he often felt that they made fun of the way he would speak. He could never ask anyone for help because he thought people may think that he was not smart enough to take on a task. Justin seemed to be trapped in his own world with his own ideas.

It seemed that as much and as hard as Justin tried before, he was never good enough to be better than anyone else. When he would get his test results returned to him, instead of passing with a good grade, he would always be one question away from failing. If only he would have scored two more points on his exams, he would have achieved a passing grade. Somehow, he was downtrodden and could not figure a way out. Somehow, whatever confidence he had at one time was lost along the way. It's a possibility that he started to believe that all his efforts may never amount to anything. I was determined, at all costs, to find a means to an end to come to a conclusion with all the struggles he was going through. It would be two weeks left of the third marking period, and I decided to meet with him after school in the presence of his grandparents to discuss possible motives for his behavior. At the end of the school day, when all the students in the class were dismissed, I asked him in front of his grandparents exactly what contributed to the change in his performance.

"Justin, do you know why you are here right now?" I asked. "No," he said. "Listen, the reason you are here is because of the grades you have been getting in school. Your grades have been going down in all of your classes, and you are not showing any desire in wanting to get better grades. Do you know how you can achieve better grades?" I asked. "Yes, I know how to get better grades," he said. "OK. Tell me how you can get better grades?" I asked. "You can get good grades by having the right answers in class, doing good on tests, and doing all the homework," he said. "So why are you not doing those things?" I asked. "Well, Mr. Moffatt, I tried to do those things, but I could never do enough to be number one in this class.

"I try very hard, but it's not enough. Someone always gets higher than me on a test. Someone always does something better than me on a project and outscores me all the time. It is not fair. I want to be the best, but you give higher grades to other people in the class. Those people I know are not better than me," he said. "Oh, I see! You seem to be upset about a lot of things in school, especially if it does not go your way. Justin, do you know I like to achieve my own goals in life, but do you know that I can never achieve them if I stop trying? Just because you have something that does not go your way, you can't just give up on it. You have to realize that you can't stop until you get what you want.

"Winning or losing is a close call sometimes. Sometimes you can pass by two points or fail by one point, but just because you fail does that mean you throw your hands up in the air to surrender. No! You can't. You have to keep fighting until you find a way to overcome what you are going after. Your success and attitude toward it are measured by what you do each day. If you can do more than what you did the previous day, you can set yourself up to succeed even when it looks like your victory is out of reach." "Mr. Moffatt, I have done that in the beginning when school first started," he said. "Yes, you did, Justin, but somewhere down the line, you stopped. Let's face it, if you study more than you did yesterday, and you keep that habit going where each day you put in one more minute of studying more than the previous day, you will see the results turn in your favor. I don't believe you gave yourself a chance, Justin, but if you do and have that attitude, you will see a drastic turn around in all of your grades," I said.

Justin took the conversation to heart, and the following week, he came to school still lacking the desire to participate and engage in any of the class activities. To Justin, it appeared that I was still not being fair by not providing all the chances that he needed in terms of being successful in the class. It was not until Friday of that week, a switch went off that triggered a spark in Justin's mind that enough is enough. It seemed he got tired with himself. He got tired of fighting with his emotions and decided that it was time for him to turn the page to a new chapter. It was that day he decided that he was going to fight through all of his struggles and overcome his battles of failing.

He finally came to terms with how he was going to change his behavior and attitude toward getting better grades.

Two weeks had passed since my discussion with Justin, and each day I noticed that he kept making slight progressions. Every day, he seemed to do a little more than the previous day. Whether it was staying five minutes extra after school to ask a question about a topic he was not clear about, or coming upstairs from lunch to set up his classmates' worksheets for an assignment, his level of interest in school had reached new heights. What became an ordinary individual in the beginning of the school term grew to an ambitious student who excelled on all the tests I gave him in science. Each score he received in succession was higher than the previous score. He averaged a 90 percent on all the tests that were given to him. In addition, for every writing assignment and science project he was assigned to in class, he zoned in on completing it all in record timing. Justin had a comeback spirit where he refused to let his emotions through all his efforts fail him.

After successfully making it through the third and fourth marking periods in the seventh grade, he later went on to graduate from high school where his high grade point average granted him admission in one of the top colleges in the United States. Justin's extraordinary work ethics and academic excellence continued to gain higher grounds as he was awarded scholarships and dean's honors for his outstanding performance in college. In all of his endeavors, he is now in relentless pursuit to become a medical doctor who wants to specialize in internal medicine. Justin became a true example of a scholar who kept pushing in life to succeed. He was one who kept improving himself each day and an individual who gained momentum to overcome any margin of failures in his past.

# I CAN ONLY BE ME

## CHAPTER 5

**The Core of My Heart**

Nobody understands me; maybe it is because I am created differently than everyone else. Everyone expects me to be who they want me to be, but I can only be who God created me to be and who I am destined to become. I can't be you, and I can't be anyone else. All I can be is me. I can't be a part of someone else's destiny when a moment has been specifically designed to help me capture my own destiny. I can't be part of anyone else's dream and goals when a specific moment in time arrives to help me accomplish my own dream and goals. Life, in essence, makes me realize I wasn't born to rise in another person's moment other than the one designed to rise for me.

When a significant moment arises, I must be willing to face my challenges and overcome the battles in my life to succeed in that moment so that every other moment is also successful. I have learned to fight my own battles without trying to fight the ones other people supposed to fight for themselves. Each moment must matter to me so that I can use each moment to create a momentum for other rising moments.

After all, there are moments that matter in everyone else's life, so why can't each moment hold significance and matter to my own life? Crossing the bridge to success has not been easy, but I realize that nothing in life is ever handed to you. Once a bridge is created, it has to be crossed; and once a match is struck, it has to start a fire. Each step I had to take, it was taken in stride to help me overcome other steps I needed to take. For every step, I am either destined to cross the line and overcome my obstacles, or I am destined to fall back with no significant improvements or accomplishments from the obstacles placed before me.

Up till now, I should know what it takes to win. I wasn't born a quitter, neither was I born a winner. Everything I had to gain in my life has been and will always be about overcoming an impossible situation. I had to learn from my mistakes when no one else could correct it for me. I had to overcome all the negative forces whenever I would try to keep the positive ones alive. I had to find out on my own all of what makes me fail and the very things that would make me succeed. I had to learn why winning conquers failure and why it makes me forget what failure is and why failure existed.

I had to learn that winning makes me look forward in life, while failure constantly makes me look back at why I have failed and what I will do to correct it. To me, it is proven that when I fail, it makes me remember I did not achieve anything special in the moment. When I win, it makes me remember how special each moment was for what I set myself to achieve. Obviously, winners take the bus, while losers take the long road home. Oftentimes, when I lose, I was left with no choice but to reflect on all the challenges I faced and the mistakes that made me pay the cost for not overcoming my challenges. After much frustration and disappointment, I vowed that I would return refocused and reenergized on achieving my dreams and goals.

That is the only way I can claim something in life that belongs to me, and that is to take it as if it should be mine without expecting it to be for anyone else. Truly, I strived to achieve possible goals with impossible dreams through which I wanted to make a believer out of so many people who thought I was incapable of achieving an impossible outcome. It was only a matter of time before the struggles I had in the past and the present will come to an end in the future. My time was coming. It may not arrive as fast as other people's time, but when it arrives, anything that was not achieved in a prior moment will also come with it.

After all, my moment was closer than my time, and my destiny would be next after my moment was fully maximized. Once my destiny was made clear, time was all that mattered in allowing me to reach my destination.

Once my destination was set, all the moments that failed in my life will be wiped away by ones that will generate enormous success. All the scars that I have had will heal, and all the tears that I had will be wiped away. No more will I suffer in the hands of circumstances that spin my life out of control, but rather I will be controlling the circumstances that will swing my life back into its appropriate direction.

I could not live expecting people to please me knowing that my personality has always been geared to please other people. I am who I am; I can't change myself to anyone else other than who I am supposed to be. I can't change who you are, so how can you change me to be someone else. This is me; this is who I am. You have to accept me for who I am or reject me for who you expect me to be and for who you want for me to become. If I accept you for who you are, why can't you accept me for who God created me to be? I think what some people don't realize is when they live by their wishes, they will die for what they wish for. In the same vein, when some people live with other people, they can get buried by other people's ideas, weaknesses, and downfalls. You get to see the best and the worse come out of them at the same time. The best comes out at the time you least expect it, while the worse comes out at a time you never expect it to come.

The worst, at times, has a tendency to come out more than the best. However, it is sometimes the worst situations that bring out the best in people. When life changes, you will realize with others just how much your relationship with them also has changed. Through people, I am either going to be accepted by them or be rejected by God or be accepted by God but rejected by people. Once you become part of God's world, it is nearly impossible to be part of everyone else's world. The future to me will be more important than the past, but the present to me will make every difference with what I want to accomplish in the future. I should never settle for less. I am more if I want more, and I will be less if I expect less. Apparently, what I focus on is exactly what I will get. Therefore, why not focus on the things that matter so that all the things that don't matter can be weeded out of my life. After all, I have only one life to live, and all I can be is myself to live it to its fullest.

***Your moment may be closer than your time, and your destiny will be next after your moment has been fully maximized.***

## My True Potential

Potential is having a look at something, not knowing what it could become but expecting it to bring the best possible results. Many people will look at others and not know what potential lies inside another individual until time reveals and releases all of the potential that was internalized within that person. Reaching self-actualization is when all your potential in life has been utilized and applied to its maximum capacity. That is why one must know what lies inside one so that it can be unleashed to others to achieve something that is backed by a purpose. Potential is inside all of us. The reason it has not been discovered is because there is no one or force that has the power to unlock it. Potential, by all means, stays in the corner of your four walls until you find a way to release its energy in the world. Once its energy is released, and the power of it gains momentum, it becomes an unstoppable force that surges an individual toward self-actualization.

Attaining self-actualization for anyone is not easy. Self-actualization, to many, is the highest mountain to climb and the farthest distance that anyone can reach. It is only until one climbs and reaches self-actualization that one's potential in life is fully revealed through intense passion and purpose. Personally, I wanted to reach self-actualization, but before I could reach it, I needed to release my God-given talents and potential to the world. It could never be unveiled being stagnant. Potential, by all means, must be activated by motion so that its energy can be channeled through my desired dreams and destiny. Releasing it over and over again would be having a desire that knows no boundaries and having an ambition that knows no surrender. Not knowing how hard potential was and how much time it would take all that mattered to me was finding a way to tap into it and project its energy at all possible cost. Once all of my potential had been exhausted, I would give myself every meaning to achieve and exceed all of my limitations in life.

Achieving a level of self-actualization would mean I would have fulfilled all the dreams and goals I ever wanted to achieve. Personally, I tried extremely hard to reach the highest level I could possibly reach, but various circumstances would come into my life and block me from achieving its possibilities, letting me know it may not be my time or moment to achieve them. No matter how hard I tried to push for it, I kept getting pushed back and pulled away from my dreams and goals. It just seemed that there was a greater force that blocked me from reaching my true potential, and the only way that I would ever stand a chance to see a break through happen is when I break down the walls that have prevented me from making it become possible.

As a youngster, I knew I always had great potential. The one thing that I often lacked was to make my potential actualized. I just wanted to believe that I can reach a point in my life where I can not only reach it one time but also reach it over and over again. I wanted to believe my efforts and hard work were not a mistake, and that they were talents that were held inside of me so that a greater dream can be accomplished, and when that one dream or goal would be accomplished, another dream and goal will also be brought into reality.

Through the midst of it all, it would never be easy because I faced many challenges. The one challenge I had was tapping into the energy and power into making my dreams possible. I had dreams, dreams that made me imagine what my future will be like if they became a reality. I had visions of creating a successful business, visions that would range from being an ordinary student in school to eventually someone who would grow with all the knowledge and experience to rise to a successful entrepreneur. I had an imagination to create a legacy where I can be remembered by millions of people across the world. I had a voice that I wanted everyone to hear, but I needed a medium through which it can be channeled to others. I needed to have the heart to inspire and change the lives of others, but I needed a vision to make that dream possible. I had to be strong, focused, and faithful that no matter which direction I turned I will never steer myself away from my targeted destination. Even at an early age, I was often business-minded with whatever I wanted to do. When it would come to starting a business, I thought of ways to make it happen in every direction I thought possible.

As a youngster, my mind was wired for business, and my motives were geared toward making profits. If I bought something for fifty cents, I would try to double or triple my profits in selling it back to people.

All that mattered to me was making money and saving whatever money I would make and watch it grow. In school, I knew I had potential in my classes, and I strived continuously to set goals that I challenged myself to reach so that I can be the best that I can possibly be in class.

My potential at times arrived at some crossroads when it was thwarted by other people outperforming me to make it to the top. It just seemed that this continued till I became twenty-six years old.

Every task that I ever put my hands to was outshined or outhustled by someone else working a little harder than me. Whenever I would get back my grade from a test taken, I would normally feel that I had the highest grade in the class, only to realize that I would round out to the top five people in class, landing oftentimes in the fourth or fifth place. Most times when it came to writing, I felt the same way. When an essay was written in my English class, and I received my results, it would round out to the top three. It made me feel that whatever I did, no matter how hard I tried, I could never be number one.

My potential would be reached, but it would never be actualized. No matter what I did, it would never be acknowledged as the best by others. My potential, thus, would never be actualized in the sense that it can outshine and outperform others who were also taking on the same tasks that I took on. There had to be something different about me that made my capabilities and talents in the world unequal to them. The only conclusion that I could draw was that they had something that I did not have. I said to myself, *Maybe if I keep trying, one day my potential will be actualized until it reaches a point where it will be fully maximized. And when it becomes maximized, all the efforts and dreams and goals that I once envisioned in my life will no longer be unattainable.*

The problem for me was that it was taking too long for it to happen. One fact that is certain is that life can't be the same for everyone all the time. One day the time will be right, and when it is right, the right action must be taken. I never had anyone to measure up to my potential because I didn't live up to anyone else's expectations but my own. The problem that I had in dealing with my potential was that the nail kept becoming difficult to drive through the wall. One day I will be strong, but another day, I will face a challenge to never finish what I started. It seemed my determination was strong, but my focus did not match my determination at times.

Instead of becoming stronger, I kept getting weaker. I was weakened by distractions and the circumstances that placed limits on my life. I was on a roller coaster ride not ever to see the end of where it would take me. I was left with no other choice but never to stop trying and fighting until my potential was actualized and eventually maximized. It came to a point where I would never stop to believe in myself when no one believed in me.

> ***You must know the full potential a project holds before you take it on otherwise your actions toward it will shortchange your own potential in the process.***

**Not Your Typical Hero**

Oftentimes, I have mistaken the idea of what it means to be satisfied. After I became a Christian, I felt in order to be satisfied, I must be a hero to others by meeting other people's needs in order to maintain lasting friendships in the world. Though there is nothing wrong in being a hero and serving other people, it is the fact that sometimes I would get so engaged in serving others that I lose sight of my own goals.

Being there for others didn't mean the world to some people as it did for me. I could not imagine living my life without doing right in other people's eyes. I had to serve others, meet their expectations, and in turn live up to my own responsibilities.

Satisfaction to me was bending my schedule for everyone. However, what took me some time to realize was that not everyone was alike. What many people should realize is that it is just nearly impossible to satisfy everyone. Sooner or later, you will fall short of people's expectations, and they will also fall short of your own expectations. If you can't meet their needs, along with living up to their expectations, some of them will have a different mind-set toward you. Some of them will expect nothing less from you, especially when you made a promise to fulfill an obligation for them.

Sometimes what you value in a relationship is not necessarily what the next person will value. I have held so many people in high regard without them having any regard for me. Maybe that is the reason for my taste for dissatisfaction at times. Maybe it is the fact that people make promises to me that they could never keep. Maybe it is the fact that everyone expects me to be their hero, and for me to take on the responsibilities of being a true friend when in all true measures, it is nearly impossible for me or anyone to take on that role. Before I became a Christian, I often felt if I was there for some people, then they should return the favor to also be there for me. Some people don't mind that you come to their rescue in times when you need them the most. At any time, they can call your name, and when they do, they expect you to be right there at their doorsteps.

These are the people who know you will surrender to their needs. They are the ones who hate to take no for an answer. They are the ones who expect extraordinary things from you. If you have committed to them before, you have no choice but to continue to commit to them now.

You are left with no option but an obligation to be a hero for them. In some cases, these are the same people who feast on the ones who are weak and the ones who are forever dependent on others. They use your services for what you are worth, and when it comes time to move on, they would not include you in their plans. I know this because people who do not have an agenda will be around others that will make him or her part of their agenda. It is a prime example of how people willingly prey on the weak and take away any possible strength they have left.

It is similar to Randolph, a soccer player who has to leave the game because of a recent injury. In doing so, he will have to rely on each of his teammates to play well enough to win the game without him.

Strength then comes not only in what people feel they can do for others but how they in turn can utilize the strengths they already have to produce dynamic results for themselves.

I know I could never rely on the next person to pull me out of a situation if I have not pulled myself through other situations. I was at a point where I had to face and handle my own challenges before I can handle anyone else's. The objective is, in a game, you must be able to play well enough to combat any circumstances that arise. If the entire team relies on their best player to win, when the time comes to play the game without him or her, they will never find a way to win for themselves.

They will be defeated by their own poor performance and excuses of not placing sole emphasis on how they could perform well enough to win when the time and moment arise.

Imagine being a person who has no aim or direction in life to the point where they don't hold an identity for their own selves in the world. Their mind is everywhere. Their hearts are everywhere, and in the end, they end up nowhere. They can't figure what happened to their lives because they failed to plan the days ahead of them that could have made them successful. These people fail to focus on their individual outcome because they have been focused on achieving other people's outcome.

There are people who will always be concerned with what you can do for them, and in this world, it is only right to serve others with the right heart and mind-set. After all, God called people to serve others in the world, and you should make that sacrifice just as long as you have conditioned yourself with the right heart so that your actions do not cause a strain on other people. Why?

If you have not conditioned yourself with the right heart, how can you possibly serve and give yourself to others with the right intentions? You will be serving people for a good cause, but the motive will all be for the wrong reasons.

**Once a Child, Now a Man**

Looking back, I remembered how special some moments used to be. Moments when I was a child, a child who grew into the world learning what was right from wrong, moments where I also had the intelligence but did not have the power to do something special in that moment. I was on the inside always looking outside to see the different types of people that made the world evolve.

I saw bus drivers, mechanics, tailors, teachers, construction workers, doctors, nurses, and lawyers. I saw every occupation I could have possibly seen under the sun and in the realm of possibilities that existed among them were some that sparked my interest, while there were others that did not drive me to believe my dreams will be fulfilled by their titles and ambitions.

I needed some time, time to discover what the world meant to me and what my life meant to the world. I was much too young to battle through it on my own. However, if I had to get anywhere and be someone, I had to learn to fight for what I wanted in life. After all, no one would respect my ideas unless I become my ideas and bring them into reality. I can tell anyone I would like to be a lawyer, doctor, or engineer, and they would complement me and wish me the best.

However, wishes by anyone means nothing if I don't have beliefs and actions to stand up to my projected desires. There came a time when I would not allow anyone to put a limit on what I can become in this world. Some people will believe that the possibilities to become someone in this world are endless. This is primarily because there are so many titles and professions that one can take on. I can believe in all the dreams and ambitions in my heart the moment they have all been conceived, but if I don't have a plan of action to back my beliefs, my efforts will be rendered futile.

That is why I believe having hope can only carry you so far when hope, in reality, is a fantasy in one's everyday world, unless it is backed by action to become a reality in one's everyday life. I grew older, and as I grew out of being a child, I became a teenager. I became a teen who wanted an identity but did not know where to find it. I searched and questioned it through others without having to define it on my own. I thought maybe people gave me as much insight as they could possibly give me, and when their insights became limited, I had to figure out what mattered in my life must also matter to what I wanted for myself. At times, I looked to their interests, approvals, ambitions, and guided paths without looking into my own desires, ambitions, and line of direction. I wanted to aim for something, but no one around me made me feel that life gave me something to aim for, let alone talk about.

With all the shots that I wanted to fire, I had the guns in my hand but didn't have the bullets to fire the shots. The chamber was cold and completely empty. I could not aim for something unless I had a target for what I was aiming for. I figured time and timing in the world must be different for everyone. The time I wanted to accomplish something in my life was just not the appropriate time for it to happen. I believed that in a matter of time, I would ultimately figure out my destination in life. Because my destination lacked purpose, it became weak in the moment; but I knew in time, it would grow stronger as long as I developed the right passion for it to cross into another moment. I endured my life as a child and passed through a series of moments as a teenager, and now I am living each moment as an adult. Through it all, I saw many young people become successful actors, artists, entrepreneurs, and ones who would win scholarships to major universities.

These individuals had something in life that set them apart from other people. They had an extraordinary skill level that made them special. They had the very things in life that I wished my life was based on. At least if a moment never happened in their lives, they had the gifts to make it count for them at another time. They would accomplish much more in a short span of time than what other people could accomplish in their lifetime. I would often ask myself, *What is it that makes their time and moment in their lives special, while for me I could not make the moments and time in my life special?* Surely, if one moment in my life had enough meaning, it will transcend into another moment that will be more meaningful and dynamic.

Every stage of my life, I took it in strides figuring, contemplating, and hoping for some breakthrough experience. However, in that moment, I will learn that a breakthrough was never possible if my life was not designed for it to happen at the time it was meant for it to happen. I was left as a child who had grown into a teenager to figure out that what I was living through was exactly what was meant for me to go through. It was in an impossible moment that was clearly not my time where my destiny in life could be defined.

Maybe all I needed was to become an adult. Maybe by me crossing through the moments in my childhood, years as a teenager have prepared me for all the steps I needed to take in my life. This may just be what will bring all the pieces of the puzzle together. After crossing through the stages of childhood, I was now an adult left to figure out life on my own. I reached a moment in my life where I wanted all of my struggles to come to an end. I wanted a fresh new start, a start that would erase all the moments I never had into ones that will make every special moment that was lost become born again.

## Letting Go

There is no use in hanging on to the past. I might as well just let it go and prepare myself for the future. There can never be a hopeful future if one is not able to overcome all the setbacks experienced in one's past. It seems as long as one strives to achieve more in life, no condition or circumstance can be permanent for one's future. Chains are not the strongholds. Once the chains are broken, so are the links that bind that chain together. The links are through which the strongholds are connected. Once the strongholds are broken, so does the ability for any circumstance to lose its grip on making your condition in life permanent.

Despite all the difficulties and setbacks I have had, I knew the future will be different from the past, and the painful memories of my past will never define my future. Oftentimes, as a youngster, I was considered an emotional person. I would do right in other people's eyes, but when I was done wrong by someone, it would be hard to forgive them. Sure, I can forgive, but it will be at times hard for me to forget. I held on to the pain without having the power to let it go. People who were supposedly ones that I could trust were no longer people I could rely on. I had to find new friends that I could trust and be there for me when I needed them the most. In order for me to find new relationships, I needed to let go of the ones that kept pulling me down. People who I respected thought less of me when I thought highly of them.

The moment in time was different for me, but it all gave the same result of separation and alienation that I felt in being around people who had different intentions in mind.

As much as I want to hold on to the pain and put everything behind me, I believe it would never help me propel in life if I never found a way to forgive and let it all go. No more would I think about all the promises that were made to me that many people could not keep. No longer will I rely on someone who was not there to pull me through a difficult moment. No more would I be looked down on others because of my profession and the quality of my character. I just felt it was time to let go of the grudges, resentment, and disappointments I had with others and focus on the things in life that would solely matter and have meaning to my future.

I thought about the reality that I will never be blessed if I hold malice in my heart toward others. I know God can't bless anyone who has grudges and unforgiveness in his or her heart. I knew there would come a time I would need to let it go. Sometimes the pain and damage from all the tragedy that took place in my past were so strong that it became hard to overcome it. However, I needed to let go of my emotions and turn to a higher power that could change me into a better person. Soon enough, I would get the power I need to love, which will conquer all the feelings of doubt of not being loved. I would learn what it is to fill the hearts of others without expecting others to fill their heart for me. When I filled the empty space in someone else's heart, the space in my heart also became filled. In the same likeness, the only way a treasure is going to be found in this world is when you make the effort to get up and look for it without expecting anyone to find it for you.

## Fall Early, Rise Late

I have taken many falls in life. The falls that I have taken sometimes made me wonder how I got back up again to continue to fight for what I believed in. I recalled many of them. For one, I was handed defeat when I would lose a race against other runners in school. I would practice consistently against other runners, but no matter how hard I tried and how fast I thought I could run, my speed just was not enough to pass my competitors. I could not outlast any of my opponents on the track.

They often held the upper hand when it came to them being faster and more skilled than I was in practice.

I encountered other obstacles where I could not make the basketball team because my shot selection and ability to gel with other players on the court was not sufficient to get selected. I would make all the shots I needed to make in practice, but when it came down to a game, there were other players who were more skilled and talented than I was. I seemed overmatched by their talents and physical strength, which made me look like the weaker individual. Once again, I felt my talents failed me. Once again, I was left to figure why every time I had a moment to rise; it was another one where I continued to fall. I thought what I had was enough, but I did not meet the mark to exceed other people's expectations. I would often do well on exams, but when I thought I had the highest grade, someone would score higher than I scored to be at the top of the class.

Everything that I desired to do, I had the expectation that I will be number one. I wanted to be first and everyone else to be last. I wanted to come out on top, while everyone else was at the bottom. When people were acknowledged for their abilities, I wanted to exceed anyone's opinions of any doubts they had in their minds about me.

I believed in myself, and I never short-changed my confidence or any of my abilities when I needed to prove myself. I had every intention to succeed because I believed as long as I have a heart, mind, and desire to attain my dreams, nothing can stop me from achieving what I wanted to achieve. It just seemed that no matter how much I try and how hard I kept trying, I took on many falls. But I knew a time would come where I would rise much later in my life. Everyone's moment is never destined to be the same.

Maybe it is your moment to pursue being a doctor; maybe it is your moment to be married, get out of debt, buy a house, and drive a nice car. Maybe it is your moment to rise from all the falls you have taken. After all, every moment that was my moment to fall would also create another moment for me to rise. In every fall that I have taken, I knew the time will come where I will be set for success at a later stage in my life. Obviously, there were so many timely downfalls, but every time I took a fall, I found a way to rise. Every time I rose, I knew a moment in my life would come where I will not fall again so easily. Time and time again, I would fall because the moment never belonged to me. When I thought I owned the moment, it was handed over to someone else that could own up to it far better than I could. Apparently, the light seemed to shine on them before it shined on me. Through it all, I remained positive that my time was destined to surely arrive like everyone else's.

**The Right Time Is Now**

No one, including myself, can ever be a bearer for change if I don't snap myself out of a cycle that repeats itself day in and day out. In this life, it is so easy to be mundane where you do the same things you did yesterday, and you do it until the day ends, the month ends, and the year ends. Suddenly, your life slips right through your hands, wondering where all the times you could have achieved anything could ever be brought back. I got caught in the web many times. I had to realize that change would only come if I expected it to come at the expense of taking action to do something I never did before. I had to break a habit that was so hard for me to let go, which is being in my own zone of comfort. I had to gather myself and think my whole life through and reroute how my mind has processed the information that it has been fed over the years.

I worked at a full-time job, and after work, I would come directly home to watch television, or hang out with friends, only to go back to work the next day and start the process over again. I knew my life was much better than that.

I knew I had to do something I never did before so that when I start it, I can weave myself into a pattern until it becomes a new habit I develop to see change and different results in my life. It was something that no one could tell me; it was just the pain that I experienced in my life that let me know that the time in my life was running away from me.

If I don't catch up to it, the end will be near, and I will never see life the way I would have wanted to see it differently. I was angry that I didn't see what I needed to accomplish any sooner. If I did, so much time would not have been lost. I can't reflect on things that took place in the past that I can't change. Now is the time to make a difference, and there is no better time than now to start with the things I can change.

Each day, I approach it and wake up with a plan of all the things that I need to do that day. Nothing matters more than what I need to do to follow the plan and make it work so that I can adapt to a whole new pattern that is different from the way I have been conditioned and programmed in living on an everyday basis. I looked back and thought to myself, *I really must have been insane to think my life was going to change doing the same things every day.*

That is impossible! No one's life can change if one doesn't expect to create a plan for how one wants it to happen. After all, the definition of insanity is doing the same things over and over again and expecting different results.

I can never get different results with an insane mind-set, but I must be truly insane to think I will get different results living the life of someone who is not driven to desire something different. That is all I needed for my life to be; I needed to flip a switch that has not been flipped in a long time. I needed to stop taking the same route and try going in a different direction so that I can get different results.

# ABSOLUTE POWER

## CHAPTER 6

**Achieve What Never Fails**

There is nothing like having absolute power in this world. Once you get it and maintain it, there is nothing like it! Having absolute power makes you have no weaknesses when everyone is strong. It gives you all the strength to control what you want to do, why you want to do it, and how you want it to be done. Anything and everything that you desire to take on becomes a success, while it is a struggle and roadblock for other people. You will watch others fail, while you find a way to timelessly succeed and exceed in your goals and expectations. You will have abilities and capabilities beyond the capacity of other people. It seems people just respect a powerful person. No one likes to lose, and if you happen to lose consistently, there has to come a point in your life where you have to get tired of losing. For once in your life, you deserve to be in a moment where you can become unstoppable.

Too many times, you have been down and under, not knowing if you will ever rise again. What you don't realize is that God exalts who he wants to exalt and blesses who he wants to bless. Once you are blessed by him, no man can curse what he has blessed. He will continue to scatter your enemies and make you rise higher than the circumstances that try to derail you in life. Everything that you ever failed becomes an absolute success when the right amount of power is harnessed in your direction. It brings forth everything your life desires. It eliminates all the frustration, conquers every defeat, fulfills all the passion, and promises that life is supposed to deliver.

Every doubt and negative thought that ever crept in your mind can be filtered out immediately when you have absolute control of how you want your mind and soul to be fed. Power is the true definition of strength and the ability to overcome and to keep overcoming. Futility is the true definition of failure, which demonstrates no ability to overcome, and living a beaten and defeated unsuccessful lifestyle. Power gives you victory after victory, while the lack of it gives you defeat after defeat. Once you are tired of being constantly knocked down where the hits you take leave you in last place, you make a decision by channeling a massive amount of energy to no longer be second fiddle in the world. For once, you have to be the person that is tired of being dragged along in places that you never expect to find yourself in.

Now is the time that each person demonstrates the ability to wake up and take control of his or her life, take responsibility for his or her actions, and stop making excuses about the things that he or she can and cannot do. You will never stop the rain from falling, the sun from rising, and the clouds in the sky from moving. It's time to overcome and take action from all the frustration and pain that life has caused you to not excel in life. You must push and power your way to your future; otherwise, you will be disrespected and left in the dust. How essential it is to have power and how the quintessential of the lack of it destroys your inner and outer core in life.

When you have enough power, people can hear it in your voice; they can see it in your walk, your talk, and your actions. You will see people get knocked down, but they have the ability to get back up and rise to an extraordinary level after every assault.

Power is indeed an element that one has that enables one to fight back when something tries to destroy one's destiny and destination in life. Just exactly who has this absolute power? Who has the strength to overcome circumstances and get extraordinary results in a short amount of time, while others have to struggle to get what they want? And who has the ability to maintain what has been built for so many years that no matter who comes along, it can't be touched or destroyed? Just who has this absolute power? Answer? Everyone! Everyone has the ability to sustain what he or she has built and has the strength to overcome any situation or condition that desires to destroy him or her. Life sometimes is a matter of choice; however, most times, it is a matter of the example that you can set for others. When a significant moment has come into your life, the only power you can have that can channel it through that moment is to continue to rise and silence all the people who believe you never had what it takes to make it in this world.

## Indestructible Forces

In power, there is no failure or formula for denial. Failure in life is never final because once you work hard for your dreams and continue to chip away at them, you will achieve them at all possible cost. At times, the challenges will come and outweigh all the efforts you put forth, but in spite of what comes your way, you can never take a step back. You must continue to charge at all the forces in your path that dares to break you down and make you fall apart. Some forces are destructible by nature. There is the force that a person's job is on the line because the company is not able to maximize their profits. There are other destructible forces that deal with one's present condition in life.

Destructible forces such as changes in one's health, unexpected accidents, disease, and other manifestations, it seems whatever conditions there are in this world, when it comes to the human body, it has always been susceptible to destruction. Life, income, health, relationships, and all the breakable things in this world are all targeted at some point to come to an end. How, in the midst of all what was just mentioned, can someone be indestructible such that they can take on all the challenges and forces that life throws at them and still have the power to get through one challenging moment after another? Answer? One must find out how to create an indestructible reality such that there is no fear when it comes to overcoming the laws of nature that set out to destroy him or her.

This indestructible reality is a channeling force that can only happen through a greater power than the one you already possess. It is a power that is unstoppable, unwavering, and unchallenged by the complexities of the temporary world that people live in. It is a power that you can find and try to fight on your own, but it will be a battle that you can only win for so long. Sooner or later, you will use your efforts, and those are the same efforts you must continue to employ so that you can sustain what you have built in the past so it can last and continue to be useful in the long run. Power, as far as human strength is concerned, can only take you so far.

Once you decide that you have tried many times but have not gotten where you need to get to, you need to tap into an infinite power—one that will last and give meaning behind the lack of success you've had. Look at the indestructible forces in the world such as the earth itself, which can fall prey to earthquakes, floods, hurricanes, tornadoes, weather-related issues, and natural disasters. Only the people who have already died have no need to worry about dying to any of those trying disasters. However, for the ones who are alive have no other choice but to fall victim to any of those indestructible consequences.

Power, thus, is a great asset that anyone can have. It gives you the ability to protect, the freedom to live, the right to be free, the encouragement to speak, and the talent to rise above any effect or force that tries to overtake you. Even as much power as one dares to seek in this world, power can only belong to those that God wants to surrender that power to. Only if you are able to transfer your energy to him will he transfer that energy back to you by giving you an indestructible and untouchable spirit in this world. It has to come through one force channeling through another force so that the two forces can unite and ignite a higher energy.

> *Lack of power makes some forces destructible in human form, but a massive amount of power makes some forces indestructible by nature.*

## Break What Needs To Be Broken

You are only a slave to whoever your master is. If you have a master to obey, you will follow the instructions to please your master all the time. Once your body and mind feeds into a habit, it becomes part of that habit that feeds itself over and over again until it becomes hard to break away from it. For so long, it is so easy to sow a habit, but later, once people continue to sow it, they have no other choice but to reap the results from what has been sown. How many times have you seen something so devastating that it oppresses people to a point where they can't unlock themselves out of it to create a moment that will ride itself into a momentum for change? Hence, your battle with oppression is summed up in two words: master and slave. The master tells the slave what to do, and the slave does what he or she is told by his or her master. After all, slaves are indebted to their masters. They surrender their power to whoever their master is. A slave is frustrated when he or she can't break free from his or her master's control, so in an effort to be at peace, he or she does what is told by the commands of his or her master.

Unfortunately, when it comes to freedom, some people don't have the power to break free from what oppresses them in life. Most of them have given up the battle to break free from imprisoning themselves to smoking, laziness, being in debt, and other negative conditions that enter their lives. They have become powerless to break the chains that have put a stronghold on their lives from being free. How interesting it is that some people can make a prison cell their own home and be used to it because that is all that they know and see. Outside of it brings no realm of possibilities to change. All they live for is what they feed and feel on the inside. Their lives have been a broken wing without finding a way to fly. The wing has become so detached without having any idea as to how to put it back together again.

If only they could develop the power to find a way to break themselves free, they will no longer be bound to the chains that have limited them in life. If only they use their minds to make a single decision to look inside of themselves of what they need to change so that the outside can also be transformed. They, just like many other people, have not developed that power. Thus, the lack of it allows them to be a slave in life to whoever their master is. The master is constantly at work to oppress the slave. When the slave does his or her duties, the master is still not satisfied until he or she gets every drop of energy and power that the slave has to do other things to serve him or her. Thus, the master has more power than the slave.

The slave never displays a power over his or her master, unless he or she has a plan of attack that will help him or her find a way to break free from the master's control. Life, then, goes on for the slave. He or she has been imprisoned by the master's command and is fully powerless in his or her master's presence. Every day he or she has to wake up being in debt, mistreated, beaten, and overtaken by the demands of his or her boss. It is all because there is no way for the slave to figure out what steps to take in life to break free from the chains that have entangled him or her. As a result, these individuals become oppressed by their oppressors, looking for ways but not having the power to find the ways to make the changes that they need so that they can overcome what has taken over their lives. All in all, oppression is a single word of futility in a moment that one has to deal with in one's life until one finds a way to overpower it in that moment so that it no longer dominates one's life. Finding and tapping into it gives you the power to break free from that moment and other moments of oppression. It is a power that you need to unleash so that your mind can break free from whoever your master is in this world. Look at the very nature of how some people's lives are situated in the world. Most of them are slaves to lenders where they are indebted to spend most of their lives paying off six-figure loans or credit balances. Examine the fact also that many people are trapped in their own world filled with negative habits and life-threatening addiction. The addictions that these people have are so strong that if they are unable to break free from its control, it can later destroy their health and ruin their lives. Look also at the fact that many people are oppressed in a relationship where they are dominated by their partners. Take note of the fact the sins mentioned in the second chapter of this book and how it also places a stronghold on people's lives who have not demonstrated the power to overcome its barriers. It proves the master never stops telling the slave what to do because he or she expects him or her to follow instructions.

If the master is dissatisfied with the slave, he or she will unleash a relentless unmerciful attack on the slave. The master will do whatever he or she needs to make his or her slave powerless. The less power that the slave has, the more power the master has to control what the slave wants to do and will continue to do. Some people unfortunately are unable to break themselves free from the master who has oppressed them in life. Why? Most people have been oppressed all their lives. They live and die to an old age, not having the ability and power to change and overcome the conditions and circumstances that have oppressed them in life. Surely, it is essential to overcome your master so that you can develop the power to break free from what he or she binds you to do consistently. How can you, as an individual, develop this power?

How can you set free when it seems you are forever in chains, forever doing the wrong things when you are supposed to do the right things for the right reasons? Only your mind can give you the power you need to break yourself free from your master's control. Only when the mind has developed a way to break what needs to be broken will it find a way to free itself and never be in chains to a master that tells it what to do, how it should be done, and when it should be finished on a daily basis. If you are in prison, the only way you are going to get out is when you break yourself free. It is time you wait for your master to sleep so that you can climb over the fence, run, and escape to never be seen by him again. When he wakes up, he will try to find and chase after you so that he can lock you back into your oppressive state. However, once you served enough time, and it's time for you to be free and break free, you have come to the decision where you reach the power and point of no return.

**Get What You Want**

Jesus says, "If you are hungry, come to me and I will give you something to eat. If you are thirsty, come to me and I will give you something to drink." Therefore, those who desire to eat will eat, and those who desire to drink will drink, only at the expense that individual has a desire to be fulfilled. When you have a desire, you will do whatever it takes to go the distance until you find a way to put that desire to rest. Desire gives you the power to get what you want, even in the moment others have tried but could not find a way to make it happen.

It is desire that gives you the satisfaction that you need so that everything you want to accomplish in your life gets accomplished. Challenges are different. Challenges are forces that stand in your way of achieving a possible outcome. Your ability to achieve your desires and unlimited desire to excel past your challenges makes you go above and beyond to get what is burning inside of you and use it such that it radically changes your life. Every person that underestimated you will no longer be an opposition to you. Every battle you face will no longer undercut and overtake you because you have a brewing desire to attack than be attacked. Your desires, thus, become a replacement of the reflection you want out of life. You reflect what you want to see in the mirror because you believe what you see from it brings exactly what you will get back. Each person is born with a desire. The desire he or she has gives him or her the power to accomplish impossible goals and incredible outcomes.

Every step and inch in life is bent on the desire you have and want to have in getting what you want out of it. Having this desire is an innate trait that no one else can impart on you. It is something that can only be imparted from what you possess on the inside. Having it makes you go the distance to never be satisfied being comfortable in life. It makes you believe that you will never lose and give in that easily to opposing forces. There are moments that you must be able to get what you want in that moment; otherwise, when another moment comes, it will not carry the same magnitude it once had.

## Having Absolute Power in the Moment

There is no failure in power. Once you achieve it, you have no reason to feel it won't carry you through any difficulty. Power, when given enough of it, breaks down every wall that needs to be broken and shatters every glass that needs to be shattered. Nothing stands in your way when you have power. When you desire that power and you achieve it, nothing can stop you from getting more of where it came from. Power, when it develops, builds until it becomes a force that can battle and fend off any attack that tries to break it down.

Each person supplies him or herself with a power to achieve extraordinary outcomes and accomplish impossible dreams. When the moment comes, you must harness its energy by tapping into all the forces that make you strong so that you can oppose anyone who dares weaken your force shield and strength. You have to have the power to accomplish great things, but how many of us feel it can be done? How many of us feel that nothing can hold us back no matter how impossible something may seem? Once you find a way to break that shield you will never have to worry about it holding you back again because once you break through it one time, you will keep breaking through it all the time. Isn't that what having power takes? After all, people enjoy challenges because nothing comes easy, but what happens when the challenge has become so extraordinary that it just makes you look weak because you are unable to get through it?

You now have an immense obstacle that is placed before you, and the only way that you even stand a chance of overcoming it is to constantly attack it until it becomes weaker so that you in turn become stronger. When enough attacks are released then it gives you the ability to gain the strength that you need to achieve what you desire to go after.

Nothing can stand in your way because the strength that you have in releasing this power is demonstrating the ability to conquer your obstacles and overcome all the challenges and tests that is placed before you. After all, challenges come when your first or second try at something was not successful. Now you have something to deal with until you find a way to break through it. Not having it over power you is extremely important. You must be so diligent at what you do that even when you fail you know just how to come back. That is the demonstration of never giving up, never giving in, and constantly believing that you will cross over to the other side eventually when you keep attacking your challenges and never stop believing that one day your challenge will no longer be a challenge, but it will be something that was left behind in the moment.

*Greater things come with power, but lesser things come to people who don't know how to harness its energy.*

## Speak What Needs To Be Spoken

There is power in your words—power to change your outcome and power to change other people's lives by the way you speak. A single word when spoken in the moment, with the right or wrong intentions, can trigger a memory that will last a lifetime. Singers have sung songs that have changed people's lives just by the very language of their lyrics. Speakers have held meetings and presentations where they imparted their wisdom, lifestyle, and experiences to educate and inspire other people.

Words, thus, are vital to change the destiny and outcome in an individual's life. How essential words mean to someone when promises are made, but the very promises that are made become broken by the same person later on. Words hold the true significance and meaning to someone when it is used in the right context, but how destructive and conflicting it could be to others when it is used for the wrong purposes. Consistent words of love in marriage can restore a marriage that is falling apart.

Words of honesty and commitment in any relationship can enable relationships to withstand the situations that it has to go through over a course of time. People have even used what they have spoken in words to inspire others through their writing to also impact and change the lives of other people. At least, if you are not able to see these people physically, you have access to the sound of their voices through various mediums of radio, Internet, and audio disc. Truly, no one has seen God and heard him speak, but his words are living and active in the Bible. The power of his words used in the scriptures has the ability to dynamically transform the life of any individual who believes in him.

Words hold the potential in one's life. They create the ability to harm or heal someone. Imagine the words you have to use when someone is in pain or is dying in the hospital. The tone, the language, and the context of the words are altered in that moment to provide the conditions necessary for healing. Each moment that transcends in life is meant to transform your life and another person's life once the words used in that moment are intended to impact the moment that emerged during that time. Consequently, how devastating words can be when someone is unable to sustain their emotion in a critical moment in a relationship.

The anger and hostility of the person's words gush out with fury, not caring about the destruction that it will cause in the long run. Just imagine when you are faced in a moment of despair when you realize you have been lied to by your spouse, or your partner was living a double life outside of your relationship. Will you use words of resolve, peace, and amendment, or would you use words to tear and destroy what you and your partner have spent so many years to build? Poor choice of words in a heated moment can steer someone in the wrong direction.

The right choice of words in a heated moment can turn away wrath and deescalate anger. How essential and vital it is to control your emotions because once one loses one's emotion there is no self-control over what one wants to say and how it will be said. We have the power to control our language. It is one that we use in every changing moment to make a difference in our lives to prevent ourselves and the very conditions around us from falling apart. When the situations become more than they can handle, prayer can sometimes be the only answer for the challenges that life hurls at everyone.

There is power in prayer—power that is emulated when you read God's word and understand the life and language that he wants you to live. Even as powerful as God created human life, he knows that each individual has been created with flaws in his or her language. There are flaws in our language that if left uncorrected will determine how effective our relationship will be with others. Language and developing it in a way that can have a positive impact where you can influence others is not an easy task. If it were easy, there would be no broken relationships and false promises made in the world. If language was also spoken with kindness and compassion for a lot of people, there will be no need for crimes or acts of violence.

The Bible says that every person has fallen short when it comes to acknowledging and obeying the word of God. Therefore, this ability to change the choice of your words and acquire a language that when spoken is kind and compassionate can hardly be done through human strength, especially if it is not innate. The only way you can change your language and the power in which you use your words and how you process your information is when you abide by the power of God's word through his scriptures.

There is absolutely nothing that people can do when it comes to them operating on human strength. If they rely on themselves and their own power to change, they may never change. However, if they rely on God and his power to change, there is every possibility change can occur. Every day, our mind processes information. What we think about and how we process our information is what we live our lives by. Thus, for those of us who are Christians, when we don't think about God and what we need to do for him, our mind is processing what we need to do for ourselves. Therefore, your needs either revolves around what the world wants you to process, what you want to process individually, or what you want to fulfill for your creator.

It is so easy in life to drift away from what you are accustomed to doing because the mind has a tendency to lock itself into the information it wants itself to process. Truly, there is power in prayer, but not many people believe in that power so because they don't believe in that power they don't pray. And without prayer, there is no way of proving if that power really exists. Look at how practical life can change for someone when he or she decides to use God in prayer. God needs to hear your voice so he can know how to react and answer you in times of need. When you speak to God, he can speak to you and guide you in ways you would never expect. When you pray, you don't worry about anything because you should pray about everything that you have no control over.

## Comparisons

Life is like playing a game. If you change the rules in the beginning of the game, you affect how the game is supposed to be played. However, if you play the game the way it supposed to be played (i.e., you play by the rules), you have a chance of winning the game. You can't compare yourself with the next person who is playing the game because you have to do what you can to make sure you create the best opportunities for yourself to win. You have to be comfortable that no matter which moment and time in life you are in, you are never created the same as the next person. Your DNA in life is not linked with anyone else. You just have to be comfortable with who God created you to be and what your dreams are created to become. This world lives and thrives on comparison.

People compete in this word to be someone else other than their own selves. They try to match their skills and talents, believing it can be just like another person's gifts and talents, not considering the fact that each person is unique and different from the next person. This is a great downfall in one's character because it does not free you from who you are because you should celebrate how God has created you to be by utilizing the unique gifts and talents you were born with. You just can't view yourself as inferior when compared with the next person. Suppose that other person has abilities that no matter how hard you try, you never seem to have enough power to come close to what he or she can produce. Do you need to be happy to do the same thing that someone else is doing? Obviously not! When you start comparing your relationship, your position, your home, and your image with others, you are looking at idols that God did not create for you to worship. God created you to run against the voice within you. It is the voice within you that at times create the unhealthy comparison you don't need. It is the voice within you that at times tells you that you don't have to look at the blessings and the gifts that another person has when he already has your own blessings and gifts that is lined on your path.

Inside of you, just like myself, is a competitive nature that is burning to overcome all odds. But you have to realize that God gives you everything you need for what you were created to be and created to do. If the first part of your life was not powerful, transform and let the second part of your life speak for itself. Sometimes you see God's blessings on someone else and begin to feel disappointed that you are not where you need to be in life when you compare yourself with that person. However, when you do this, you are only drawing negative energy to yourself and the people around you. Why?

The reason is when you feel you are not where you need to be in life, the material possessions of others can rob the very joy of your relationship with God and your family when you lose focus on what he has given you. You have to believe that God made you differently than everyone else, and he imparts his power in a unique way to everyone. Sure, it is easy to be discouraged when you look at your friend's life, and he or she has a nice career and home with a few children. You wonder why your life can't be like the one he or she is living. It is also easy to look at someone else in a higher position at your job and feel as if time has cheated you in every moment where you used all the power and energy you had to making your life count for something, but it was not enough to achieve and advance into anything extraordinary.

How easy it is to compare yourself with the world and what your friends and other people have accomplished. How easy it is also for one to be free but also feel cheated living a life of freedom. How passionate one could be at times to get power or wait for that power to be given to someone else. Truthfully, there is nothing that you can't accomplish in this world once you put your mind to it.

You can't compare your life with the next person and try to accomplish what he or she has accomplished. Instead, you should try to compare your life with whatever talents and gifts you have so that you can use them to make a difference with the life you are living. You may do something greater than the next person all because your ideas and mind-set are different from his or hers. So many of us have the power to accomplish incredible dreams, but we shortchange our dreams by feeling defeated when we feel that others around us have the ability to make their dreams come true, while it becomes a struggle for us to make our own dreams a reality.

Notice that there are so many billions of people in this world, but not one person will look like you unless you have an identical twin. It shows you that you are unique in God's eyes. You are who you are created to become in his power and time that he wants you to become it. I heard my wife tell me about a woman who got married to a doctor she met on the Internet. She is not working, and the man told her she can stay at home and be a housewife. He already has a house for her to live in at the time they got married. Thereafter, she will start to have children and raise them at home, not ever having to work or rely on a babysitter to watch her children. So my wife told me who would not want a man like that. Sure, I am positive many women would not mind to have men where they do not have to work and stay home and watch their children. However, how many relationships in this day and time are set that way?

Apparently, every situation in everyone's life is not the same as the next person. Therefore, who knows the future and what life will bring for anyone. Some people have the power to put themselves in situations that creates some form of comfort, but if it is not sustained properly over time through love, finances, structure and nurturing, it can all fall apart at any given time. At any moment, your life can change for the better or the worse. What matters in your relationship matters to what you must do with your family to sustain it with the one that God has provided for you. Different people create different circumstances that all lead to different outcomes with ultimately different principles of power. We can't compare our relationships with anyone else and what other people are doing. That is a powerless sign of faith and trust in your own relationship.

The truth is you don't need to be someone else other than yourself to be satisfied. Truly, I can be all things to all men, but what good would that do for me? Will that bring out the best in me? I am who I am, and I can't change that for anyone else. I am content on the inside and don't need to be fulfilled by the things I see on the outside. After all, look at the doctor's situation with his wife. How do you know that the doctor and his wife will be in a relationship that will last?

What type of relationship will they have, and what are the standards they will hold in their relationship? The problem that some people have when they look at another couple in their initial stages is they will see what is in front of them without seeing what lies ahead of them. That is why, in spite of all the things happening around you, there is so much power inside of you to change your outlook on life. If you tap into it the right way, you can be free from everything and anything that pulls you into a negative direction.

The truth of the matter is the outcome of other people's lives attracts other people to sometimes make a decision with their own lives. Some people then delve into that mentality, "If it works for you, why can't it work for me?" I just see that it already worked for my wife, so why should it not work for me? It worked for my cousin, so why can't it work for me? My best friend became a millionaire without going to school, so why can't it work for me? Those are the voices inside most people that tell them to take action in their lives. However, before the outcome of anything, there are the obstacles that one must go through to bring that outcome to fruition. Each person has an idea of what he or she would like to achieve. Therefore, your ideas and where you stand in this world must cross that imaginary threshold of impossibilities if you desire to ever accomplish your dreams without being compared with those who have already achieved it in their lives.

**Built on a Rock**

No matter how hard the rain falls, how strong the wind blows, and how extreme the temperatures gets, the ones who are built on a rock will always find a way to shelter themselves from a storm. A bad weather is never easy for anyone to predict. Not everyone knows when a storm is coming. When it arrives, one can immediately prepare for it or be caught off-guard by its tremendous force such that it is hard for one to find the time to prepare or turn away from it. Indeed, not all storms are intended for everyone to survive. Some of them will claim lives; some of them will also take all that you worked for and quickly bring it to an end. Quite evident for some people, in the midst of facing these storms, some people will have to eventually get wet and have their house, cars, and belongings washed away.

Apparently, when it comes to a storm, no one can stop the inevitable from taking place. What was meant to happen will happen and take its course. Thus, how many of us can actually see the storms life brings before they arrive? How many of us also feel we stand a chance to withstand the forces it brings when it comes? That's why it's important to know who you are and the foundation you have built so that when the storms come, you will not be blown away by its strong winds. If the house you made was built on a rock, you will withstand all the forces from that storm because your house was laid down with a strong foundation. Foundation, of course, is an important aspect when it comes to building. Even the Bible knows how important it is to build something that will not easily fall apart. It talks about how strong one's house needs to be to hold off a storm. It says your house can't be made from straws or sands but must be laid with concrete blocks such that the house never crashes in the event of a bad weather. How important it is when you look at your life if the kind of house you are building is not strong enough to weather the storm, prepare yourself to experience a natural disaster.

Some people don't realize that everything in this life requires you to solidly build on something so that in the event of a storm such as loss of jobs, challenges in your relationship, personal and financial setbacks it can remain standing. If it's a relationship, you must build your relationships. If it is a job, you must build your skills so that you can advance at your job. If it's your education, you must build on what you know so that you are knowledgeable and marketable in the world. Even with all the talents you have, you must build and maintain your talents for it to impact the world so that it can be a greater place because of you. Consequently, there are many individuals who don't build on anything, and it makes me wonder what are they living and dying for? There has to be a greater reason for their existence and what they want to build on. After all, if one can't sustain what one has built, it can be destroyed in seconds.

It proves when one builds, one must build one's house with a strong foundation. A house can only survive so long on pure sand, but it can stand the test of time if it was built on a rock.

Obviously, for any house that is built on sand, you can expect the storms to come and dismantle that house. All the treasures and hopes you also placed in your property will be washed away and taken by the wind because no foundation was laid correctly for what was built. Even as a witness, you will be running after your belongings to save everything you have, but you will also be taken away by the high winds because you were not able to set your feet on solid ground. Unfortunately, it is not just the storms on the outside of each individual that has a tendency to destroy what took him or her so many years to build; it is the ones that are at work inside of people that limit their own progress in the world.

Sometimes their negative personality and moods are the storms they create in life that leads to their own downfall. Surely, there is a dark lining for every cloud that hovers above them. Others who live with these individuals can predict their forecast every day of the week because they know the type of weather that is displayed by them throughout the week. Some have a tendency to rain on Monday, change to snow on Tuesday, have a hurricane warning in the forecast on Wednesday that spirals into a tornado on Thursday with high winds on Friday that ends the week with dark clouds on Saturday until the sun finally comes out on Sunday. After a week of bad weather, this person finally comes to terms with calming down. However, no matter how calm they get, they will almost always find a way to repeat the storm that they themselves have no way to control. That is why internally, as individuals, we must be strong and have our foundation firmly planted on the ground such that no matter what comes our way, we are not easily shaken and taken off course by its circumstances.

## Cross-Pollination vs. Self-Pollination

Cross-pollinators are often the ones who bring big ideas to the table. They are credited for their open mindedness. They possess the ability to be the game changer that other people are not. For the most part, power does not mean anything if it can't be transferred to help make a difference in another person's life and the lives of other people.

Examine the life of a teacher and how he or she imparts his or her power of learning to his or her students. A teacher is a cross-pollinator in the world, creating more of what is around him or her, spreading and building better communities that make changes that are larger than life. A teacher is one who uniquely impacts the lives of individuals so that they can transfer that same impact to others.

If you are a cross-pollinator by design you are one who intends to broaden the scope of your horizon by stretching yourself beyond your capabilities by making others better around you. How often power is given but how well it is received when each individual who has it knows how to effortlessly impart it to others through wisdom and lessons of experience. Even the very fruit trees in nature exhibit this example of pollination by relying on cross-pollination from other trees to produce larger crops. Some apple trees are self-pollinators, which mean they could produce apples without cross-pollination. Self-pollinator power is power that is only vested without crossing it over to another source. In spite of an apple tree's self-pollination, their production will still not be able to produce large fruits if their sources are not derived from other varieties.

These trees, hence, are better pollinated if they receive cross-pollination from other sources. Do you see yourself achieving something without believing you can achieve anything else? At any point, do you have power that was given to you that enabled you to make more income, have an elevated status at work, church, or in an organization, only to lose the power that was given to you all because you did not successfully know how to impart it to others? If you surround yourself with other people who have undergone the process of cross-pollination, you can receive a greater power by being a student to the lessons that many of them offer to teach.

This cross-pollination is a type of influence where you don't compare yourself with anyone but you tap into your own power to be something greater than you already are, making everyone else even better around you. Comparing is when you look at another person's life and wonder what your life could be if you go in the same direction as that person has gone. Cross-pollinators are people who have nothing to compare themselves with. They are individuals who extend themselves to others through service, commitment, and attitudes of justice. They tend to make others greater around them, producing more greatness and yielding more than what has been expected. What efforts have you produced through cross-pollination and has it made the impact necessary to transform yourself and others around you for the better?

## Battle Tested

With all the challenges one faces in this world, it is proven that life can be equally a mental and physical battle. Each point in time creates a moment and method for its survival. It can give people moments where they were left unproven in their battles till they have to work themselves all the way back to the top where they need to prove themselves to others all over again. When situations come at you that set you back in ways that you least expect it, how many times are you supposed to get hit before you realize it's time to start fighting back? It seems that the blows that one takes have a way of leaving its scars unchanged through time. The attacks wound people in such a way that if they don't have any idea or way of fighting back, they have no power of demonstrating their ability to overcome an impossible situation.

However, no matter what challenges life brings and no matter the setbacks you have with all of them, it is time to come to your senses where you salt your wounds, put the patches on, wrap yourself up, and get back to work! You are down, but you are never out. Being down does not mean you are defeated and stay defeated. You have the power to change any moment and circumstance that tries to overtake you. You could be injured; however, through your injury, as long as you can move your arms and your legs, you still have the power to change your outcome. Once you live to see tomorrow, all you live for is today and wait for what tomorrow brings.

In each stage of your life, you are battle-tested in a moment that by passing it can shape your character for the better. Experiences in life create the greatest test for you to pass. You are tested at every stage and moment in your life, moments where you can continue to fail or moments where you can continue to succeed and overcome your failures. Whatever moment you are in, each moment creates a test for you to pass. Somehow the test can range from fighting a disease that has taken over your body. Being in a car accident where you have to go through physical therapy to regain the strength in your arms and legs, even relationships that end in divorce. Each test is a battle that makes one battle-tested that is intended for his or her survival. Every moment that you are in, there is no telling how you will be tested in that moment. It could be a physical or a mental test. Whatever tests come your way, all that matters is if you demonstrate the power in that moment to overcome any circumstance that is placed before you.

## Battle of the Titans

David and Goliath were considered to be two of the greatest titans ever to go to war. In the Bible, Goliath, a great giant who stood over nine feet tall, challenged the Israelites to go against him in a fight. He intimidated the Israelites with his size, power, and strength. Many who looked at him felt there was nothing that they could possibly do but surrender and live in fear of this towering force that stood above them.

For more than forty days, Goliath stood in full armor and terrorized the Israelites. One day, David, a young teenager, stood up to Goliath and challenged his authority over the Israelites by telling him that there is no way that Goliath can defy the armies of God. Goliath grew angry and challenged David to a fight. Having no fear but the power of God at his side, David took on the challenge of Goliath.

Standing toe to toe with Goliath, David was clearly overmatched. He was nowhere near Goliath's capacity in size, strength, and power. On the day of battle, Goliath carried with him swords, spears, and a javelin to use against David. David, who probably did not stand more than six feet tall, brought with him a pouch full of stones, a shepherd's staff, and a slingshot along with the power and faith he had in God. Goliath looked at David and hurled insults at him; he thought that the young boy had come prepared to die in a battle that won't last even a single minute. All Goliath would need to do is unleash his merciful attacks, and the fight would be over. David looked up to the sky and said to Goliath,

> *You come against me with a sword, a spear and a javelin, but I come against you in the name of the Lord Almighty, the God of the armies of Israel, whom you have defied . . . today I will give the carcasses of the Philistine army to the birds of the air . . . and the whole world will know that there is a God in Israel . . . it is not by sword or spear that the Lord saves; for the battle is the Lord's, and he will give all of you into our hands.*

The comments David made only annoyed Goliath, and as he charged at David and appeared to move in for the kill, David immediately pulled back his slingshot with a heavy stone that struck Goliath directly in his forehead. The forceful impact from the stone caused Goliath to immediately collapse to the ground, where David went over to him and took out his sword and beheaded the great giant in front of a crowd of stunned Israelites. From that day forward, no longer a giant would stand before them and oppose his will toward them.

No longer would they be powerless in someone else's presence. Goliath appeared invincible to many. His size and power intimidated the Israelites for more than a month. He used his size to rule over others. How incredible is the fact that someone of a much smaller size came to fight him with no shell of armor but a slingshot that when used allowed him to prevail over a towering force. Not even one Israelite aside from David had the courage to face someone taller than they were (New International Version, 1 Samuel. 17).

Obviously, this story is no different from the goliath that many people like you and me have faced in our lives. Everyone has a story of a goliath that they need the power and the courage to face and overcome. Look at the goliath in people's lives that deal with a turning point in their career where they must ultimately make a decision to stop living their lives under a mediocre salary where they struggle to support themselves and their family. Examine also other goliath's that include obstacles in marriages that deal with issues of compatibility that end in separation and divorce.

What is more telling are also the challenges one must face in one's health when it starts to deteriorate. It is a process where some people have to battle a condition that limits their potential health-wise to do more than they would normally expect. Facing legal issues in life is also a goliath that people battle with, where people are constantly taken to court for the injustices that they may have caused on others. It goes to show that when it comes to health, marriage, debt, and all the legal problems that crop up in life, you will encounter a goliath that will test your heart and will power to stand against it. Surely, whatever the goliath is, you must find a way just like David did to prepare yourself to overcome it.

At first, the battle may seem overwhelming. In the beginning, it may look as if there is no end to it because the obstacles have been mounted too high. However, we need to come face to face with our battles and place them below our feet. We need to trust that whatever we come in with to battle we will still have a chance to succeed. Why? Sometimes we overthink the battles we need to face because we are so concerned with the goliaths that have confronted us that we put on as much armor as possible to prepare for a battle not even knowing if we stand a chance to win when we decide to take it on. Look at David, how he went to battle with no armor and how he fully trusted in God to fight his battles. That should also be our very mind-set. A mind-set that knows the only armor that God provides is the power he gives us through his word and the faith that nothing can harm us through his Holy Spirit. Sometimes we look at giant problems and impossible situations, not having any idea of how to break through them, but once we become fearless and take them head on, the results instantly change our perspective in that moment.

Change could, at many points, seem impossible for even a relationship to improve, for a family to be more unified, for our health to get better and to get the miracles we need to find a satisfactory job that will improve our income and status in the world. However, when enough faith and power is displayed, you, just like David, must take a string and knock down any opposing force that defies any possibility of change. Moments can change someone's life for the better or for the worse, but each moment was designed for a decision to be made so that we can power through the changes that are necessary to overtake the goliaths in our lives.

**Unwavering Passion of the Heart**

Only God has the power to make your heart new again. Only he could take a broken heart and make it unbroken. If your heart lacks passion, he can give you the power your heart needs to enable the passion you must have to succeed. The heart is constantly tested because it searches for a reward that is fueled by a relentless purpose to go after what it wants to achieve until its desires are fulfilled. Once the heart is backed with enough power, it will continue to fight its way through various circumstances and conditions that will enable it to succeed. Only he has the power to make you overcome death so that you can experience life and the way it was meant to be lived. However, in spite of God's power, he can do so much to regenerate you because in times of crisis, you must take on the responsibility to maintain what he has generated in order for you to forge ahead.

Apparently, God can do so much to supply the power if you don't supply the effort for the outlet of how that power is generated. Thus, your willpower matters. The heart has an ability to be broken, but though it is broken by disappointment, it can be repaired through a never-ending passion of attaining fulfillment.

> *Greater things come with having power.*
> *Greatness comes when you can use that power*
> *from someone and make it your own power.*

# THE ULTIMATE REWARD

## CHAPTER 7

**Accomplish What Matters the Most**

In the moment, rewards are based on an accomplishment of a desired dream or goal. Each award achieved has a date and time line for its achievement. No award or accomplishment of recognition can be achieved if it is not etched into a moment and time of its achievement. Look at any award achieved, and the time in that specific moment is linked to the very accomplishment of its achievement. Historical banners are raised every time a team wins a world championship in a given year. When it is raised, the time of its accomplishment is also raised in front of thousands and millions of people across the world to see so that they can witness a symbolic moment merged into the history of its accomplishment. Even trophies, plaques, certificates, medals of honor, titles, and championship belts are also given to achievers; and as they are given, they too are acknowledged for their moments of achievement.

Apparently, there is not one individual who highly competes in a game or outperforms another opponent without feeling he or she deserves an award for his or her performance. Performance, thus, is vital to one being in line to achieve a necessary reward to sustain a commenced and deserving effort. Achieving an award in a specific moment can take months and even years to complete. However, finalizing it makes the time in achieving the reward worth every effort and time spent working for it.

It seems once a signature moment comes alive when an individual's day and time has come to achieve a monumental accomplishment, a moment in time is also etched into history it was accomplished. It is much similar to degrees and licenses that all have a specific period of time of their accomplishment. Some of them take years and months to complete, and when one finally achieves either of them, one also achieves and capitalizes the rewards given to one in that moment. It goes to illustrate in a moment designed for you, there is an award waiting for your name to be etched and carved into the wood, gold, or paper for which it will be given.

Every line that is crossed and every extra mile that is taken allows someone to establish opportunities for his or her success. Once a reward is achieved, there is no doubt in the achievers mind that another one will be attained. As long as this person has an intense passion matched by incredible work ethics, he or she has every possibility to excel past any obstacle so that one reward is reached and can be built on until he or she achieves his or her ultimate reward. Think about the first time you stepped foot on college grounds. Did you ever have any hindrance or doubt that you will not obtain a degree? Many people who attend college have an end goal in mind, which is to obtain and be honored with a college certificate. The time, of course, that each person spends in college will be linked to a set of classes that he or she has to undergo a major and minor to complete. Thus, the greatness of one's performance is essential in those classes because it determines one's overall grade point average and if one is successful enough to advance.

Most likely, the more classes you pass, the greater the likelihood of your advancement to other classes, while the least amount of classes you pass, you stand a chance of not achieving your ultimate goal that will lead to your ultimate reward. Doing all that you can do to succeed, each moment seems to define the stages of one's life that with enough sacrifice a single effort can allow one to transcend into another moment that will be the next stepping-stone to one's destination. Thus, the small achievements in life matter because the little things you do to accomplish the small achievements seem to go a long way to accomplishing bigger dreams and accomplishments.

College is not apparently for everyone because not all people can walk in a classroom and be disciplined enough to learn and succeed at learning. Some people dislike the fact that they have to expend countless amounts of hours and days studying, not knowing if they will ever achieve what they set out initially to accomplish. Hence, even with all their desires and drive to accomplish an expected goal in the moment, when challenges come, they drop out of school and lose the very momentum that they came in with. Their reward to pass one out of many classes to achieve and move closer to a college degree has all yet been defeated by distractions and circumstances that override any hope or dream of them becoming successful. How vital it is that when one takes on a task or a desired goal, one must drive it to completion if one wants to meet and exceed one's desired expectation.

How vital it is also that purpose and passion can also disintegrate if the reward of what one wants to accomplish in the moment suddenly loses meaning and momentum over time. For many who desire to achieve a college education, there is no area of futility that is lacking in their lives as long as they have a beginning and an end goal in mind. Achievement and fulfilling it over and over again is an innate desire that fuels them into attaining one reward so that they are one step closer to their goal of getting a degree that when reached allows them to achieve their ultimate reward, a career. Rewards should matter to people. After all, you have to have something to work for that makes you want to look forward to what you will eventually accomplish. If you are going to invest in something, there has to be a return from your investment; otherwise, there is no reason to put your time and effort into it. Indeed, every moment that you spend in wanting to reach a goal is another moment that you will spend in trying to make the effort and sacrifice in the moment to make it a reality.

Just as students go to school to achieve a college degree so that they can achieve their ultimate reward, a satisfying career, players on teams also employ their skills and talents effortlessly to achieve their goals in a season by winning as many games played so that they can get their reward by being in the playoffs where it gives them a chance to achieve their ultimate reward, a championship. Championships mean a lot to individuals as well as every member of a team. To the coach, it symbolizes all the plays that were drawn, the motivating words that were used to inspire his or her team to win. It takes no exception as well to the players who play for their coach. To them, it polishes every practice session, time in the weight room, and their ability to analyze and prepare for their opponents. To the managers and owners of the team, it is all the sacrifices that were made monetary-wise, bringing in the right personnel and investing into the right players that would make a difference in making their team competitive enough to win and be consistent at winning.

To the fans that stand by their team emotionally through all the wins, losses, and draws, they pay their tickets to a full season and playoffs in hopes that their team has a chance to achieve the very goals of winning so that they can celebrate the ultimate reward, a championship to the city. On a much larger scale, examine the individuals across the world that come to churches that are impacted by God's word to change their lives. Many of them, who are tired of living a meaningless and empty life, feel that by repenting and being baptized can change their direction in life for the better. Hence, their baptism and commitment to follow Christ is rewarded by them having a relationship with God as true Christians where they can become believers that can lead others to Christ. Surely, there are rewards in one's heart and soul for every good deed that one produces while one is here on earth. But for every action taken or not taken to receive it, each Christian strives to achieve the ultimate reward in his or her relationship with God, an entrance into heaven. It is proven in honor of good deeds, service, hard work, obedience and determination, rewards are given to people who are worthy of its praise.

Just as many of these individuals strive to achieve in life, people from all walks of life such as actors, singers, dancers, musicians, and humanitarians to society also effortlessly work to achieve rewards based on their performance. Their effortless work and constant endeavors pushes them to obtain the highest achievement possible. Life and living it in the moment with a purpose makes each of them have something to look forward to knowing in the end that there will be something waiting for them to receive.

> ***Moments that are designed for you to fail are also moments that are destined for you to succeed.***

## The End Goal Is All that Matters

Belief in *Merriam-Webster's Dictionary* is considered a state or habit of mind in which a person places trust or confidence in a person or thing. One can't easily impart one's beliefs onto anything if one is not inspired to believe what one is shooting for in one's life will become possible. From start to finish, one's belief must start with nothing but end with a reward. Obviously, in the beginning, any goal or ambition that you aspire to take on will oftentimes present roadblocks to determine how strong your levels of beliefs are in your quest for them.

If at any point you are weakened en route to your ambitions by circumstances and distractions, you will face life's greatest battle, which is your ability to battle to the end even in times where the fight to the finish line does not seem so promising. Thus, all that you achieve and aspire to believe you can achieve will not matter if you fail to capture and attain your end goal. The end, apparently, is always vital in life because only the end matters when it comes time to achieving a reward.

Rewards are less likely to be given out in the beginning of a task. Any individual who decides to take on an ambitious goal will capture a reward if his or her levels of beliefs in life are passionate enough to carry him or her all the way to its completion. Indeed, even at the very expense of achieving a reward, as long as an individual remains passionate, he or she will never see the end to that reward until he or she achieves his or her ultimate reward.

Truly, that is the mark that will complete true satisfaction from all the ambitions that one has gone after in one's life. The fact that he or she can not only reach a level of achievement one time, but their ability to get that achievement and build on it until something greater can arise from it. Rewards matter when it is linked truly to one's destination. Success and fulfillment matter when one has attained that reward and maximized it to its fullest capacity.

Think about how many people have gotten college degrees only to work in a different field of interest from what they majored in school. Though they achieved their rewards, the only satisfaction that will allow them to feel successful in life is if they are creative in bringing maximum results to all that they achieved by accomplishing something far greater than what they have already achieved.

Look at how many people also that have gotten their degrees only to leave it by the wayside without doing anything to capitalize on their intelligence to do something greater than what they have accomplished. Sometimes even when a reward is achieved, it is not the road to your final destination because once one is passionate with strong beliefs in what one can achieve in life, one will keep driving oneself further and further to higher level of rewards that will maximize one's needs for achieving fulfillment. Rewards in life only bring you satisfaction, but maximizing what you can build on from achieving those rewards provides the ultimate fulfillment.

That is why only the end is what people evaluate to see if you were able to leave your mark and have an impact toward your destination. After all, what is the sense of starting a project if you can't carry it past its final mark? Being defeated or coming up short was never meant to bring you to your knees. Look at how many people have opened successful businesses without achieving a college degree. Their dreams were not written off for not getting a college education. Just because these individuals were not able to graduate from college, they still made productive use of their time by turning their lives around by embarking on their passion of being an entrepreneur. As a result, these individuals ignite their passion by putting their time, energy, and effort into a business that has the potential for them to earn higher revenues than they could earn working for anyone.

It so happens also in the process of them achieving those rewards that it gives them the satisfaction necessary in the moment to believe they can go on a much higher scale of success to duplicate that reward by opening other businesses across the world. It proves for everything in life that one aims for, one constantly strives to achieve an ultimate reward that will bring forth a high level of fulfillment and greater moments in one's life. To the individual who is passionate about life and never stops believing in what he or she desires to accomplish, his or her mind and heart will always see an open door to ones that have been closed. The true power to achieving anything big in life is to never dream small.

Dreamers in the night dream big, while dreamers in the day dream small. Daydreamers only dream of the possibilities of what could be or happen in a temporary moment, but real dreamers dream of the reality that life-changing dreams can happen in every changing moment. So what in life are you dreaming for? Are you dreaming for something to happen in a temporary moment, or are you dreaming for something to happen in every changing moment? Just imagine how often in life you wake up from a dream, and no one can truly remember how it starts. All that one can take hold of the fact is how the dream ends. The end, thus, is the memory and the moment that people hold on to. All the efforts that could or could not carry them to their mark will be the ones that will change and alter the course of their direction for a lifetime.

What you go after in your dreams is important. When you accomplish what you have gone after holds true significance, there is no reason to stop your progress from making another dream possible. One single moment of accomplishment is a moment or minute of satisfaction, but every changing moment of an accomplishment brings on achieving ultimate rewards that leads to one's overall fulfillment. Knowing the end goal to one's destination makes it matter to reaching higher destinations in the moment.

Look at teachers and the examples they set to have end goals with their students. Teachers evaluate their students the minute they come in the classroom, yet their students are not given a grade until they prove themselves by meeting and exceeding the necessary expectations essential for them to pass. Hence, teachers habitually predicate themselves on hard work to sacrificially impart their wisdom and experiences of teaching to their students.

Their reward is for their students to achieve a passing grade where ultimately it can lead to many of their students venturing on with the principles and practices learned in their classroom so that their students can apply the same principles and practices to life. A teacher's diligence comes from his or her ability to persevere with students who learn at various levels.

Their efficiency at what they teach comes from years of experience of teaching in the classroom. The same tangibles that some teachers have used to impact their students are the same ones their predecessors have used to impact their lives as educators. In the beginning, it is never easy for a teacher to establish a common ground. From the onset, he or she must establish the rules of the classroom and the goals that must be reached for his or her student to be successful throughout the course of every marking period.

The teacher has high expectations for his or her students to reach, and, in order to succeed, each student has no choice but to meet his or her teacher's level of expectations toward that goal. The beginning of a class presents many challenges for a teacher as well as a student, but in the end, the expectancy is a reward to look forward to on both ends. Knowing that performance is a grinding effort, students who passionately commit themselves to daily class work, weekly tests, participation in projects, and presentations have every chance to receive successful grades and overcome all the challenges set before them.

The end goal, thus, is all that matters. The beginning never counts as much as what should matter in the end. For this reason, in the end, one's status in life is known, pass or fail, lose or succeed. Either way, a verdict must be handed out in the form of a report that displays the desire of a commitment or the lack of a committal to a life-changing lesson that could be the key to achieving not only an end goal but also a reward that leads to one's ultimate fulfillment.

**Moments of Transformation**

Several years ago, I heard a story about a person named Zena who had a malignant skin condition when she was born. The condition left marks and scarring that covered nearly 75 percent of her body. The result left Zena's parents to wonder how their daughter would cope with the condition of being around other children in school. As a result, they were determined to find a way by any possible means to correct their daughter's skin disorder. At a young age, even before reaching her first birthday, they took their daughter to several dermatologists where she received biopsy and skin treatments. Zena's parents were optimistic that the outcome overtime would be a positive one for their daughter. However, several months would go by and still there will be no signs of improvement. Unfortunately, to many of the doctors who treated her, seeing the severity of her skin ailment, made them draw a conclusion not to perform any surgical procedure on Zena because of her age. Several of the doctors advised Zena's parents to wait a few years before making a decision to have their daughter's skin condition corrected through surgery. Thus, her parents endured. They continued to care for their daughter and use any prescribed medications from doctors' visits that would provide little relief to her condition. Nine years would pass and not much improved with their daughter's appearance. Zena's parents were desperate to find an answer. They would visit other skin specialists where they would also prescribe various antibiotics and skin regimens to see how she would respond to medications and treatments used to enhance her appearance. Apparently, days and weeks would pass after Zena's treatments; and to no avail, the medications and treatment had little effect on improving her skin condition. What looked as an improved condition only worsened in a matter of days after her condition showed no significant enhancement to the treatment she received from the doctors.

Zena's parents knew they had no other choice but to take the chance of having their daughter go to school and struggle through the criticism and alienation she may face because of her condition. As a young child, Zena, herself, was not fully aware of the impact of her condition. She carried herself through life as any normal child would. Unfortunately, it would be advancing to other grades in public school that increased her awareness of her current debilitating skin disorder. It was at that time Zena would notice how she was secluded from being part of any participating activity with her fellow students. In school, at a young age, she would be looked at scornfully and called names based on her condition by other children. People around her even stressed the fact if anyone comes too close to her that they might inherit the same condition that has destroyed her skin. It seemed oftentimes when Zena would go to school she would be at the center of disrespect by other children.

The pain of being insulted by other children would go to the extreme when Zena would come home from school in tears as her parents would watch her emotionally ripped inside from all the hurled criticism she had gone through on many school days. Zena, with much discomfort with her image, had a lot to overcome. She was no longer nine years old but would now become a fourteen-year-old teenager who still searched for an identity of where she would fit in with others.

She wanted to feel accepted by everyone without facing rejection from anyone. It seemed as if all the criticisms each day presented a challenge of its own for Zena. Despite the criticism she faced from others, throughout the course of several marking periods, Zena had excellent grades. Many of her teachers praised her ability to participate in class discussions and her tireless efforts to be involved in taking on many of the challenging science projects. Performance and being an achiever in school was never a concern for Zena. She was gifted in her academic abilities. Consequently, the only obstacle that she was confronted with was the constant setback of not being appreciated by other people. Her image was an ongoing issue that lowered her self-esteem around others. She thought that as she grew older, as long as she stayed with her debilitating skin condition, no one would marry her.

Going to school and seeing all the other girls in her classes made Zena completely aware she was not one of the best-looking girls in school. As a result, it was difficult for anyone to be friends with her because of the way she looked. Even the boys in school would never ask her out, and the girls would rarely have her around in group conversations. She was isolated in school from others, which caused her to feel a common disposition of unfriendliness toward other people.

She felt despised and rejected by her peers, and the only way she felt that she would be able to deal with it was by treating others differently than the way she was treated by other people. Evidently, when someone is hated and ridiculed enough, the common reaction that he or she has is to treat others the way he or she has been mistreated. Even though this could be the case in a number of scenarios with people, the type of reaction that Zena had toward others was different from the way others treated her. Throughout the times she had a negative interaction with others, she had a heart for people who oftentimes never had a heart for her. Thus, overcoming and going through the hardship of her appearance was an obvious lesson that was hard for Zena to learn. The only people that truly accepted her for who she was as an individual were her parents. The challenge for Zena was how it was going to be possible for her to get the same type of acceptance and respect from her peers, all while aspiring to achieve her goals in school. As difficult as the circumstances were for Zena, she managed to do well in many of her subjects.

The issues of her appearance would be ongoing, unfortunately, as she would later move on to graduate from high school and attend college only to go through the same issues of rejection by adults. Zena surrendered to the fact that life would just not change for her no matter what moment in time she was in. She had to swallow her pride and continue to stay focused on achieving her goals in life. She would stay optimistic and hoped that one day her skin disorder will become a distant memory. Deep in Zena's mind, there was nothing wrong with her as far as being a student in school and a member to society. The only challenge she faced emotionally was connecting to people after she was constantly rejected by them. Over time, as much as she wanted to connect to others, constant years of rejection made her lose trust in people. Ultimately, through it all, Zena felt emotionally scarred by the torment she had gone through, being looked at scornfully by others and having to see the same reflection of herself every day before she walked out the door. Ideally, she felt that she was a good person at heart, and it would take time for other people to see it. Surely, if only some people can look on the inside of a person instead of judging what they see on the outside, the world will be able to withstand the issue of discrimination that is alive and embedded in today's society.

As emotionally painful it would be some days for Zena, she surprisingly remained optimistic that one day her life will change, and when that happens, people's opinions about her will also be altered. In 1993, she attended college as a freshman and was on the honor roll every semester for her outstanding grades. She participated in many of the student services where she raised funds for the homeless and strived to create workshops for freshman, sophomores, juniors, and seniors who were struggling to make the grade in their classes. In addition, she also became a spokesperson in building a better, cleaner, and safer community for all the students who attended the school.

After three years of hard work, in her final month as a senior in college, her outstanding grades in school earned her the reward valedictorian of her class. She not only received the reward for her academic excellence in school, but she also received other awards for her time and dedication in making the community and others better around her. Remarkably, after much objective criticism regarding her skin condition, she achieved a moment in her life that many people could not accomplish. Almost one year after Zena obtained her bachelor's degree and reward as valedictorian, she would now face a formidable challenge of finding employment with a company she hope would accept her for who she stood for as a person.

Through all her efforts, it would take nearly nine months of constantly attending job interviews before Zena decided that she should take a series of different approaches to her job search. On her resume, she decided to add more to the awards and experiences she had in school. In addition, she was fortunate enough to also get some positive leads from her previous professors. Fearless of the outcome, Zena's confidence kept improving day by day. She knew it was a matter of time before she received a job offer. Despite her excellent grades in college, it made Zena wonder if her condition played a role in her not being accepted by interviewers and people in the world.

In the midst of being turned down by many interviewers in the past, it would take nearly eleven months for Zena to finally gain acceptance and find a full-time job where she stayed and grew with the company for more than four years. In her efforts to treat her skin condition, Zena had to live with the fact that whoever was going to accept her was going to appreciate her for who she stood for as a person. After four years of being on the job, Zena became a spokesperson who constantly spoke and donated part of her income and time to researching the cure for certain skin disorders.

Her outstanding contributions to science have allowed her to become a heroic figure to many women who battle with skin conditions. Life, in essence, rendered a constant battle for Zena. She had opposing forces at the turn of every direction in her life that repelled her from achieving job opportunities and maximum respect from others. Though Zena was an intelligent and giving person from the heart, she never felt cheated in life because of her malignant skin condition. If anything, she worked effortlessly to achieve her rewards on the inside as well as on the outside that made a difference in her life as well as the lives of other people. Her satisfaction was chiefly based on the rewards that she received in the moment, but her fulfillment in life would be based on the value of achievements she would generate over time.

In her pursuit to correct her skin condition, it would take a single decision of Zena visiting a specialized dermatologist to see if she could get help in getting her skin condition corrected. At the time of her doctor's visit, the dermatologist offered much hope of support by informing Zena the advancements made to medicine. She would later be referred by her dermatologist to a plastic surgeon who specializes in skin repair. Suddenly, Zena's window of hope of having a new life and future took a dramatic turn.

After visiting the dermatologist and taking on skin corrective surgery and its regimen, Zena's life was transformed two years after receiving all the treatments. Instantly, what looked like a person that at one time had no hope or resolve for her condition became an individual who was transformed in life with a changed and remarkable new image. The surgery would deem to be a success as it lessened the visibility of any scarring on the outside surfaces of the skin.

A few years after her surgery, she would later get married and become a mother to three children. She has taken the initiative each time to be a public spokesperson on her battle with skin disease. It would take ten years of going on speaking engagements and making timely contributions to science before she was given a humanitarian award in her field. Zena's life quickly became not only a story of constant tragedy but also of life-changing rewards where she helped thousands of children and woman overcome intimidation and inferiority complexes because of damages to their skin as well as challenging strides toward achieving their desired dreams in this world.

> *Sometimes you can't believe what your life will become until it is transformed into what it is intended to become.*

## Hitting the Highs and Lows

Rhythm is a tune that often repeats itself in a series of periodic segments in a song, dance, or lyric. Some rhythms are patterned high in tune, while others are patterned low in tune. Apparently, for any movement, pattern, arrangement of words, or tunes to be in rhythm, they must be in an appropriate sequence to be in harmony with one another. One dislodged sequence in a word, tune, or movement in dance, speech, or song can alter the performance of the individual or people who are performing. Thus, every note that every person hits in life will either be a high note or a low note. The higher the note, and the better it is performed in rhythm, the greater will be the performance of the performer. Consequently, the lower the note, and the less it is performed in rhythm, the greater the likelihood of that performed output being subpar and one that is orchestrated poorly.

It becomes evident how being in rhythm with your goals and dreams will carry you to places you never imagined. How evident is that the greater the person keeps on hitting the note with a high degree of accuracy and precision, the higher the chances that he or she will receive a reward based on his or her performance. Obviously, the same practicals are applied in life when people perform in and out of rhythm whereby the consistency of their performance determines how far they will get. How important it is in order for one to receive a reward in life and achieve an ultimate reward later on, he or she must find and connect themselves to a rhythm that will bring on consistent results. After all, it does not make any sense to start an artwork if the artwork lacks a consistent pattern that will drive it to its completion.

It does not also hold any value to be a singer if he or she can't sing to a song that brings on a harmonious sequence where the tone of the words are executed and incorporated with enough talent to win praises from a crowd of people. Every ambitious goal laid out by any individual must be sowed into a consistent habit that leads to him or her to properly execute and develop it into phases and patterned sequences to receive an award. Once the pattern breaks, you lose all the ties that formed your rhythm, taking you out of your element and out of your line of ambitions.

Much to no surprise, just look at every failed dream in a person's life where he or she was not able to make it to his or her destination, and you will see a breakage in the tune of his or her performance. Somehow, down the line, his or her rhythm was broken. Somehow, he or she was on target with the task of writing and singing a perfect song, but a song is only as good as it is sung as long as it is orchestrated with practice. Evident is the fact that everything that you want to do in life gets better and better once it has been performed on a consistent basis. Repeated performance and practice during an endeavor is essential to anyone's success. Every task and endeavor you take on requires you to be in rhythm to achieve its rewards. The more you are in rhythm to receiving a reward, the greater the chances that you will achieve other ones to reach your ultimate reward. In rhythm, you can never get too high, and you can never get too low; you must always manage to stay in tune with what you desire to achieve.

Just imagine how important it is for the heart to be in rhythm. For the heart to beat regularly and in a normal pattern, that is a sign of good health. Electrical signals are sent from sections of the heart to another section of the heart to beat in an appropriate sequence. However, once there are any signs or breakage in signals, an arrhythmia occurs, driving the beat of the heart completely out of balance. Once the heart is out of rhythm, serious complications may develop as a result of it not beating properly for it to survive. Surely, it becomes a life-and-death situation when the heart is not beating in proper sequence. Even God knows how essential it is for life to be in rhythm. That is why he created the heart. No animal, human, or life-form that possesses this organ can accomplish anything if the rhythm of their heart is out of balance.

Cardiac rhythm, thus, is essential for life and essential for the way blood flows through the heart. It goes to show that nothing in life can happen without the heart playing a role in bringing that dream and goal into reality. Just as the heart beats in rhythm, every action that an individual takes on to be successful must also take on a pattern for it to come into reality. One can't expect to pass an exam and not get into a rhythm in studying for it. Likewise, one can't play any sport and expect to be in the rhythm of playing that sport if one has not consistently practiced and patterned one's habits and attitudes into the game. Rhythms are indeed good when they benefit you for an acquired and fruitful purpose. However, rhythm can indeed be detrimental if its intent has not carried you to reach a common goal where it solely defines your achievement.

Practice is essential to achieving and receiving any reward. Rhythm is necessary so that practice is sustained and the awards that can be achieved from it are attainable. Obviously, one should know the burning passion of not stopping something once it has started until one gets what one wants. Once an endeavor or desire is in rhythm, it must also be in sync with all the dreams that the individual desires to achieve so that the rewards from it can come to fruition. No matter what levels of disappointment, obstacle, and setback there are, they will be overridden by the power of an unbreakable tune.

That is why when you are in rhythm, each year should be better than the last year, and each day should be better than yesterday. You live your life knowing the present has to be better than the past, and the future has to be greater than the present. Surely, the only way of getting something done and getting what you want out of it is to practice consistently until it becomes fused and immersed into your desire.

Knowing this, you can't possibly aim your life looking for perfection without looking for a sense of direction. That sense of direction exists when someone has decided on the destination of his or her path. Once that destination is set, a formulated rhythm must also be established to accomplish an empowered dream and goal en route to that destination.

> *Making a sacrifice is something that will not last forever but it is the rewards that come from it that will last forever.*
>
> —Chinwe Okeke-Moffatt

## An Entry with No Exit

Imagine how someone falls into the same patterns of giving up stuck and overloaded into a series of circumstances that repeats itself over and over again. To some individuals, life sometimes is not a matter of finding a way in but finding a way out of a situation that is not getting them anywhere. For example, look how many people can't establish a pattern where it is harmonious at certain jobs because they are not compatible with the people they work with and the content of the job. As a consequence, so many of them quit or consistently get into conflicts when they are not compensated for their efforts and performance. These are the same people who stay at their jobs for months and years, never to receive an adequate raise in their salary or acceptable promotion to other advanced positions. It seems no matter how hard some people work and do their best to follow what is required of them by their boss, they sometimes fail to get out of a position that has left them high and dry with no form of advancement.

Job dissatisfaction is not the only struggle that people go through, because even people who are in relationships that are not getting anywhere, they also have a tendency to free themselves from something that holds no promises in the long run. Imagine how some spouses have to go through being the one responsible for paying a good portion of the expenses because nothing financially has changed with their partner. Having this type of relationship may make many spouses feel it does not create the balance that they need for their marriage. Consider the fact that also many of them have lost the so-called intangibles that at one time made them feel loved and in love with their spouse. Some spouses go through phases in a relationship where they are constantly belittled and verbally abused by their partners. Sometimes no matter what they do to try and please their spouse, it ends up never being enough to satisfy them. How vital it is that when one commits to something, one must take the steps necessary in making it last or be removed from a situation that is less than likely for one to go anywhere with it.

For all obvious reasons, people try to put themselves in the best possible way to win. However, there is a fine line between winning and losing. People desire winning at times to be their ultimate reality in the moment, while losing oftentimes is a reality that people will like to let go of in any moment it happens. Losing and being in a situation that leads to nowhere is an individual's true motivation for escape because he or she feels by continuing with it leads to no intrinsic rewards in the end.

However, life is not based on all the things you see and judge at first glance. If we ever take things for face value and judge our businesses, relationships, jobs, career goals, places where we live with an immediate negative impression, we will oftentimes shortchange ourselves with the rewards it has in store for us. Thus, for some people who go through the daily grind in life, it is all about their ability to persevere instead of finding a way out of a situation that holds no guarantee what magnitude the next one will hold. Obviously, when things go wrong, most people will like for a tradeoff to happen because some of them feel the exit to enter into something else should be far greater than the entry that was initially taken. However, the unknown oftentimes project itself to others when people don't realize the next thing they are getting themselves into. Surely, there will always be defining results, positive or negative, that will come from the choices they decide to take on.

Indeed, if the results are negative for some people, and the obstacles become too extreme, escape to them is the easiest way out. But the escape tactic doesn't offer the best solution at times for people who want a level of resolve. Apparently, that is not the case with all people because there are some who believe that what starts in their lives must carry itself through obstacles to determine whether it is strong enough to last. After all, that is what builds us in life—the ability to be shaped by what we can overcome over a period of time. There is a reward for people who always find a way to persevere in their relationships, businesses, school, work, legal problems, and other situations that crop up in everyday life. How quickly some people jump the gun without riding out their challenges to see what the true outcome will be? Many relationships, job opportunities, career endeavors, relocation choices, and businesses have failed because of people's inability to exercise their patience, perseverance, and belief to see the rewards that would await them if they are willing to grind it out to the end.

*Getting through and changing your history is not enough. You have to be determined to punch through and make it happen with every changing moment so that a new moment in history can be born.*

## Dream the Impossible

I remembered how success in life was a distant dream until I opened my eyes and realized that my imagination and memories could very well make my dreams possible. Every ignited thought and inspired hope that was driven out of my life would find its way back to make the most impossible moments come alive. There will be times I would be pushed to the edge only to have everyone believe I had no chance of winning. There will be moments I would find myself buried in mud with no way of finding the strength to climb out.

I had to prove everyone wrong who thought I could not make it in life. I had to show them that even though dreams are created and obstacles are created from those dreams, nothing will stop those dreams from becoming possible as long as I believe and have the passion for my dreams to come true. Thus, it became evident to me that there is a truth for anyone who burns with a desirable intent to be successful. Apparently, once an individual has a passion for something, it will keep burning in his or her heart until that passion is fulfilled. No one can underestimate the power of the heart when it is backed by a person who knows no surrender. Each time he or she is knocked down, he or she will effortlessly find ways to rise after he or she has fallen. There will be times in life where the answers to my dreams will be fleeting, not knowing which route or avenue to turn that will steer me toward a rightful destination.

However, in moments of despair, out would come a second wind that would ignite my desires and make me believe I still have what it takes to turn my life around. I knew, for the most part, I wasn't an individual who could exactly make a believer out of everyone if I couldn't first believe anything was possible in my own life. I could no longer meditate on disappointments of the past. Instead, I used all my current talents and skills to change and create a new script and outcome for my future.

Apparently, life and every changing moment that comes with it makes me realize when someone speaks of an impossible dream, it can be challenging to watch other people live out their dreams, not believing the same possibilities can be attainable in my own life. Evidently, no amount of achievement or dreams in one's life can be rendered unimaginable. As long as someone feels the same possibilities exist for him or her, he or she will continue to attack every shortcoming he or she faces in life until he or she reaches one step closer to making his or her dreams a reality.

After all, every dream that burns inside a dreamer has a purpose for why no circumstances can put out its fire. The fire inside a dreamer will remain lit because its intention is made clear from the onset that dream has come alive. Only extensive, progressive action toward an impossible dream enables that person to channel his or her intentions in life that burns a hole through many challenging situations that block him or her from achieving its possibilities. Once a dreamer is fueled by what he or she can achieve in the moment, there is no negative situation that can write off his or her desires from accomplishing it. To a dreamer, going and getting through a goal is not about being conquered but being a conqueror.

He or she must be an individual who hold a set of collective ideas of how to withstand any opposing force that dares to conquer and destroy the dream he or she desires to keep burning. Therefore, challenges that are presented to the impossible dreamer becomes not about experiencing a magic of overcoming them in the moment but making magical moments come alive from the visions that is sustained in his or her heart and mind.

Look at the amount of times that people lay their lives on the line because they are uncertain if they will be able to continue to pursue their dreams. There are many rewards that one can obtain in daring to dream. However, there are ultimate rewards that are given when not only one dream is accomplished but also other dreams are materialized. The one who dares to dream must be active when it comes to taking a risk toward starting one dream to finish it and start another. That is why the one who continues to dream must be active in keeping one's dream alive no matter what challenges and obstacles stand before it. How many dreams live and die is incumbent on an individual's overall ambition and passion to see it come through one moment crossing over to other moments.

For a fact, you have to be strong enough to dream, and you have to be even stronger to believe no matter what crosses in front of them, they can still be achieved. The weak lets their dreams fall by the wayside when they let distractions and circumstances override their faith and beliefs. However, the strong realizes that if one needs to dream, one must land oneself out of the zone of disbelief and into a zone where unlimited beliefs and possibilities exist from zeroing in on all the potential and maximum potential one must release and keep releasing to make those dreams happen. Once an individual finds a way to release it, he or she must exercise his or her power to release it again and again without having any excuses to hold back anything in the moment. That is why you have to continue to release the possibilities so that its momentum in the moment will be all that will be necessary to attain other essential rewards.

Clearly, in my years growing up, I knew a person by the name of Darren who oftentimes had been an impossible dreamer. In many of the conversations Darren held with people, he would oftentimes dream of the possibilities of what his life will look like in the future. He had a strong vision for what he wanted to become and where he wanted to take his life. He had a dream that one day he will get a masters degree in engineering and have an impact with it on the lives of others by building memorable architecture. Some people who heard Darren's stories thought his imaginations were rendered impossible.

Most of his friends had doubts in their minds toward him. No one believed that with all the challenges he had in his life where he was raised by foster parents because of the death of his mother and father he had any chances of becoming someone special. Darren loved his mother and had a strong relationship with his father. Distraught over the emotional and physical loss of his family, the challenge of not having his parents by his side took a dramatic toll on his life. Knowing all of what he had gone through made him have a difficult time connecting with people. In school, it would be no different as many of the teachers regarded him as being a troubled child, whose focus seemed to be somewhere else outside of the classroom. He would often struggle academically in school, where his grades and performance were not up to the school's standards.

Darren always stood on a shaky ground through which no matter how hard he studied and applied himself in his classes, it was never enough to get a satisfactory grade. Disappointed and overwhelmed by his reality, something in Darren told him to never quit in life because one day his vision of becoming an engineer would be magnified. In spite of his low grades and failing performances in school, Darren never stopped finding a way to battle with the setbacks he experienced in life to achieve a reward that will override all his past failures.

It was not until his eleventh grade in high school, at the age of nineteen, that a voice from within inspired him to rise and stand against all the setbacks he experienced in his life. Despite all his failures in middle school and early years in high school, he never stopped believing in himself. He always dreamed of the possibilities of what his life will be like if he could let go all the situations and circumstances that was holding him back. No one, ultimately, in this world would be more proud to see him make it than his father. Even as a youngster, Darren's father always had strong dreams for his son. His father as well was an individual who wanted to be a civil engineer. Unfortunately, as a result of a life-threatening stroke, his dreams were cut short. Before he died, Darren's father had high expectations for his life and the life of his family. Whether it would be swimming, riding a bicycle, martial arts, or swinging the bat to hit a homerun, Darren's father never saw any impossibilities or hindrances in any of his son's actions. His vision in his son to achieve all that he wanted for him remained constant.

Knowing this, no one could ever dare to tell Darren his dreams were impossible because all the principles of accomplishing an impossible dream have been ingrained in him from childhood. Though he was not the scholar that he wanted to be in school, he knew that no dream could be real unless it gives birth to an imagination. Once an imagination is placed into Darren's mind and heart, he continues to dream about it every day until he achieves and makes it become part of his life. Darren would later graduate high school at the age of twenty. Though he had somewhat subpar grades in school, it never diminished his hopes to one day turn his life around and become a widely respected engineer. It would be five years after graduating from high school, Darren went onto a technical university to get his bachelor's degree in engineering. Three years following, he would further his education by pursuing a masters degree in the same field. Soon afterward, he would be employed with a respected engineering firm, designing bridges and buildings as part of his task.

Suddenly, all the setbacks in Darren's life changed. It would take almost ten years to achieve the dream he desired to achieve. Through all his efforts, his perseverance would finally be rewarded. No longer will he rest on his inabilities that reflect his past failures and disappointments in life. Now more than ever, he has given himself an ultimate reward to look forward to. Unbending in his passion and hopes to succeed at his goals, he vows to become a widely respected engineer worldwide where he will be the architect of a monument that will have his name etched in its stone. It shows that one dream was never enough for Darren because when that dream was attained he built on it to accomplish another dream. Similarly, one reward was not enough because he kept building on it to achieve an ultimate reward. Indeed, one would look at Darren's life and believe none of this would be possible. Most people around him thought he had every intention to fail and not make his life count for something. However, the one difference with Darren is that he never stopped believing that any of his intentions were impossible. Darren may have had impossible dreams that at one time appeared unrealistic. But no one should ever underestimate the power of an impossible dreamer, and the rewards that one can achieve when those one time impossible dreams finally become actualized.

> ***Sometimes we have so much foresight with what we want, but those visions never become possible if we never have insight into taking the actions to make those visions a reality.***

# NEVER SAY NEVER

## CHAPTER 8

**The Uncommon**

There is a special moment that is designed to come into a person's life. It is a signature moment that doesn't happen very often to everyone. However, when it happens, it opens a moment of rare and unexpected occurrence. It is one that is embraced and designed to give that person the acknowledgment and the deference he or she deserves for his or her achievements in the world. It is one that releases all the energies of hard work, perseverance, tenacity, and ambitious power to knock down any opposing force of failure and disappointment that threatens its course. It is an energy that desires the affinity to be successful and achieve success at all costs. It is one that projects not only the power to achieve, but also the power to overachieve and superachieve anything and everything it wants out of life. Such an individual who harnesses this desire is relentless in his or her passion to make a name for himself or herself in this world. It is the same fiery passion that one uses to create history when no history could be created by anyone else.

It is also the same intense passion that generates all the opinions by others to make one's deeds appear unrealistic and uncommon because of the unspeakable talents and gifts one has yet to display to the rest of the world. Interestingly, because of the challenges that life brings and the negative forces that arise from those challenges, this individual has a burning passion in his or her mind and heart that is ready to overcome any opposing force that feels his or her dreams in life is rendered impossible.

After all, it is the very passion that stems from one's desire so that one can get what one wants. It is the same burning passion that forms a habit that produces the results necessary to never allow an individual to go below ground. Applying this level of action becomes the very measure and altitude of that individual's desire to never fall and settle for the lesser things in life. It is when this individual burns with this desire, he or she goes above and beyond the call of duty to exceed his or her dreams in this world. Truly, such a moment in one's life is deserving, rightfully called for, yet less likely to be reborn or reincarnated by anyone else other than the person it was given birth to. Such a moment is one where it faces the actuality of time, by which it surrenders itself to each individual in a moment that is regarded as uniquely special to others in the world.

It is one that becomes an unwavering force in a person's life who is acknowledged for all his or her efforts and contributions imparted to society. Interestingly, what makes an individual quite unique in this world is the ability he or she has to accomplish his or her dreams and goals on a much faster and broader scale than anyone who may or may not be traveling on the same path. A moment, then, is one where it should be credited for experience, experience that can only happen once, never to arrive in that person's life again. Thus, the past, present, and future, when that moment gives birth, is no longer the same. The moment, for all sense of reality, becomes an energy that was trapped in the past but becomes a power when it releases itself in the present and becomes a memory when it unveils itself repeatedly in the form of memories to everyone in the future. Whatever the moment calls for, it is intended by all purposes indeed to present itself as an uncommon entity in the lives of others. There exists a special moment designed for a unique person. This person is a young lady by the name of Stephanie.

In countless steps toward achieving her goals, Stephanie is an individual who illustrates what it means to be an uncommon achiever in this world. Being an achiever has been the background and foreground to Stephanie's hallmark of accomplishments. Even as a youngster, she was ingrained with the principles of higher education from an early age. Most people saw an unlikeness in Stephanie that they had not seen in other children. Some people thought by the way she developed and the speed of her development that she was bound to achieve things in life at a much faster pace than others. Even at the very age of one, born on the first day and month of the year, Stephanie never liked to be in second place. Her family remembered when she was just a toddler, she started speaking and confidently, in a song, recited all the letters in the alphabet.

Her mother was impressed by her intelligence, so impressed that she consistently challenged her daughter in every stage of her development to keep learning and work hard. Each day would go by, but not one day would slide without Stephanie learning something important that she could apply to her life. Eventually, when Stephanie reached the age of eight, her mother sent her to boarding school. The school would be one of the top boarding schools in the country. It would be regarded as academically challenging and intense; however, knowing the capabilities Stephanie already possessed, she confidently carried herself forward to the challenges she faced and felt there was nothing that she could not do or accomplish in any moment she wanted to belong to her.

In just a matter of weeks after undergoing many tests and intense practices in her subjects, many of Stephanie's teachers praised her efforts in the school and regarded her work ethics and performance as remarkable. She was a student who scored a 100 percent on many of her exams. Incredibly, even with the separation of her mother and father, she was not deterred in life by any circumstances when it came to excelling and surpassing all her challenges. She was focused. She knew exactly what she wanted and when she wanted for it to happen. The grounds for achievement belonged to everyone else, but the uncommon grounds for extraordinary success were owned directly by her.

With numerous achievements growing up, at the age of eighteen, she was able to receive a bachelor's degree from Texas University and is currently five years away from becoming the first medical doctor in her family. Looking back, her mother has been a key figure who has been instrumental to her daughter's success and development. Every step of the way, Stephanie was pushed and encouraged by a greater good and avoiding a lesser evil of finding the avenues to her destination. Nothing, as much as circumstances and the obstacles that exist in the world from them, was enough to conquer her in her moment. She was determined to push through and make it through in moments where she needed it to count more than anything. The projected story of her success and achievements in life is one that inspires the hopeful and the faithful to never stop aspiring to go after one's dreams.

It shows no amount of accomplishments he or she creates for himself or herself in life can deny the stage that is set for a special moment to occur in his or her life that will outshine every moment of disapproval and disappointment. Much to the enlightenment of her journey, she received numerous awards for her outstanding academic performance in school, which ranged from honorary academic achievements, Phi Beta Kappa, and an outstanding GMAT score. In every endeavor that Stephanie took on, she possessed every capability and talent to succeed. There was nothing that she would put her hand to, and it failed. She constantly found a way to overcome difficult moments where it channeled her way to success. Maybe, just maybe, it is part of God's plan that her life defies no gravity.

She will continue to overachieve and be this way until her impact in the world is gone. Incredibly, despite her rocketed efforts to success, she was intimidated by other people who were not on her level of intelligence. Throughout her time in middle and high school grade levels, she would encounter other people who were envious of her success. Most of them would do anything to sabotage her performance by being unsupportive with group projects and providing helpful information that she would need that pertains to her studies. It seemed that she would make friends as well as enemies on her path to excellence. Many people who were unfortunate as she was desired to see her not make it. However, through the midst of all her challenges, she still found a way to keep rising to the top. In all her endeavors, she did not allow anyone or anything to ignite a setback on her path.

Ultimately, it shows the highlight of a person's life, in a time of his or her achievement, symbolizes the countless efforts and performance he or she has had in this world. Moments that rendered an individual's accomplishment and historical measures and endeavors taken are ones where it has crossed over into unprecedented boundaries that not anyone can cross. Stephanie, still vying for her ultimate reward, never chooses to surrender until she has accomplished all that she needs to accomplish in this world. Each day, she continues to walk on an uncommon ground where she diligently strives and moves one step closer to her dreams and desired destination to become a doctor at the tender age of twenty-three.

*The moment becomes an energy when it is trapped in the past. It becomes a power when it is released in the present, and it becomes a memory when it is timely recalled in the future.*

## The True Element of Karma

Karma is defined as a force generated by a person's actions held to perpetuate ethical consequences. It is the total effect of a person's actions and conduct during the phases of his or her path in life. All the principles of justice that determine a person's state of life and the state of his or her afterlife is permeated with suffering or enlightenment obtained through the right conduct and wisdom that he or she releases from his or her desires. Thus, it is whatever energy that is released from this desire in the moment that will transcend other moments to come. Through it all, it is proven there is a magnetic field in the air that traps all the energies you send out. It propels forces in your direction that can either bring positive results or negative consequences.

No matter where you are in life, all the energies that you ever exhibited in your past is somewhat trapped right into this energy field. This energy then is transmitted back to your life and through the rest of the world. It displays telling events of how your past will be recalled, how you will live in your present, and where you will be in the future. This, essentially, is the karma in one's life. In all of its ethical consequences, it determines a person's inner being and his or her actions and conduct in life. Every area of justice that permeated through this world that determines an individual state of life, state of mind, and the state of events held will inevitably happen in the future through how a person's life has been lived.

It is similar to an antenna signal that transmits radio waves. A signal is set, but it relies on every frequency that is transmitted back to its starting point to bring a radio signal back to the world. It is the moment that everyone anticipates. It is a moment that let's one know that one can send something off to the rest of the world and hope that the signal and message is strong enough to relay positive feedback. Every moment in a person's life is set up by all the energies he or she has ever exhibited in the world.

Some people believe that certain forces in the universe must be linked to some psychic energy that let's one know that whatever one does in one's life will either propel one to success or leave a result that is marked by one's failure. Knowing how justifiable one's actions are in the world, it only makes sense that one channels a force of positive energy so that the same energy can be returned to one's life.

The world, thus, operates in a cyclical fashion, giving you what it has received from the energies that you have transmitted in the world. Whatever it is that you need, you give it, and it will be returned to you by the same measures of your heart. If you need love, you give love, and it will be returned to you by the same measure it was transmitted. If you need kindness, you give kindness, and it will also be returned to you in the same likeness it was transmitted.

Even for those who desire affiliation, they need to give to others so that they will not only be shaped by people in the world but by the personal relationships they have with them. Each word, thought, action, and decision that you made releases its intention in the universe to prove your true passion, destiny, and desire in life. These are indeed what makes moments last and what equally makes them special. If all the intentions are weighed equal, the results and energy that return to you will be dynamic. However, if your intentions have been somewhat negative and unequal in the eyes of others, the energy transmitted back to you will bring on destructive results and mounting consequences.

Growing up, Julia was a girl who was never born with a silver spoon in her mouth. She grew up having to work hard for everything she ever wanted in life. For everything Julia desired, nothing came easy for her. Her life from the day she was born was all about overcoming trying situations and hardship. As a youngster, her parents did not have a lot to give because they also encountered many of the difficulties that dealt with finding the right jobs and being placed into the right situations. It seemed that whatever signals they transmitted through the world was bound to be returned in the form of a positive or negative feedback from others. They gave all that they could give to have a better life for themselves and their three children.

Of all the children they had, Julia took special interest in their hearts because she was their first child who was eight years older than her siblings. They figured if they could at least get her in a good high school where she could take college courses, she would have a great chance of graduating early where she would become someone who could make a difference in the world. Other than Julia's parents believing in her, Julia also possessed strong confidence in her abilities by believing in herself. She knew it would be those very capabilities that would enable her to channel her way through the obstacles she would eventually face in her life.

Although Julia was the first born, most of the troubles she had in life was exactly what her parents had to go through. Her parents would work hard but would often come up short when it comes to achieving anything they desired. Maybe Julia's path in life was by the same design. Maybe it was the way the energy in the universe had been established for her. Because life was hard for Julia's parents, life for Julia would also in turn be difficult. What would make the real difference in how Julia's path in life would be defined was knowing that because all of her endeavors would be equally challenging because of the imposing and compelling forces that her parents had to go through, she would have to be an individual who would have to work two and three times as hard to get the results that she wanted in her life. Julia knew that she can't just go to school and try to achieve. She knew she had to go to school with the mind-set that she will achieve.

Trying, for all obvious reasons, is good in the world, but trying is not good enough if one can't capitalize on achieving the mark to succeed. Sometimes it is because of negative forces that have been transmitted in someone's life that he or she would have to continually find ways to battle through it to find a mark for his or her own achievement. In her years in college, Julia passed all of her classes. She was considered to be well rounded in many of the subjects that were part of her curriculum. She believed in all her heart that she had what the world needed for her to make it and get over the edge she needed in life.

Apparently, what she did not realize after she graduated from college was all the difficulties that she would encounter when it comes to finding a job and sustaining one in a declining economy. Julia would go through an intense uphill climb, trying to find a satisfactory-paying job one year after getting out of school. When she found one, the job fired her for poor performance only six weeks of being employed with the company. Julia's next job opportunity was not any better than the first. Desperate for income and a chance to make ends meet, she found a commission-paying job where she had to work in real estate, showing clients different properties working more than fifty plus hours a week. After four months of being a real estate agent and working with a potential buyer where her efforts would have net her a $12,000 profit from the property being sold, the buyer pulled out of the deal because of reasons unknown.

Julia was devastated. She knew for sure that the deal was going to go through, but it seemed just when she wanted to make something happen in life and have something going for her, another moment had slipped right through the palm of her hands. She felt defeated and disappointed. She figured that maybe there was a supernatural force that was out there that just didn't want her to succeed. She prayed to God to find the answer, but as many times as she prayed, she would be left to find the answers on her own.

Julia worked as hard as she possibly could to maintain her integrity by continuing to be faithful and confident in her abilities despite the obstacles and challenges she continued to face in life. In a matter of weeks, she tried to sell another property. The deal all appeared to be moving in a positive direction, but certain factors with down payment and loan payments resulted in the same situations where the property could not be sold. Soon enough, Julia became dissatisfied. Life put a taste in her mouth that left her appetite sour.

Poor-paying jobs, missed opportunities, working hard but never to see the end from all the sacrifices that she made almost made her surrender and give up on life. Julia's parents watched her daughter struggle as they battled through struggles of their own. It seemed everywhere Julia would go, she ventured on an avenue that took on many surprising twist and turns. When she aimed for higher-paying jobs, they required her to pass a certain test to be employed. No matter how much she studied and how hard she tried to pass, she began to fail every test that shunted her from any opportunity that would lead to satisfactory income and employment. En route to her journey, Julia's struggle reached her fifth year. She knew that something was wrong. There had to be an external force that was holding her back from succeeding.

She took a few steps back and asked herself some questions to see if there was something that she needed to change in her character. She knew it was not the college she graduated from because she went to an excellent university. She also had quality referral letters from professors and previous employers she worked with in the past. Still, there was something else that was far deeper than all of that. All of Julia's efforts were not convincing enough because she reached a point in her life where she continued to battle with certain obstacles and challenges that decided to come her way. Julia began to realize that she had to take a step back in life and realize that her moment in time may just not come at the time it was supposed to arrive. She tried her best to live good with people, but obviously, there was something out there that apparently did not want her to succeed. Was it the energy that other people have sent from bad relationships that she or her parents have had in the past with others? Was it the energy also of not being able to produce one successful outcome so another successful outcome will follow? Or was it simply the fact that repeated disappointments and failures have transferred an energy into the world where it would transcend into other disappointments and failures?

No one knew for sure. All that mattered, in spite of all Julia's setbacks, was to turn to a new chapter in her life. After having undergone years of challenges, she met a young man in her church with whom she became very good friends with. In a short span of time, it seemed both of them were a perfect fit for one another; and at the age of thirty-three, she got married with the intent that her life would take a turn for the better. She would take on an entirely different approach and mind-set toward life. She would now have a clearer mind with a rejuvenated spirit that would hopefully erase and overshadow her past disappointments and struggles.

For the first year, everything seemed well in her marriage. Julia was able to find a suitable-paying job, where she was able to assist her husband in most of the household expenses. In addition, she was focused on the possibilities of moving and buying her own personal property in the future. All was going well until both Julia and her husband decided it was time to have children. After three years of trying to have a child and not being fertile, Julia decided to see a doctor. On the day of her doctor's visit, the doctor examined Julia and told her she has a condition that causes her body to produce low follicle-stimulating hormones along with fibrosis, which are normal precursors in women that are not able to have children.

The doctor advised Julia that she would need to have a procedure performed in order to remove the fibroids. Moreover, she would also need to attend a fertility clinic to see if a specialist could offer any kind of remedy to her situation. Without hesitation, Julia attended the clinic where she was able to get treatment regarding her situation. The specialist prescribed medications along with intravenous injections to increase her follicle-stimulating hormones. Over time, the treatments worked, her FSH levels increased, and the doctors gave Julia a choice to perform a method called in vitro fertilization if she desired any chance of conceiving. Being challenged, desperate but hopeful, Julia was willing to try anything that would bring her passion of being a mother into reality. She expended $5,000 of her own money saved, which would be the cost of the procedure. She agreed to perform in vitro fertilization where the doctors would physically remove the eggs from her ovaries and mix the eggs with her husband's sperm where it would be fertilized in a fluid medium.

After doing so, the eggs would then be implanted back in the uterine wall where she would wait several days for the results to see if the procedure was an overall success. It would take a week where Julia would use her pregnancy indicator each day to find out whether she was pregnant. After repeatedly using her indicator and finding the results to be negative, Julia returned to the doctor to find a solution as to what went wrong. Apparently, the doctors explained that even in the event of in vitro fertilization there is no guarantee that the procedure would be a success.

It would be a fifty-fifty chance of performing the procedure and it being successful. Ultimately, if anything would add meaning and joy to Julia's life, it would be the sense of having a child that belonged to her. Defeated and desperate to find a solution to her futility, Julia was relentless in her efforts to try a different doctor who could possibly bring a different result. For one week, she searched vigorously on the Internet where she would find a doctor who had a proven track record of delivering successful pregnancies to his patients. She would go to the doctor's office for a visit and would set up an appointment four weeks later to perform the same procedure. The procedure would be performed, and after one week of checking her results on her pregnancy indicator, Julia had finally gotten pregnant. It was at that moment everything that she had gone through had suddenly been overshadowed with joy and happiness.

Julia and her husband shared in celebration the expectancy of a new child in their home. It was indeed a moment of relief as well as victory for Julia to treasure. She would be two months into her pregnancy while maintaining regular doctor's visits to monitor the growth of her child.

She would go out to shop for unisex clothing and create additional space inside her home to make way for her newborn; even friends offered as much support in any way possible to assist Julia in her growing state of pregnancy.

Ultimately, it would be her fourth month of pregnancy until Julia noticed something unusual was taking place inside her body. She would start to feel signs of weakness, sharp cramping, and abdominal pain. Added to all the effects Julia was experiencing, she began to experience bleeding in her cervix. The elevated signs would get so severe that she thought that she was in labor. She immediately sought medical assistance and was driven straight to the emergency room by her husband.

Julia, in intense pain, was treated by the nurse and doctor in the ER. Given acknowledgment to her sudden onset of complications, the doctor claimed that she must not do any heavy lifting and engage in any sexual activity. She would also be advised to stay on bed rest until the bleeding subsided. Julia decided not to take any chances. She would not go to work for a week. In her time spent at home, she was on bed rest for the majority of her days spent indoors. In her mind, she fought too hard and too long to surrender to any of the complications she was experiencing. Ultimately, the symptoms would subside, and Julia returned to work in two weeks. It appeared that her life returned to normal. She religiously kept to her habits of heading straight home from work where she tried to get as much rest as possible. All seemed to be going well until three weeks of working at her job, she returned home one evening only to notice that the symptoms worsened.

This time, she was left in complete despair. She would come home at a time her husband was at work. Therefore, she had no one at that time she could rely on to drive her straight to the hospital. Julia, in obvious pain, was nervous and alone in her room. She laid on the floor in severe and obvious pain. It would be moments after the onset of her pain, heavy bleeding would develop. Frantically, Julia dialed her husband at work, where he assisted her in contacting emergency services to have her rushed to the hospital. The emergency attendants came to the scene and quickly rushed to her attention, and she immediately was given treatment in the hospital. Julia's husband quickly left his job to attend to his ailing wife. The heavy bleeding continued in the emergency room where there was no sign or stoppage of relief to all of Julia's ailing attacks.

The doctor, in the event to save Julia's life, had no other choice but to abort the child and remove all the undeveloped and developed parts of the baby that took place inside her uterus. In her utmost distress, Julia screamed and cried in intense emotion. It would be at that time, her worse nightmares have come true. Ultimately, there would be no way for the doctor's to deal with the situation other than to perform all the measures necessary to save Julia's life, even if it meant for her losing the one she had inside of her. The surgery would be performed, and Julia would remain in the hospital for the next several days.

She would spend consecutive days in the hospital inundated by the recent events that had taken place. Each day, her husband would visit, and he too would share the moment of a stressful and devastating loss that occurred in his life. On the day of her departure, it all came together that she would have gone to the hospital pregnant, but she would leave with her dreams shattered of not leaving the hospital a mother. Both Julia and her husband for weeks grieved the loss of their potential newborn child. Julia's life was in complete turmoil from all the devastating consequences that unseeingly kept happening in succession. Just when she expected her life to take a turn for the better, it took another turn for the worse.

Julia had strong hopes and dreams that were suddenly cut short by an unexpected outcome. It appeared from the inception she was born, her life was and will always be about being a survivor where she constantly had to overcome the challenging forces that have been projected in her path. Julia would ultimately take on the pain and loss of her newborn by taking the time she needed to reflect back on her life. She would reflect and wait for the next possible action that would be necessary to turn her life around for the better. All of this made Julia saddened by all the challenges and suffering she continued to experience in her life.

Through it all, she felt maybe her destiny in life in every moment was marked for failure. Maybe she would never find a way out when she constantly fought to find a way to open many of the doors that have closed.

Maybe it would be the challenges that her parents have gone through in their lives that have filtered right down into her own life. Julia wanted the best things in life, but those things became blocked by the challenging forces of nature. It was a nature that would overall determine when a moment in time would arrive for someone based on the amount of energy he or she has transmitted to the world. When the moment arrived, it would either be destined for success, or it would be designated for failure.

Julia constantly battled to have a positive outlook on life. She had to undergo countless obstacles where she faced a world of challenges. The challenges she had to overcome dealt with many important moments in her life that she could not capitalize. Life, thus, started to become frustrating and meaningless to her because at every angle there seemed to be something that reversed all of her efforts. Unfortunately, it became something that was beyond her control. Julia would eventually move on, and through the process of moving on, she would make several further attempts to conceive a child; but to no avail, her efforts continued to come up short. For the next few years, Julia would settle for whatever jobs she could find when situations would arise where she would be laid off or fired from work because of a decline in business sales. After more than ten years of marriage, Julia decided to adopt two children, a boy at the age of two and a girl at the age of one, all while purchasing a five-bedroom home in a small Florida county. The decision would be one where she and her husband would feel a sense of newness in their lives.

Apparently, the only driving force Julia had going for her was her years of experience being destroyed by the forces of nature and the results of unexpected outcomes. She had to battle within herself to find a job when searching for one became a challenge to get one and sustain it along the way. She would also overcome the pain of emotional and physical loss of her own child to have two foster children of her own. She would sustain her marriage with her husband despite all the obstacles and emotional challenges it faced.

She is a true example of a person who would never be undertaken and undercut by past forces. In any and everything she would do, she displayed a relentless passion to never give in and surrender to the challenges she faced even when she experienced timely downfalls in life. Because of her past failures, no one believed that Julia had what it takes to make it.

However, at no point did she ever surrender and give into the challenges that were brought on in her life unexpectedly. Indeed, circumstances will constantly find ways to press you against the wall, but you must consistently see that life is a series of moments that when you are pressed against a wall, you have to find a way to get your back off the wall and move again. One moment can change your life, but it doesn't write your destiny. In no way shape for form can a single moment define the way the rest of your life should be lived when you have enough time to create a new channel of moments that can override the ones that have failed in the past.

*If you keep on winning in life, there is no element to losing; but if you keep on losing in life, there is something that you need to break through so you will not be blocked from achieving anything deemed impossible.*

## The Power of Resurrection

It is inevitable you can make people stronger, or you can make them weaker by the personality you exhibit in their presence. One's personality alone is one of the key determinants as to who and what flows in and out of one's life. Much to the dismay of many people with personalities that clash, they can never find a valid solution or formula to hold on to the relationships they have built effortlessly in this world. Every step taken forward is another one taken backward if they can't bring any solution to the changes that they need to make so that their lives can emerge with progress.

Thus, for every calling in one's life, in order to rise from a lower to a higher ground, one must bury all of one's ineptitudes that is stifling one from moving forward with a new purpose and passion in the world. Surely, no one can live for himself or herself too long if he or she can't find ways to coexist with others. Something has to burn inside of him or her that will be far more fitting and rewarding than all the experiences of having failed and missing the mark in his or her past.

Ultimately, there are so many people who chase after a vision that the world has planted in their hearts and minds only to lose the vision that they should have planted in their own lives. Without having a plan, they build a connection with what other people see for their lives without building a connection with what they should see for their own lives. Through it all, there comes a time when someone must die to his or her old self so that he or she can live again. No one will ever be a believer out of someone who is not taking his or her life anywhere. In order for people to believe that you are worth something in this world, you have to prove to them that no matter how many times you have failed, there is a moment that can still emerge that will be destined for you to succeed.

How easy it is for other people to despise others who have not achieved much success in their lives. How often is it that they look down on these individuals that have missed their mark in life by not living up to their potential? It just shows that many people only respect you for what you have rather than for who you are as an individual. Why? To these people, they only see that person in the moment because they are not focused on what can be transformed in that person when that moment has passed. It goes to prove in life, you will always face criticism because the world is filled with people who don't believe in transformation. They focus on the reality but never dream of the possibilities. How evident is it that one can look at the life of someone who has suffered with missed opportunities, setbacks in relationships, constant ailments in health without considering how he or she can demonstrate an ability to overcome them?

Biblically, one can clearly envision the suffering and life of Jesus before he died. He was a man who was brought to this world to save the souls of others. He was an individual in pure likeness of God. Many believers who followed him knew he was the way and the truth to life. Others who did not follow him believed otherwise. No matter who was for and against him, Jesus remained focused on his ultimate commission, which was to get people saved so that they can live changed lives as his disciples. By then, many will also get to experience the power of life over death and what it is like to have a relationship with God. At the expense of his passion to change the world, he suffered intense scrutiny and hatred from unbelievers who wanted to see him suffer and have his life taken at all costs. As a result, Jesus would be beaten and nailed to the cross to die. In the midst of his death, it was clear that he knew that his life and time on earth was short.

However, he already knew that even though he would die, he would rise three days later and come back to life. Many people who doubted him didn't believe in his transformation to be resurrected. Unsurprisingly, Jesus had a life where he was vulnerable to death because of his passion to serve God and his life under the living flesh. He was ridiculed, beaten, tortured, and hammered to the cross. Surely enough, in the last minute of his death, it was all part of God's plan that his son Jesus would take on the sins of the world, which would be bored to the cross.

Indeed, it was a moment in the Bible that no one could forget because it is that very moment that Jesus would also use to help many like-minded Christians in the world today reflect and remember the sacrifice that he made so that we can have a relationship with God. Death, essentially, is all part of life, while life, essentially, in many cases, can also give rise to death. All in all, in the moment of Christ's resurrection, he would be united with the body and spirit to show the world that he, just like you, as long as you have a relationship with him, can overcome death for life.

Obviously, the resurrection of Christ was one in which many people stood in fear and joy. Evidently, many believers doubted that Jesus can be resurrected in a body that was already deemed perishable. However, God talks about the fact that for anything to come back to life, it must first die so that it can grow and rise again. For example, examine an individual who plants a seed in the ground. Once a seed has been buried in the ground, what people see is a new body that arises from that seed in the form of a plant. No one ever thinks about the seed afterward because all that is seen from what has been examined is what develops after that seed has been planted.

As it is written in the New International Version Bible, 1 Corinthians 15:36 states the following:

> *What you sow does not come to life unless it dies. When you sow, you do not plant the body that will be, but just a seed, perhaps of wheat or of something else. But God gives it a body as he has determined, and to each kind of seed he gives its own body. All flesh is not the same. Men have one kind of flesh, animals have another, birds another and fish another. There are also heavenly bodies and there are earthly bodies; but the splendor of the heavenly bodies is one kind, and the splendor of the earthly bodies is another. The sun has one kind of splendor, the moon another and the stars another, and star differ from star in splendor.*
>
> *So will it be with the resurrection of the dead. The body that is sown perishable, it is raised imperishable; it is sown in dishonor, it is raised in glory, it is sown in weakness, it is raised in power, it is sown a natural body, it is raised a spiritual body.*

It is proven that everything you do in your life is not only prone to destruction but also prone to be resurrected. Nothing good can stand and last forever. Vanity doesn't last; material possessions, talents, gifts, achievements, and life on this earth do not last. Everything that you gain and acquired in this world is bound to grow old and die. However, God can always bring back to life what many people thought was dead. With him, there is always a new beginning—a new healing that takes place in one's heart once the resurrection process has taken effect. Imagine for the people who doubt your efforts and contributions to life, you have to plant a new seed in their hearts and minds so that they no longer see the old seed that was there.

It is up to you to alter the course and direction of their mind-set. Only you have the power to bury all the failures that people saw in your life so that you can resurrect a new mind-set of victory that is what people need to see in your new life. Just as Jesus was resurrected from the dead and took on the spiritual form, people can only reflect on how he was raised in glory from all the suffering and pain he had gone through in the world.

What are you doing to rise and comeback from failure in your life? What do you need to do to make your life transform for the better? Do you have the power to bury the past seeds that were sown in weakness and dishonor in the eyes of others to plant new seeds that will be raised in power and glory to the world?

How evident is the fact that many people miss the mark in life when it comes to believing they can make a comeback from all the setbacks they experienced? Life has yet buried them with circumstances and hardship that they have no way of finding a solution or method of transplant to recover. They have all but given up on life without giving themselves a chance to rebound from past mistakes, circumstances, and defeats.

No longer can they become a victor from their circumstances because each day they fail to realize that life draws a new victim to its element of success or web of destruction. Thus, it becomes essential to have passion in what you want to resurrect and bring back that passion with purpose so that your resurrection is lifted with power. In order to have purpose, you must have a passion that fuels the purpose you want to exhibit in the world. Having purpose without passion only makes your intentions and power in this world futile. When you have purpose that is reinforced by passion even at the expense that dream dies, it will always carry itself to make that dream rise again.

It becomes vital to any individual who is driving through challenging moments not to be paralyzed and thwarted by its setbacks. How important it is for one to die to one's past so that one can find ways to reemerge and create a successful future. Interestingly, imagine how much better life will be when you make a decision whereby successful moments will not be written off and left in the dust. You just have to believe you still possess the capabilities and talents to make those moments rise again. Once too many times, we let our talents and capabilities in life die without finding a means to resurrect them and bring them back to life. Ultimately, everyone has had to face limitations in life. However, once those limits are no longer limitations, they become a stepping-stone to climb toward a greater good, destination, and moment in our lives.

> *The ultimate measure of a man is not where he stands in moments of comfort and convenience, but where he stands at times of challenge and controversy.*
> —MARTIN LUTHER KING JR.

## Battles and Wars Are Never Setbacks

The times in everyone's life presents many altering moments. One moment can transition into another moment, not knowing the results or impact it would bring. Sometimes when a transition is made, its intent for all purposes is to create the necessary tools for change and the necessary remedy for justice. Unfortunately, in a conflict between two people, change can only emerge if both parties are willing and able to make a sacrifice for that change. Over time, if one party is willing, but the other is not willing to accept, a choice must be made by one party to surrender or fight for everything he or she believes will continue to make that relationship last. As a result of one party's continual resistance and another party's willingness for change, he or she can either go the distance in life to fight for what he or she believes or will not believe will be a worthy cause for progression. Incredibly, when the indifferences are repeatedly discussed, but no resolution comes into action, the result from continued unresolved conflict is an imminent war.

Ultimately, it is not the first or last time that people have to go through a battle in their relationship to resolve conflict. Battles are always being fought in this world. No one can dishonor the fact that he or she has not taken the initiative to battle for something he or she wants. It is when he or she consistently loses the battle that the result ignites the mind to take on a higher level of action to go to war. A war, thus, is not born unless the battles that stem from that war repeatedly end in defeat or go uncorrected. Obviously, there are many challenges as to how one can overcome the life of war to exchange for a life of peace. For example, look at the constant battles a relationship goes through where two people continually argue never to resolve their indifferences with one another. Look at the damaging effects also from a war that can lead to violence and separation by people who don't have any intentions of fusing the broken pieces back together.

There are battles that make or break everyone's lives, but it is the constant battles that lead to war that destroys people's minds and hearts for one another. Recovery from being separated is difficult, but it is even harder to recover when there is nothing to separate from. It is different, however, for the ones who battle for peace. There are individuals that have to fight to restore the values in their marriage and relationships with their children. Life is a battle for them, but it is a battle that will never lead to the possibilities of being in a war. Those individuals in life seem to have a different DNA than other people because their bloodstream is battle-tested with all the difficulties and circumstances of the past that has enabled them to overcome and channel their way through future obstacles and situations. It is amazing, in the heat or the event of a continuous conflict, that the aggressor never hears that person's voice because he or she is solely focused on the voice he or she hears from within that is making all the demands.

Thus, fighting for a purpose to obtain power and respect is ultimately one of the many reasons a war is waged but not the lasting solution for how a war should be won. Truly, it is a battle that is fought in the moment until that moment dies. Surely, it is a war also that begins unexpectedly with no expectations of when it will come to an end. For some people, the experience of continuous conflict will always be a defining moment in their lives where it can make a relationship stronger if it is mended, or it can be the very one if not mended can destroy all the relationships that one has created. Creating peace, ultimately, that has stemmed from war is not an impossibility, but it is one that takes time for two parties to reach in agreement so that they can live in harmony with one another.

Sometimes the fight to prove a point brings on so much intensity that it leaves a devastating scar to those who survive its attacks. Just imagine coming home and getting into an argument with your spouse about something miniscule that could easily be corrected in a matter of minutes. Is life all based on trying to prove a point where you slam the other person's ideas and heart against the wall? How often are the little things that start a battle can magnify and escalate on a much bigger and unnecessary scale? Just envision the possibilities of also coming home on a different day only to have another argument about something else that goes unresolved for a few weeks and a few months. The words and messages that are delivered in the heat of a battle can leave scars that are not healed so easily. Indeed, it takes time to dwindle it away, but even as much time has passed, some people still can reflect on the intense moment that led to all the damages they experienced in that time. Obviously, a battle can get so intense that a message is sent with anger and volatile language that either side refuses to back down from one another so much that the arguments in the heat of the moment go unresolved. Thus, the fight increasingly continues, and the war that has emerged from the battle rages on.

Quite evident is the fact that no one can bring a war to an end, but somehow there has to be a greater purpose and reason beyond the people who are battling with one another so that it can eventually come to a resolution. A war can take on extreme hate that makes an individual forget how to love, encourage, and honor the things he or she values the most in his or her relationship. A war can take on all the small things in life and make it seem as if it is the most important things in life that matter.

Fighting battles are all bent on the fact that one's emotion has gotten the better of oneself. It is an emotion that he or she battles with to prove a point despite the opposition or conflict he or she has faced in his or her life. When it comes to two opposing forces that have continuously battled, there is no telling when a war will end. Some people can fight a war for months and years in hopes to channel their way through conflict to bring satisfaction and peace to their lives.

Sean and Marie were one such couple who have been married for several years to one another. The relationship they had with each other was one time based on love, trust, honor, and sacrifice. In the beginning of Sean's relationship with his wife, he had obvious conditions with his health where he had problems with blood pressure, lungs, and would constantly suffer from periodic migraines.

Sometimes the pain of his conditions would be so extreme that he would need to be rushed to the hospital for treatment. Through it all, Marie figured his chronic health condition could all stem from a complicated childbirth and poor smoking habits he developed as a teenager. For all reasons obvious, Marie overlooked her husband's condition and was willing to see in him the greater good that no one else saw. When he was challenged by his ailments, she constantly found a way to support him in any way she possibly could to overcome them.

In many ways, Marie had to offer her support for Sean where his condition would at times cause him to take a leave of absence from work. The outcome led to Marie paying majority of the bills and assisting her husband in every measure possible until he was able to start working. Through all her efforts, it seemed just about everything that Marie would do for her husband, there will still be constant indifferences in their marriage. Despite all the conflicts and battles that would range from communication breakdown, lack of compassion, understanding each other's needs, and financial instability, Marie constantly found ways to overshadow all of what she experienced in the past by being optimistic of the life that will possibly change going forward. In spite of it all, it would be three years into their marriage, and although Sean and Marie had disagreements in the past, most of their disagreements would come to a resolution by the day's end. At one point, it appeared their marriage had made some improvement. It seemed that their relationship was built on a foundational strength that repeatedly plied its way through bitter situations and conflict.

Indeed, the battles that appeared to look unsustainable many times found a way to be sustained so that their lives can be stabilized in that moment. Over time, they reached a point in their marriage where both of them became battle-tested. Life was now in the fourth year of their marriage, and the moment took on a different turn when Sean and

Marie decided that they wanted to start having children. Marie agreed, even though she had already seen the worse sides of her husband in the relationship.

She believed that she would be a good mother, and he would make a great father to a child in this world. He became a willing party, and she became a willing participant who was willing to comply with him to ensure that both of their dreams of giving birth to a child will be brought to reality. Marie, in retrospect, thought about all the battles she has had in her life with Sean that has now brought her to this defining moment that may make or break her relationship with her husband.

Deep inside of her, something was buried under her exterior. The armor that she once held in her relationship was being chipped in every instant she encountered a battle. Something that at one time symbolized hope, peace, love, trust, and encouragement became broken over the years. In spite of all the arguments that she had with her husband, and the negative thoughts that came to mind, she would continue to hold strong and overlook all the flaws in her relationship. Somehow, the fifth year approached, and Marie successfully delivered a healthy baby girl. Despite the blessings of having a child, the arguments and tensions between Sean and Marie grew worse. Sean's temper toward his wife had gotten to a point where it grew uncontrollable. Tempers would start to flare when Marie could not hold to her husband's expectations, and she could not maintain his level of expectations in the relationship. The arguments became so intense that it even progressed to them physically hurting one another. Marie struggled to find a meaning and purpose to her relationship. For many nights, she cried and meditated on the possibility that it would one day come to an end. She was a mother of a newborn, who was fighting for a sense of peace and direction in her life. Inevitably, as time progressed, the vision and hope that she once had and placed in her marriage were suddenly torn to pieces in her heart.

She fought and battled with her husband when all she wanted from him was for him to love and honor her affection. When Marie was unable to have her needs met, it transformed her into an entirely different person. Apparently, her husband also had needs. The one person who seemed to fight with his wife about everything suddenly started to withdraw when he no longer felt he had the power to mend a relationship that was destined to fall apart. Sean, ultimately, was an individual who was solely focused on other people meeting his needs without demonstrating the ability to do things for himself.

He felt he would give his wife all the attention that she needed, but when that attention was given to her, it was still not enough to please her needs. Marie started to feel Sean was at times too insensitive and inconsiderate to her emotions. Through all her emotions, Marie was at the tipping point in her relationship where she reached her limit for dissatisfaction in her marriage.

Sean was no different toward Marie. Out of anger, Sean would think that his wife no longer had the love and respect that she once had for him. She would withdraw from preparing his meal, communicating with him, and doing household chores. It all but seemed her motivation and passion that she once had in her heart for her husband had disappeared. The foundation that his relationship was built on had all but fallen apart with the battles he faced with his wife over the years of his marriage. As he became more and more irritated with her, she became more irritable with life when she felt that her fight for a relationship had no clear meaning for resolve since the inception it was brought together.

It would take years of battling with each other's indifferences before it came to a point where Marie felt it was time for a change in her life. Marie decided to confront Sean about her feelings, and after a heated discussion on feeling that her relationship with her husband was not going anywhere, Marie decided it was time to let Sean know that she wanted a divorce. Instantly, in the moment, Sean reacted in a way that made him not care about what his wife said. However, after a few days, when she began to pack her clothes to head elsewhere with her child, Sean pleaded with her. He asked her to give him a second chance. Through the discussion, he would struggle with his wife to find a solution. However, after several hours, Marie gave it a second thought. She felt a possible turning point in her relationship where she may start to have her needs met. She decided to unpack all her clothes the following evening and anticipated a new beginning with her husband. Apparently, two months would pass, and after weeks of not seeing the changes that she needed to see, her decision of getting a divorce was final. This rational decision by her led to an ongoing war in court that ended with both of them parting ways after many years of marriage.

No longer would Marie tolerate not being loved and cared for in a marriage that she at one time had a strong vision for. No longer would she also have to worry about her emotions being crushed and stepped on by her husband's insensitivities. Surely enough, Sean wanted his relationship to last, but no matter how hard he tried to bring it back together, it was not meant to continue when a moment in time had come into his life that brought it to an end. The decision ultimately led to Marie and her husband living miles apart from each other in different states. After three years of being away from Sean, she decided to get married to an individual who would treat her with the utmost respect and compassion.

Unequivocally, it would seem that Marie and her new husband would become a perfect fit and partner for each other. Sean, on the other hand, would be challenged to live a life building on other relationships with women. He would focus his ambitions on improving his health and achieving a higher level of education.

All of which he was not able to do with a relationship that had constantly gone through rigorous battles that has led him to being stifled at many points in his life. The difference between the past and present in Sean's life was that he was challenged by constant battles where he was not able to see neither himself nor his insensitivities toward his partner. It became a battle that led to other battles that eventually and ultimately spiraled into a war that led to a divorce.

Even though he was able to come to his senses later on, it was already too late as the decision that his wife made to leave him had become final. Sometimes there is no telling from a constant battle that has emerged into a war which way a person's life will turn. It took eight years for the lives of Sean and Marie to go in an opposite yet positive direction. That is why it is important that one should never lose a vision one has for one's future in a destructive moment that has elapsed. The aftermath of a war can never finalize a person's life. He or she has every possibility to come out greater from a drudging battle that other people would destructively see as a fitting end to his or her path in life.

As an added fact, constant battles in relationships are not the only conflict that one must go through in order to find a resolution for victory.

There are also wars that people deal with emotionally where they face abuse, hatred, and abandonment in their surroundings. Each person faces a battle that he or she must go through if change is an outcome he or she wants to produce in his or her life. When a battle is unresolved, the mind and heart can engage in a war that brings about unsettling consequences. The point is not everyone deals with it the same way another person would; however, all conflict must be dealt with in order to bring about any desire for peace and resolve. People constantly go to war when it is a challenge that they must uphold so they can create a change that is necessary in this world. A battle can't last forever, just like an opposition can't stand in front of anyone forever. Sooner or later, the battle will be over, and it will be one that will suffer in a loss or result in a victory. The battle at times all starts in one's mind, but when it's over, it ends in one's heart.

Sooner or later, the war that rages on in your body with a disease will find its way out of your system, never to return and regenerate in your life. Soon enough, the conflict and feeling of being unsettled and lack of being in love or feeling loved will have a period of time where it goes through one's ability to conquer its attacks. Though in many cases that is possible, note that for everything you want in and out of life, you must be willing to go the extra mile if you are willing to fight for everything you have to fight for to get it.

If you realize that there is a war occurring in your surroundings, the only way you can win it is to be prepared to go to battle and make meaning of what it should stand for. People often say a war in anything can bring on more negative consequences than positive results. However, no individual can ever tell the outcome of a war even when it holds a purpose as to why it is being fought. Sometimes the battles become so intense that mending the ties between the two sides waging it becomes irreparable.

More people are concerned with the outcome of a war than the justice it can serve to others when that war is won. The end of a war is never immediate as it can take days, months, and years to win. Victory can never be claimed in an instant because when a moment and time of war has started, it must go through a rigorous battle until it drives itself to completion. No one can ever rule out the outcome from the experience of a war and being involved in one that brings on continuous battles. Wounds are inflicted, and the scars never seem to heal; but in spite of it all, life still presents every possibility that the reason for its emergence clearly creates a change for the better.

> *The experience of war does not need to be an outcome for destruction when its outcome and purpose can be channeled for the development and greater good of others.*

## Rise of the Fallen

Every moment was destined to have a shining star in someone's life. The brightest star is the star that outshines the other stars in the sky. The one that shines the brightest has to emit the most light that makes itself conspicuous from other stars. There are billions of stars in the sky, crossing into many billions of galaxies throughout the universe. It is difficult to separate and know which one is the brightest star in the sky because so many emit a high polarized amount of energy to give light to the rest of the planets. Of the greatest star, there can be none greater than the sun that gives light to the day.

No star could ever outshine this star because it is responsible for giving light and life to all life-forms on the planet it shines on. From the very creation of this star, it projects a light that will never lose its power. Its energy and power in life is endless in the world. No matter what happens when it goes down, it will always find a way to rise again. It does not matter where you travel and where you are in this world, everyone can't escape the light that is transmitted from this powerful source of energy. Surely, how many can take on and be the star that they should be in life so that they can shine right through life's problems? How many people can actually rise in life, fall, and rise again?

There are not that many people who possess the same qualities as the sun because once some people fall in life, their lives can never emerge with the same impact they have had before they took a fall. There are other superstars in the sky that can have their lights taken out only to find a way in a matter of changing moments to make it rise again. Examine the life of many sporting figures that have climbed to the top only to fall because of poor decision making. Even people who are star politicians are no different when they easily can have a slippage in decision making that can leave their marriages, career, and relationships with their children destroyed. Stars are constantly born. There are many of them in the sky, but a star is only as great as the light and power it transmits when it has the power to change the world for the better.

Examine the life of basketball superstar Kobe Bryant who won three championships with the Los Angeles Lakers in the years 2000, 2001, and 2002. At the start of Bryant's career, he became an early phenomenon. He had a large fan base with sneaker endorsements and plenty of recognition as a superstar player by other stars in the league. As a star player in basketball, Bryant had a strong drive and passion to play the game of basketball at an extraordinary high level. His abilities and talents would be acknowledged by others as probably one of the greatest stars to play the game of basketball. It would seem through all of Bryant's efforts he was respected by others as an individual and champion with competitive passion and power to succeed at anything he pursued. Even though winning three consecutive championships was the highlight of Bryant's career, after his third straight championship with the Lakers, many teams zoned in on the possibilities of dethroning his chances of winning a fourth title. Consequently, it would be in 2004 when Bryant's hopes of winning a fourth championship were derailed by another formidable team. The experience of losing a shot at winning the championship that year and the dismantlement of the team trading away other star players along with the resigning of a hall of fame coach stunted any future possibilities of Bryant winning another championship. That year was a memory in his life of frustration and complete devastation by missing the mark to be a champion. It would also be that very year he would face sexual assault charges by a hotel employee for an act he felt was purely consensual. The outcome affected his marriage and overall image as an individual.

As a result of the incident, Bryant lost endorsement deals with major companies. The effect also took its toll on sporting jerseys that generated a loss of sales. It appeared in one changing moment everything Bryant achieved in life was overtaken by a tragic mistake. It seemed that a powerful star that at one time emerged in the world took a mighty fall. Incredibly, in the midst of all his setbacks, Bryant was relentless to rebound his image from what has been tarnished. In September of 2004, Bryant agreed to come to a settlement with his accuser. The case was suddenly dropped, and he would be left to rebuild an image that had been devastatingly scarred.

During that difficult moment and time period, Bryant's wife stood in his corner and supported him every rest of the way. In 2006, his wife would give birth to his second daughter. He would then go on to excel at even a higher level as an athlete by scoring a record setting eighty-one points in a game, which is the second-highest-scoring performance by any athlete in a basketball game.

A year after his historical performance, he would receive the most valuable player award in basketball and lead his team to the championship finals in 2008. Though he would go on to lose the championship that year, he would return to the finals in 2009 and 2010 and win the championship with the Finals MVP Award on both occasions. Life all took a turn for the better for Bryant because the image of a star that people had once seen fallen no longer became tarnished by a set of derailed circumstances. In no time, Bryant's image as a basketball star began to sparkle as he was featured on the cover of *ESPN* magazine and appeared in several drink and video game commercials. In addition, he also received several endorsements from an airline and watch companies to promote their product (2011, May 20 Retrieved 20:58 *Kobe Bryant, In Wikipedia, The Free Encyclopedia*).

No one expected such a star to fall and reach a point in his life where he would rebound and rise so quickly. Next to Michael Jordan and Tiger Woods, *Forbes* ranked Bryant as one of the highest-paid athletes. Bryant's image had all but recovered two years after it had fallen. Obviously, he was a star with a special talent that no one could diffuse. He would be down, but he would go down only to rise with his talents all over again. There would be no windows of pain, no closed doors, and no missed opportunities for what he wanted and the companies that wanted him. Every option that channeled his way to success never presented any possibilities of him not excelling as the star he already was to make his light continue to shine through the rest of the world. Just like Bryant, you were one time a star in your life. You took on many endeavors but somehow it crossed into a channel where the arrows of defeat hurled its way in your direction and shot down any of the possibilities you had in making your dreams a reality.

There are still moments in your life where the end can emerge into a new beginning. Most people can't look at past failures and defeats feeling they don't have a chance to turn their lives around. They must have a strong vision and light that actively works its way through every step in the moment to create an explosive amount of dreams, possibilities and accomplishments that many would least expect from a fallen star.

# A LEAP OF FAITH

## CHAPTER 9

It is not unnatural in the world today that people like you and me will undergo some form of suffering as we try to achieve our dreams and goals. Ideally, it is unpractical to feel that anything you do and desire to accomplish can be attained without having some form of roadblock or obstacle en route to your destination. Thus, having a meaning or purpose behind one's actual target is only fitting to know the reason why one must be passionate to bring one's vision into reality. That is why every action you pursue and every ambition that lies in your heart must have an impact on your life and the lives of others in order for it to be purposeful. Despite the hindrances that line one's path, the end goal is to always start with the ability to cross the finish line. For example, examine the life of one such man in the bible named Job who was considered a wealthy individual. When reflecting on the life of Job, one could acknowledge he was given all the riches and abundance in the world because of his love, trust, and fear in God.

Throughout life with his family, everything started out decent and peaceful for him. All was well until one day, an unknown calamity emerged; as a result, hundreds and thousands of the animals he tended to died by natural and unlikely causes. Even as an added injury to this cause, all ten of his sons and daughters died by the eventual hands of a mighty storm. It seemed after one calamity struck, another one emerged in a matter of moments. In the midst of all the aftermath, Job was in complete disarray and utter shock. He couldn't believe everything God had given to him was all taken and wiped away in one succession after another. In his mind, he thought to himself, Why me? What could I have possibly done to deserve this?

In distress over the situation and overwhelmed by grief, he immediately prayed to God and expressed his pain and emotional loss to him in prayer. Job, as much as he cried out to God, did not get an answer to all the circumstances that took his life by storm. Heartbroken, in tears from all the destructive losses he was going through, the sun will rise another day only for Job to continue to maintain his integrity and trust in God's will and plans for his life. The next day began, and Job was still not safe from all the disasters that struck his life. In no time, he would be inflicted with unknown painful sores all over his body. Soon enough, it would reach a point in his life where his faith in God would be tested. As the growing sores took over his body, he became weakened by all the circumstances that were taking a toll on him. It all but seemed Job's life was falling apart.

He was emotionally distraught and saddened by all the events that were happening to him. He became powerless in the eye of the storm that centered his life. Days would go by, and the pain in his body worsened with no signs of hope or relief. The pain he dealt with had gotten so excruciating that he took a piece of broken pottery and scraped himself as a means of wanting to find relief from all his anguish and suffering. To no avail, his suffering continued. Even his wife stood in disbelief as she looked painfully at her husband's deteriorating body. Out of anger, she said to her husband, "How can you still maintain your integrity? You should curse God and die."

"Don't be a foolish woman. We can't expect goodness from God without expecting to have trouble in our lives," he replied. Despite all his setbacks, Job knew he had to continue to trust God. Though the meaning to all his sufferings and troubles were not clear, Job would continue to honor and trust that God will see him through all of his discouraged attacks. He dared not question God, and he was not angry at him. He continued to maintain his integrity by having the faith that despite everything that was happening to him, he knew that God will never forsake him. Throughout the tenure of Job's suffering, no amount of consolation, comfort or remedy from anyone will bring his ailments to a closure. After undergoing many days of painful suffering and emotional loss over his family and wealth, he came to the realization that his life was cursed, and the day and time he was born should have never taken place. His acts of prayers and patience in maintaining his integrity and faith in the moment became shattered. Suddenly, Job became weakened and disdained from all of life's inflicted attacks. His struggles reached a point in his life where his faith and confidence in God would ultimately be put to a true test.

Clearly, in recalling this story from the bible it is not out of the ordinary for one to take on a week, month or year filled with disappointments, destructive losses, and setbacks. It happens to many of us. It shows that in life what never happened in a thousand years can happen to anyone in one single day. Sometimes some people feel because they are well-mannered, wealthy and good law-abiding citizens, calamity will never strike them. They have the right to live peaceful and prosperous lives without any unlikely situation to evolve. Ultimately, the fact of the matter is no one is safe from recurring disappointments or any natural disaster. People have to embrace the unexpected results that life brings, even though they live their lives with the least expectation or likelihood that a calamity can occur. Examining Job's life, the end seemed to be drawing near for him, and he reached a point where he felt he needed to surrender so he can be freed from all his sufferings. Job, in all sense of aspects, was pushed to his limit. He was not only pressed against a wall, but he was also crushed and in unrelenting pain. Though he cried out to God, he still was not released from all the painful torment. Through it all, Job's heart remained grounded. Even though Job did not lose his life, the challenges of holding on to his faith became tested. I am sure something inside of him kept telling him, "Don't quit! Keep pressing on! It's not over yet."

Clearly, when one examines the life of Job, he could have folded, have a negative outlook on life, and be angry with all the changes that he was going through. Instead, Job prayed and vented his emotions and frustrations toward God. He believed that one day, he would answer him. Somehow, he felt it was only a matter of time before God pulled him through his ongoing pain and hard-pressed situations. All that he would need to do was continue to remain faithful and confident that at any given moment, he would call to God, and he would be rescued and freed from all of life's setbacks.

Job's call to God in many unanswered prayers would be an ongoing battle that tested Job's faith. As much as Job cried out to God for the answers, none of them will be provided to him. Ultimately, Job had done nothing to deserve suffering in his life. Through all the calamity, he continued to stay close to God. In the height of Job's frustration, he continued to turn to him for healing. Just when you would think Job would surrender after losing all of his children and animals that he tended to daily, undergoing painful sufferings, and unanswered prayers, there was still an undying passion and faith in God that made him continue to hold on despite the horrendous attacks he had taken through life's circumstances. It goes to show sometimes life was not meant for you to know the reasons for every disappointment and setback because all the answers are constantly held back. Sometimes our situations look hopeless, but our faith and confidence in God must remain consistent and hopeful.

After all, what is the purpose of taking a test if you know all the answers that will appear on the exam? Sometimes we are tested in our abilities to trust God when we can't comprehend the struggles we face and are going through in life. Just the fact we receive tests in life, it assesses our abilities and capabilities of pulling through a trying and unrelenting situation to determine if we are capable of passing other tests. How many times we have questioned our lives when calamity strikes, and when it emerges, we become angry when it gets out of control. Truly, we don't have the power to change a natural disaster or prevent one from happening. All we can do is rely on God to carry us through the storm and keep trusting in him to deliver us as it comes. It is proven whatever comes along and attacks you in life shows how limited you are as a human being when you don't have any control over the forces of nature. However, through the power of God, he can restore any moment of calamity in your life and give it a moment of peace and order that your life needs to propel you forward. Eventually, Job would find restoration through all his sufferings when God finally answered his prayer. Through it all, God was indeed pleased with how Job persevered through his situation and, as a result of his perseverance, he restored his life three times greater than the first time he was blessed.

Job no longer suffered in pain as his wounds had suddenly healed, and the animals that he tended to came back by the thousands. He had also new sons and daughters that were much more beautiful than the first (New International Version, Job.1-42). Job was indeed rewarded based on his faith, patience, and confidence in God. One telling fact to this story is that no matter how strong the trials are in life, if you don't find a way to break through them, you will be hopeless and helpless finding questions that you will never know the answers to. You have to believe that your life will turn around when it is being tested by unlikely circumstances you have no power to control. For the most part, isn't it evident that people constantly face tests in life, but it is not until those tests are passed that the answers at that moment in time are made clear after they successfully make it through them. Isn't it clear that God allows things to happen in people's lives in order to get their attention? After all, there are so many tests in life.

There are tests of adversity such as people who have invested hundreds of thousands of dollars in the stock market in high-risk portfolios only to see all their earnings collapse by a shattering drop in one changing moment in the market. There are even tests of being in a relationship where you hope and pray that one day your partner will learn to trust, grow, change and understand you better as a person. In addition to that, people also must withstand the test of losing a job and rebounding quickly to get another one. Also to mention, people's health in life is also tested when a disease and certain ailment decides to take over and place a limit on what they normally do.

How evident those tests are always given in life, but not everyone is capable of passing the lessons that it gives. If only one can see the patience and perseverance that comes in taking the test before the frustration sets in, the answers may not be as farfetched as they seem. Suffering, through it all, is not necessarily a disadvantage if that person is open to now be obedient to God and be open to the change that he or she needs to turn his or her life around. Life can come at you in so many changing moments that you can't tell how and when a storm will strike, but you have to be prepared that at any given time, your life can change for the worse or the better by how you respond to the situation that arises. Your viewpoint toward it matters much in terms of how you can remain confident and faithful through the unrelenting storms you must pass through to overcome life's greatest test at hand.

> *Man can live about forty days without food, three days without water, eight minutes without air, but only one second without hope.*
>
> —Sasha Azevedo

## Relentless, Unfailing Desire

I was employed in a bank for several years where I worked alongside with tellers, supervisors, customer service representatives, and managers. Everyone had their roles to play individually, but even though they played their roles, most of them tried to play my boss. Each of them had a different personality, but some had an edge to them that made their tempers fuel at any and everything at the job. It later became evident to me that it was not science to realize that many unsatisfied people were working at a place just so that they can make ends meet with their living situation. When the company got tired of any of their employees, or when their employees got tired of them, a new person was hired to replace each one of them that left the job.

The relationship with the bank and its employees became like a revolving door. When one person goes out, another comes in, and when one person comes in, another one would go out.

Even though the bank implemented its own code of ethics to all of its employees, many of my challenges dealt with my experiences with other coworkers where most of them did not comply with the company's standards and policies of how to treat others in the workplace. In all due respect, the experiences I have had on the job allowed me to see I had to have great people skills in making it effectively through the day, and the rest of the time I was employed with the company. One thing that bothered me was the fact that I struggled to move up in banking.

I argued about my position as a part-time teller to my supervisor and manager because I spent so many years in one position, I wanted to see if the bank would grant me the opportunity to branch off in a different position that would pay me more than what I was currently making. However, the managers in the bank figured it was better for them to keep me as a part-time teller for as long as they could without giving me any promotion. This, in essence, was a perfect solution for them to save money. I would start off making $9.50 an hour, but when it came to getting a raise, the company only raised my salary after six months to ten cents. The pay raise got me infuriated. I could not imagine that I worked so hard to not show any differences as a teller, and my salary was raised to $9.60 an hour after being rewarded with an excellent performance review.

I recalled my first year with the bank, and how the company gave all their employees Christmas bonuses, which equated to a two-week salary.

When my birthday would fall on the day I went to work, my coworkers would even take time out to get me a cake and gifts after banking hours. Even though there were certain aspects about the job that I did not like, the hospitality of some of the people oftentimes changed my opinion on how I felt working at the bank. Though to some extent I was satisfied with the people, I had grown totally dissatisfied with the company. I would hold on to the job with the prospect of getting a college degree that I thought would help me get into a more advanced position. After four years of working in the bank, my salary increased to 10.00 an hour, and although that was enough for them, it was surely not enough for me.

I knew I was at my limit in terms of being dissatisfied with the job. I walked in every single day bitterly upset that I could be treated as if I was not worth anything to the company. I struggled with the stress sometimes of being the only teller taking care of long commercial lines with large deposits and having cash overages and shortages when the bank was short staff because of people quitting the job or calling in sick. Even though I worked there for several years, something just kept building up inside of me to let me know that I will not be able to put up with the company much longer.

I got a forty-cent raise after four years, and I knew very soon I was on the verge of leaving my position as a teller if they did not train me for a higher position with a better salary. Shortly after getting my bachelor's degree, I applied for job postings in the company to get into a position that was in line with what I studied in school. I was called in for a job interview, and the human resource manager gave me a date where I will be called in to train for the position. I waited for several months, all while going back and forth with the human resource manager to get a training date for the technical support position but never got one.

This left me with no other choice but to look for employment opportunities outside of the company. It was now the fourth month after getting my degree, and I was still working at the bank as a part-time teller with no room for advancement in the company. I needed to make choices that will get me out of the position I was in quickly, and I told myself this company will never change because they don't care about the contributions I have made and the performances I have had with them. Personally, I feel all they care about is what I can do for them. I had a choice to make in the summer of 2002. I had to let go of the current position I was in as a teller and see if I could find a job outside of the company.

Through persistent job search efforts, I was not able to find another job, but I needed to take a leap of faith to get out of an uncomfortable situation. I quit the job, even though I did not have another one in line, after six years of being employed with the company. It was a risk I was willing to take because I was tired of being treated unfairly. I would learn this decision the hard way and through the choices I made; it made me see that I wasted six years of my life trying to please a company that clearly never had my best interest.

If I had to do it again, I will never be in a position for that long no matter how promising a company may look and the level of hospitality that people displayed. At one point, I liked working for the bank, but over time I learned to see that I should take responsibility for my own life and actions because the company will never be able to do that for me. What I've learned through all of this is that when you are making a decision, look at what you could accomplish in the long run.

If you are dissatisfied with something at your job, you must make a concerted effort to bring forth a change that will make you satisfied. Otherwise, misery will evoke, and though you think being comfortable means you being satisfied, you should never be satisfied, knowing that you are comfortable in a situation that is leading you nowhere. Your job can rob you of your joy and freedom, and at any given point while you work for anyone, the very next week or day, you can be fired or lose your position to someone else. Ultimately, when you are in a challenging situation, you must rise to the challenge to overcome it and get yourself out of it so that you can ultimately move on with your life. All you will experience is pain and anger every day until you push yourself and bring your situation to a resolve. Knowing this, if you have been in a position for a longer time than expected, and you are dissatisfied because you feel that you are experiencing a lack of advancement and respect for what you have done for the company, you must get yourself out of your comfort zone because you can fool yourself into believing that you are satisfied when you're really not satisfied with the conditions and results that should bring about complete satisfaction.

*The Moments That Define One's Life*

*Moments of Doubt versus Moments of Transformation*

## Derailed

How important it is in one's life to stay on course and focused when one starts a task. How easy it is to remember all the accomplishments we achieve when they are achieved and the time of its achievement. How easy it also is to take for granted all the wonderful memories in life when one day an unexpected situation or conflict decides to steer your life off track. You used to be a star getting excellent grades, making decent income, having friends you can rely on to pull you through difficult times. Now you are no longer the star you were. Times have changed, and the changes you made shifted you into a decision that called you to make changes with your life in a different moment in time. These changes, ultimately, transitioned you into an entirely new moment where you no longer make the same income, have the same job, get the same grades, have the same friends, and enjoy the same lifestyle.

No longer can you bring back the times that were when all you can do is live for the times that are and what is to become. Personally, I remember how life was before I exchanged stability for uncertainty. I remember the good deeds I used to perform and how they had meaning to my life. I remember the letters I wrote to encourage people and the times I shared building and socializing with friends. Those were times in my life I would treasure, but when that moment was gone, it became one that would never return. Even the past reminds me of the performances I have had in my personal life, sacrificing every moment of my time to build a relationship that would lead me to finding a rewarding and fruitful partner. I recall all the works I would put in so my deeds would count for something in life. I remember how spiritual I was in my relationship with God where I prayed, read my Bible, evangelized, and would fellowship consistently. Those days, as much as I remember them, were better than the days and times I am living in now. Thus, what is important is that they will never return, but I have every ability to live greater moments with the time and life I am living now.

It seems what is special to the experiences I have had during those times is to have new experiences that will be built from the past moments I have had. Truly, when one dwells on one's past endeavors, one would wish the moments from them will last forever. Unfortunately, every relationship, challenge, and endeavor you take on has a time that it begins and a time that it comes to an end. No matter how much one wants the good old times to come back, they will never be erased, yet they can never be returned.

These are the same moments that one reflects on that derail one's personal life. These are the individuals that live off the victories of the past, not believing and having the faith that new victories can start at any moment they make an effort to ignite it. Knowing that life transitions you from one moment to the next, you must be willing to accept the transition that is presented and not be derailed believing that your life will be cut short in a new moment because you are not able to create greater moments than what has already been created in your past.

Clearly, I now realize that I no longer have the power to produce the consistency I once had that made me who I was. My consistent habits of doing, making everything possible in the moment mattered to me, but over time those habits of consistency have changed. Time, desire, and the actions of the deeds that mattered to me were no longer a characteristic I could bank on. I had to see that a new moment had shifted forward in my life, not to derail me of past accomplishments and performances but one that assures me that I have to use what I have to the best of my ability now so that greater performances and accomplishments in my life can be generated.

Personally, I feel what has engulfed my mind with ineptitude in the moment is because I would feel that the success I have had in the past can't be duplicated with the talents and skills I now have in the future. It allows me to see how each passing moment is special in my life because once the moment is gone, all that matters in that day, month, year, and time you lived in it has changed and impacted your life for the better.

Though most of my experiences in life will never return, I have to make a concerted effort through faith that I can create a present and future for myself that will only get better. The past, thus, with all the goals and task I have taken on are moments that strictly belong in the past. The present, of course, is a moment in time that I am living in now where I must solely focus on the moment of now so that the achievements I attempt to make in my life will not fail to move forward.

Apparently, whatever I did before, it would never be easy to duplicate in an entirely new moment. It is proven that life changes as you take a different step toward something. I believe so many people remember the good times when they are going good, but those times are challenged when those times can no longer be produced. They excuse the lack of sacrifices they should make to create new moments that can be channeled right to their future. It is essential that one not only reflects on one's past actions but develops the faith to turns one's reflections into a vision of greater accomplishments than what one experienced in the past. Everyone knows how great life could be when everything is in place. It is the painful memory of looking back at your life that has now changed, not knowing if it took a turn for the better or the worse. You must be able to use your talents and abilities in the present time to regenerate greater ones than the ones you have sown in your past.

It is time to break out of the past and break into a new element. You will always feel your time and the moment are gone, but the truth is you have the power to bring greater moments in your life than the ones that you feel have no chance of returning. How do you bring it back? How do you succeed when you feel others believe you have failed? The only way to get back on the train that had taken you there before is to ride a new one and start it all over again. It is now time to rekindle the relationships you have been out of contact with for so long, all while continuing to build on the new ones that you have.

It is now time to develop the attitude of taking your relationship with your partner to where it once was in the past. I believe most people don't believe those times that they used to do the things that defined their lives in that moment has a way of coming back, but with enough faith, you have to believe they are destined to one day return. Each person who was ever bound on course will face a moment where he or she will be bound for disconnection. It is challenging for the heart to sustain itself doing the same mundane task day in and day out without being weary and worn-down over time with the rituals that life has set in place for it. It is so difficult to remain sustained when the very challenges of being consistent in the world desires you to feel what life could become when an entirely new moment gives birth to it. One must never lose sight of one's destination because it is easy to remember the victories achieved in the past, but one should never fail to realize that the same victories and moments can still be brought into the present where it can also be used to channel its way into one's future.

## A New Beginning

Normally, the end of anything you commit your life to oftentimes takes on a result no one least expects it to take on. Everyone hopes in life for a happy ending, but a happy ending is never promised to anyone. People strive to make their lives better when in turn something else blocks it from making their lives take a positive turn. Imagine living in a world where no matter how hopeful, faithful, and confident you get, the results you aim for never returns to you the same way you go after them. There are tests in life that causes people to question the situation they are in. There are also battles in life that remind us what we are fighting for and what we are aiming for. In every area of one's life, there comes a time where one must take control of a situation that one has lost control.

Look at how many times people's life calls for them to take action, but by the time they are supposed to take action, too much damage has already been done to the point where it can no longer be reversed. Life calls for people to emerge when difficult and challenging situations arise. I believe if at any point the best must come out in someone, he or she must find a way to bring it out of him or her before circumstances reach their greatest point. For example, examine a time in your life where you could have made a decision to let go of something, but because you chose to hold on to it, you paid the price for its returns.

I remembered an individual named Joseph who was constantly confronted by life-changing obstacles. He would sign on the dotted line when it comes to making an investment in properties, stocks, and bonds or even buying or leasing a new car. In any action he would take on, he was always optimistic but irrational in his choices. He always had a gut instinct that whatever actions he would take on would work his life out for the best and move in a positive direction. Maybe Joseph as an individual was no different from you or a lot of people.

Maybe it didn't take much to influence him. Maybe other people could not take on the risk and challenges of the unknown, but they were rationed in their decisions. Clearly, the obvious difference between what other people wanted and what Joseph wanted was he had a strong sense of desire but not a strong sense of instinct and faith in anything he would do. Apparently, all in one changing moment, life clearly took a different turn as he saw his investment of $50,000 in a high-risk portfolio drop to $32,000 in the stock market.

Joseph knew there were many challenges with the economy, and through it all, he held on to his ideas and opinions and did not waver in any of his decisions. It would be normal to call him bull-headed and stubborn in his choices to stay in an investment that was not working, but he stuck with his guns, believing that the amount of money he invested will return to his account the same way in which it was deposited. It would take seven months of Joseph watching his investment fluctuate in the market, hoping that it would return to the same amount that was originally deposited in his account.

The market would eventually rebound where he would see an increase of $3,000, but just as the account increased, it also took hits where it steadily declined. No one could convince Joseph otherwise. Once he made his investment, he would have the highest hope that it would net positive returns. Joseph was never a rational decision maker because many of his decisions would be based entirely on impulse. Though Joseph was one who never used and practiced caution with his choices, the quick and impulse decision to invest all of his savings in a high-risk portfolio, losing thousands of dollars, took a toll on him.

It would be two years. Joseph's savings in the stock market would continue to fluctuate, and other economic issues caused his returns to continue to fall. He felt hopeless. Never again would he place all his savings into a high-risk portfolio, knowing that he should have actual savings in his bank account to work with just in case emergency situations or uncalled events happen where he would need to use his savings to support himself and his family. Joseph continued to stick with an investment that was supposed to go somewhere, but he ended losing more than he bargained for.

It is amazing that at one time everything could be normal in one's life, but there are situations, unexpected turns in life, that can drive everything that one has worked for out of control. Incredibly, Joseph had to find a way to rebound from his situation. He pulled out of his investment when his savings dropped to $26,500.

Life just became obvious to him at that point that he needed to make a decision that in the long run he would make a much wiser investment with his savings. Joseph would then use his leftover investment to save and eventually add more to it where he would buy a house. This time it would be a more tactful decision because it would be one where he received much thought and insight about all the factors that may or may not affect it. For Joseph, he waited until the interest rates were down in the market, and special deals would be given out by the government for new homebuyers. Suddenly, out of turmoil, Joseph emerged a better and wiser person. He decided he will no longer wait for a situation to spiral out of control, believing that at any point he could seize control of it and steer his life back in a positive direction.

Partners have oftentimes joined forces in business because they believe two heads are better than one when it comes to decision making. Ultimately, when one has made a decision to work alongside another person in business, the outcome may or may not be justifiable. Thus, by all means, no partner has an idea as to how his or her attitudes and mind-set toward the business will affect sales, company profits, and relationships with customers and even with one another. Over time, the course of everything changes. Competitors marketing campaign can alter the flow of customers in the market. People's lifestyle and habits also change as they no longer have the same needs and wants that were driving them in the past. In addition, the state of the economy also fluctuates, which doesn't guarantee the same monthly or quarterly sales that have been generated in previous months.

It just goes to show the state of anything that you decide to take on is never permanent in the sense that it can generate consistent results. Consistency is not forever but one key fact that one must remain consistent is one's overall ability to continue to remain faithful in spite of the obstacle that one faces. Through it all, the ultimate test comes when a business starts to lose sales, and how each partner will react to the adversity of overcoming a declining sale in business when it emerges. Businesses will oftentimes face outside challenges that will impact its growth. If adversity is not dealt with accordingly as it happens, it will greatly affect the momentum of the business. In the beginning, every business has had to go through some significant struggle to be battle-tested in the long run.

## Choices That Change the Course in Life

Several years ago, I remembered a person named Victor who constantly searched for ways to improve his life when he felt the income he was making at his job was not going to fulfill his needs in the long run. Frustrated with his current income, Victor decided to take action to improve his living situation by spending weeks looking for other employment opportunities. At the expense of his actions, he would go on job interviews where he would rally his interviews around the part-time hours of his current job. Though some interviews did not go as he expected, Victor was optimistic that if he continued his search he would be contacted by an employer. Relentless in his efforts, it took months of searching and being in a job that he didn't like to finally find one where he was able to work at an accounting firm, making $32,000 per year.

Immediately, when he was hired for the position, he did not hesitate to quit his other job. He embraced his position as an accountant. However, after three years of working for this business firm, Victor grew dissatisfied with the company. It seemed life may have changed for him to some extent, but it never propelled his life in the direction he wanted. Realizing he was still in an uncomfortable place in his life where he struggled to pay off his debt and loan expenses, Victor, as a result, was left with no other choice but to dig deeper in his soul to find the answers to his struggles. In the summer of 2005, he decided that his best option would be a career change. He went online and researched several promising careers on the Internet. After logging on various websites, the one he found the most appealing monetary wise was the field of nursing. A few days after conducting his research, Victor decided it was time for a change. While still being employed as an accountant, he reduced his hours to part time so that he could go to school in the evenings to become a licensed registered nurse. This, he felt, would allow him the leverage to save more money and earn a better lifestyle in a field that has a starting salary of $65,000 annually.

He attended the school and received all the information he needed regarding the program for nursing. Throughout his time obtaining this second degree, he would experience one of the greatest challenges placed before him. The challenges he faced would be a true testament to his faith and decision to become a licensed registered nurse. While in school, he would complain to me and tell me how difficult the program was for him. He would tell me that passing every exam in school would be the deciding factor of whether he could successfully make it through the program. Granted, if he can successfully pass, he would be one step closer to obtaining a second degree that he has made so much sacrifice paying and studying for. However, should he fail, he would experience one of the greatest setbacks in his life of having his time, money, and effort wasted.

Being in the nursing program presented many great challenges. The nursing program was strict with students who needed to maintain a certain grade point average to maintain their status as students in the school. Thus, failing a class two times would lead to an automatic dismissal from the program. Having known the requirements of the nursing school, Victor had a total of six nursing classes to take, one of which he already failed in his second semester. Victor, as a result, would have one last chance to redeem himself. A month later he would repeat the course and succeed in passing it. Afterward, his status at that time in the school left him with no margin for error. In order to successfully graduate, he had no other choice but to work hard and pass all of his remaining classes.

It would be the spring semester of the following year and Victor's final course in nursing. The course he told me would be the toughest one that would decide if he could graduate from nursing school. It would reach the last day of school and the day of the final exam.

As Victor sat in the class, the moment was drawing him nearer to the exam time, and within ten minutes before the class started, the teacher walked into the classroom. Instantly, as the instructor walked into the class, she preceded toward her desk where she placed her bag on the table and immediately instructed students how to position their chairs from one another. She also told the entire class to turn off their cell phones and for everyone to place their text books and book bags in front of the room. Victor knew at that time all the studying time he had was over. It was time to prove if he had what it takes to get through the biggest test of his life. Despite the fact the exam was at 9:00 a.m., and there was still ten minutes left, the instructor did not allow anyone else any additional time to study. It seemed to Victor that students were just at the mercy of the professor's instruction and the school's protocol.

He started to reflect on the pass/fail statistics he heard from professors who claimed that 75 percent of the students who took the final nursing course would fail, meaning only 25 percent of the students who were accepted in the program have a chance to graduate and obtain a bachelor's degree in nursing. As Victor reflected, he also thought about his own personal struggles with test taking. He would tell me the nursing exams use critical style thinking test questions which meant that he would need to choose the best answer out of a selection of all correct choices. As much as Victor tried not to focus on the past exams and statistics, he could not help but realize the class he was in got tremendously smaller because of all the people who either dropped or failed out of the program.

The time quickly reached 9:00 a.m. and the moment in Victor's life had finally arrived. The teacher handed Victor the final exam. Once he received the final exam paper, he knew exactly what he was about to face. When Victor took the test paper from the teacher, he answered all the questions to the best of his knowledge. He was confident in many of his responses. He knew taking the test was all but based on his ability to appropriately rationalize and give his own valid reasons as to why some of the choices he did not pick were incorrect.

Surely, it was a higher level thinking that he was not used to. However, it was something that he had no other choice but to tackle if he needed to be successful at it. Thus, taking and passing the course in spite of what was placed before him would be a leap of faith that he was willing to take.

The exam was two hours, and it was timed one minute per question. After almost two hours of answering questions, Victor handed the final exam to his teacher. Eventually, he walked out of the building knowing that it could be the very last test that he possibly would take in the school of nursing. Victor knew he would have to wait a few days to get the results. At that point, he figured whatever the results were going to be, it would be because of the choices that he made on the exam, the choices he made to get in the program, and the choices he made before starting the program to improve his life.

Clearly, with all his actions, Victor had no regrets with the time and effort he put into studying for the final and his previous exams. He was satisfied feeling that he did everything he possibly could do to succeed. Two days after taking the final, the results were posted on the school's website. Victor received a 76.4 in the course and was devastated by the results. He knew he needed to get a grade of 77 to pass the class. This left

Victor with his back completely against the wall. He all but felt at that moment the curtains closed and his time and effort had all but come to an end. He stood motionless for an hour and afterward gained some form of courage to contact me in the evening. I would tell him that results in life are never final and that you can never see a result and believe that it is the end of it without you believing that you can do something about it. He said, "Well, Lloyd, believe me I have done everything in my power to pass that class. What more could I do? I think these exams in nursing are all set up by the teachers to make you barely pass."

"What makes you say that?" "Well, you have to realize that the way the exams are set, there are some that you can get right, some you will get wrong, and some you have to guess. Even if you study hard there is no guarantee that you will pass." "Victor, why do you doubt yourself and your abilities? Don't you realize in life that you must always begin by having the end of something in mind. The projects you take on will never start the way you expect them to but you must have a vision that they will end the way you want them to." "So what are you saying Lloyd? What should I do about this because I believe there is no way around this?" "Well, you have to believe Victor. You must go down to the school and plead your case and fight for what you believe in. You have to take a leap of faith and expect something good to come out of this. You should not surrender to this situation." "Ok, I guess you are right. I will go down to the school first thing in the morning."

After the phone line closed, Victor could not emotionally put himself in a situation where he could talk or open up with anyone. The tragic moment all but made him remember his personal story that led him to make a decision to apply to nursing school. Part of his inspiration and passion to attend nursing school was all because of his personal ambition to change his life. After another two hours of sulking in defeat, Victor snapped out of the shell he was in and anticipated the actions he should take in the morning when he goes to see the dean of academic affairs.

Tomorrow would begin, and Victor would go down to the school's nursing office to plead his case to the dean for a passing grade. After spending only 10 minutes in the office, the dean rejected his plea and said the grade he received was final. Frustrated but hopeful, the following week Victor would return and go to other staff members of the school pleading his situation to other dean officials. After a high level of persistence, much debate and returning repeatedly to argue his case, dean officials and teachers looked at Victor's past performance and written papers in his class and determined that he deserved a passing grade for one of the papers that was not graded accurately.

Victor was ecstatic with the message of approval from the dean. He would be granted permission to graduate from nursing school and over the span of the next several months study and take his state examination to become a licensed registered nurse. Incredibly, no one other than Victor himself believed that outside of his challenges there was still a strong possibility that he could make it through the program. In every step of the way, he found a way to respond to the challenges as they arrived and found a way to never see the results of anything as final. Sure enough, he was fortunate with the outcome he received from passing the course. However, had he not taken a leap of faith, he would have never known the possibilities that lie ahead and the vision of having those possibilities fulfilled.

# THE BATTLE FOR RECOVERY

## CHAPTER 10

**Reemergence**

*When you know something is wrong, you must do everything you possibly can to fix it and make it right!*

In the year 1949, in Marshall, Texas, childbirth was a normal occurrence for many women. Medicine was not as advanced as it is in today's world, so women who gave birth to children hoped that no complications from childbearing developed. As a result, any complications, when it comes to delivering a child, would hinder their hopes from having and experiencing a successful birth. Apparently, even though many children will be born in that small town, a mother would give birth to a special child who would also be born in the beginning of that year. From the inception of this child's birth, it was clear that he would be one that would be ordained and welcomed by God. This child would grow to be a blessing and miracle in the lives of everyone that surrounded him. He would be one that would later mature in life to be an incredible athlete and successful entrepreneur. Surely, this child will grow to experience life and face the challenges it brings on many different levels. Each moment that posed as a challenge to him will be one that he would valiantly overcome. In time, he became an individual who knew how to weather a storm. He would make necessary choices regarding a series of challenging moments that would test his ability repeatedly to succeed. There will be constant tests in his life that will determine his overall passion, purpose, and ability to rise or fall in the moment. Incredibly, in no time, he would gain worldwide recognition for all of his historical achievements. This child would grow to be an extraordinary public icon. This extraordinary figure, I speak about, is none other than the legendary George Foreman. Apparently, in his early childhood years, it was evident that Foreman had a passion for sports. Growing up, one of his favorite sporting activities was football. He would at times play positions where he would be the one chasing and tackling the opponent.

It seemed from the onset of his liking for the sport, he had an explosive stamina that not a lot of people in his age group had. It was evident that through his actions playing football, he had a strong desire to win in every game he would play. Soon enough, after much exposure to the sport, Foreman grew tired. It didn't take long before a new desire breathed football out of his system and blew boxing right into his own heart. It was unknown how Foreman developed the heart for boxing, but one fact that was evident was he had a strong passion to do what he enjoyed and be successful at what he enjoyed doing at all costs. No matter what it would take and what he would take on, Foreman was willing to make the necessary sacrifices to get himself to a point where he would become an unstoppable athlete in this world. Time will only tell how his mind, body, and heart will develop toward boxing.

His effort to succeed will either be a story that will come together in his life or one that will tell tales of how it would fall apart. Fortunately, at an early age, it would all come together when he began his training in the ring. It would be at that time his mind accepted the passion that was burning inside his heart to be someone special in the world. It just seemed that God had a calling for Foreman that he knew nothing about. All that mattered was that Foreman had a burning desire, and when the passion burned deep and strong enough, nothing could stop the forces of momentum that he started to gather. Everywhere Foreman would battle seemed to leave a blazing trail of success. His rise to stardom started in 1968 when he won his first Olympic Gold Medal in the boxing heavyweight division. Much to the enlightenment of his early career in boxing, he had an impressive record, knocking out many of his opponents to surge right to the path of striving to attain the heavyweight boxing championship of the world.

He posed an impressive 22–4 amateur record, fighting a total of thirteen fights in a year and winning eleven of those matches by knockout in that year. He was clearly a force to be reckoned with. Even though he lost four times to his opponents, his drive to the heavyweight championship would not stop him from achieving what he ultimately desired. Without contest, every time Foreman would lose, he always found a way to bounce back and come back stronger from his losses. No opponent or opposition seemed to suppress his willpower to succeed. He continued his surge toward the heavyweight championship by going an impressive 32–0 with twenty-nine knockout fights. The time in his life had emerged. It was clearly his moment. He was in a zone where he owned that time and moment in history.

Unequivocally, God had a plan for his life, and all Foreman had to do was follow the blueprint to that plan so that his dreams and passions toward it will never be mistaken. Reflecting on the progress and victories he attained made him take note of the fact that many of his accomplishments against his opponents were ones that never came easy. There were boxers, like Foreman, who also trained effortlessly day and night to achieve the very same goal that he sought out to achieve. Unfortunately, their skills, strength, and talents in boxing were nowhere near his capacity. Foreman was clearly in a different category as far as his level of achievement in the sport. If you are unfamiliar with boxing and the nature of the sport, it is a twelve-round competition where an individual can go head to head with an opponent for twelve rounds or knock the opponent out once to win the match or get three consecutive knockouts in a single round to win the bout. For Foreman, boxing was indeed a sport that was not only his calling but one where he repeatedly excelled.

Many of his opponents were no match for the strength and tenacity that he brought to the ring. For years of working hard, training, and consistent focus, Foreman not only won the heavyweight championship of the world, but he executed his victories in dominating fashion, knocking out his opponents in three and sometimes four rounds to win the match. One famed fight that Foreman gained recognition for was his fight against Walt Frazier. Frazier was considered heavily favored in the match, while Foreman was the underdog. No one expected Foreman to win, especially being that Frazier won by unanimous decision over boxing legend Muhammad Ali.

However, when the boxing match started, it seemed it was all but over for Frazier. In an epic battle of two incredible heavyweights, Frazier was knocked down to the canvas six times in few of the rounds. Momentum was in favor of Foreman; he was a man possessed by an unstoppable, unquenchable, relentless spirit of power that no one was going to tear down what he worked so hard to build. He was at the prime of his career. It was clearly his moment. It just seemed when every match begun, he owned all the boxers he fought against. Foreman could not be stopped as he had all the ability, talent, and answers in his heart to succeed in a sport that he loved and dominated for many years.

**Down but Not Out**

Foreman would not only win the heavyweight championship of the world, but he refused to let anyone defeat him and take what he worked so hard to get. Many opponents would rise and earn the right to fight him, but their skills in the boxing ring was not enough as he pushed his record to an impressive 40–0 with thirty-seven knockouts.

His reign as a champion qualified him as one of the greatest boxers ever to step foot in a boxing ring. Many times, when Foreman looked as if he was going down in the ring, he would constantly find a way to get a second wind to fight back and overcome all the attacks of his opponents. Boxing seemed to be a perfect fit for Foreman. Life seemed to be all but promising and hopeful for him because no one had an answer for his defeat. Outside the door looking in, one man would stand and watch Foreman handedly defeat all of his opponents. Training and dreaming of the anticipation of a head-to-head match with Foreman, Muhammad Ali would have his day in history as his desire to enter the ring with Foreman would ignite a true possibility.

Though Foreman successfully defended his title against many challenging opponents, Ali, one formidable opponent, would be the one to test Foreman's endurance and willpower as a champion. It was the year 1974 on the eleventh day of November that boxing history would be made. Ali got the dream fight he wanted, and he was ever confident that his victory against Foreman was sealed.

Foreman was heavily favored in the fight. When the match began, instantly and with no hesitation, Ali went on a barrage of attacks, landing many blows to Foreman's body. It seemed that Ali's speed and agility was far superior to that of Foreman. Though Foreman suffered a setback prior to the fight by having a cut above his eye, he still fought Ali and did not use his hit as an excuse to not defend his title. Unfortunately, Ali had proven to be much more than Foreman could handle. He went several rounds with Ali, expending so much energy only to fall in the eighth round. Though Foreman was able to get back on his feet, the referee declared the match to be over. Foreman felt he let a good opportunity slip away.

Ali won the fight and also went on to win the heavyweight championship of the world. Foreman was shattered by the loss. After all, he won so many times in his life that he didn't know what losing felt like. The fight would symbolize Foreman's first defeat, and Ali till this very day would be the only boxer to ever knock Foreman down in a fight. The loss made Foreman reflect on his life. It was only one loss, but what also mattered was the fact that he lost something of value that he worked months and years to get. The emptiness of the loss made Foreman realize something was missing. There was a void in his life he never felt before.

Days would go by, and he would feel that there would be something eating at the very core of his heart, he wondered how he would ever move on and emerge from such a devastating loss. One year passed, and he decided after much thought and training that it was time to take back what belonged to him. In 1976, he demanded a rematch with Ali. This would signal his first comeback as a contender for the championship. The road to Ali, of course, would not be an easy one. As Foreman's first fight in the ring would prove to be one of his toughest. The fight would be against Ron Lyle who proved he had nothing to lose against the incredible boxing record of Foreman. In the fight, it would go several rounds where Foreman would get knocked down two times during the match. Unseeingly, both fighters were hungry to prove a point.

They exchanged hard and brutal hits against one another where plenty of blood was shed. Foreman placed his heart and his body on the line and got back up every time he was knocked down. The result led him to knocking down Lyle for good in the eighth round. The fight would be called "The Fight of the Year" by many people. Though Foreman would have other great fights in that year, none of them had the magnitude of the fight he had with Ron Lyle. During the quest for his first comeback, Foreman had a rematch with Joe Frazier who he also defeated along with other contested fighters in the same year. He would go undefeated that year and it seemed all the setbacks that have taken over his life will be a thing of the past. Foreman drew one step closer at charging toward the heavyweight championship of the world, but he would encounter a major life-changing obstacle in his next bout. It would be the year 1977 when he would go against Jimmy Young who was considered to be a physical and aggressive boxer. Foreman did not want to lose the match, but as the match went on, he started to grow tired, and in the seventh round, Young was badly hurt by Foreman's punches. Young refused to quit and continued to fight back. He, just as much as Foreman, wanted the victory and to prove a point that he was a strong upcoming fighter.

The fight went all the way to the final twelve rounds only for Foreman to lose by a decision. Right after the fight, Foreman became extremely ill and felt as if he was going to die from a heatstroke. It all but seemed the match was more than he could handle. Deep in his soul, however, a voice cried out to him and said, "Hang in there. It's not over yet." The fight made Foreman question his integrity for the sport. Being that he was close to death, he needed to change his life and realize that whatever he wanted to accomplish meant nothing if he didn't have a desire to do something where God could be a part of it.

In that same year, Foreman decided to turn his life over to God and become a born-again Christian. Life suddenly changed for him. Foreman no longer reflected on the setback of losing the match in that moment because whatever happened, he constantly found ways to come back. This time it was not an emergence that was taking place in the boxing ring, but it was an emergence taking place in his soul. After all, what is it for a man to gain the whole world but lose his soul if he does not have a relationship with his Creator?

As a result of his decision, Foreman's path in life would take a complete 180-degree turn where he devoted his life to being a Christian. For the next ten years, his life would be all about reform. He would walk the Christian walk and talk the Christian talk. He became an ordained minister of a church he attended and wanted to inspire others of the movement and change that God created in his life. It shows when it comes to emergence; revival can happen at any point and any moment in one's life. Foreman's revival in this moment proved to be ultimately special because he had another powering force that he could rely on that could upset and offset all the setbacks in life that he experienced.

Clearly, no one saw this coming, but the experiences he had made this moment in his life to become a follower of God possible. Though one of his desires burned with passion to become a follower of Christ, boxing would now be somewhere in his blood, embedded but waiting at any moment to rise again. The result of his changed life allowed him to open a youth center to help teens stay off the streets and do something positive with their lives. It all but seemed Foreman's first comeback in life had failed, but at the end of the tunnel, he found a way to succeed as his life took a turn for the better when he made a decision to be united with God.

Somewhere God was watching Foreman all the times he was successful in all of his fights, but just like many others who are also successful, success does not come without you paying the price for it. Thus, there will always be a need for God. At the right time and the right moment, a voice will always cry out inside you to let you know that no matter what you accomplish in this world, and no matter how much you strive to chase after success, it clearly has no meaning and purpose if God is not in the blueprint of your life.

> *For I know the plans I have for you declares the Lord, plans to give you hope and a future. Then you will call upon me and come and pray to me, and I will listen to you. You will seek me and find me when you seek me with all your heart. I will be found by you and bring you back from captivity.*
>
> —JEREMIAH 29:11

## Laying It All on the Line

Striving and desperate to find a means to an end, the first comeback of Foreman's career came up short; he was left with no other choice but to rely on his new converted life for all the answers he held in question. It would take ten years of preaching and sharing his faith of his new life. It would be at that point he stayed away from the boxing ring and the window of opportunity to reclaim his heavyweight championship was all but closing in front of him. Foreman had a decision to make. The moment in his life had come and gone many years ago. How could it be possible to reclaim that moment and make it come alive again? After much careful thought, prayer, and insight, God gave Foreman the willpower to plan another comeback to the boxing ring to pursue the heavyweight boxing title.

Clearly, Foreman, at the age of thirty-eight, was not complete with what he started. The announcement that he made to the boxing ring shocked the entire world, and many people just did not have the heart to believe he still had the tenacity, power, and endurance to capture a title, let alone be victorious again in a boxing ring. Obviously, ten years have passed, and no longer can a fighter have the same strength, agility, and talent that he had coming in the boxing ring. The world waited to see the outcome of Foreman's decision, and it was an ambitious one as he challenged to fight Mike Tyson who was believed to be the world best boxing champion at that time. Obviously, before fighting Tyson, Foreman would need to test his ability against other competitors in the ring. Foreman would enter the ring in his first fight after being out of the ring for ten years only to weigh 267 pounds and look poorly out of shape.

No matter how much he trained and sparred, he was clearly not the same individual that everyone saw dominate the boxing ring during his prime years as a fighter. The fight begun, and clearly as bad as Foreman was out of shape, he dominated his opponent, winning by a knockout in four rounds.

In 1987, he would later go against other fighters and would also win those other matches. Every match in the ring caused him to get fitter and slimmer, acquiring more speed and agility for his next opponent. He pursued a relentless quest to capture the heavyweight championship of the world. Approaching forty years of age, Foreman felt he had something to prove not only to himself but to all the people who doubted his candidacy to win. In the following year, 1988, he would go on to win nine consecutive boxing matches. In two years, he would remain undefeated.

He was drawing ever so close to the dream match with a new undisputed heavyweight champion of the world, Evander Holyfield. In his quest to obtain the heavyweight championship, a year before his title fight with Holyfield, he set out to be the brand that he wanted people to see. An idea came to him where he decided to put his name on a grill machine. The result became an instant success. He was an overnight celebrity who branded his way straight to stardom.

Foreman was forty-two years old, who, after achieving success against multiple fighters, earned him the right to step foot in the ring to contend with Holyfield. Obviously, no one expected the match to go the full twelve rounds, but it did. Foreman had nothing to lose. All he was riding on was the hope of victory. He spent so much effort winning to make this moment come alive that he refused to go down without putting his best foot forward into making it work. When the match was over, it was clear that Holyfield was the decisive winner. There was nothing more Foreman could do but continue to fight and have the end goal set in his mind that even though he lost, he still did not fulfill what he set out to accomplish.

Foreman would go on to fight other great fighters, where he would win but suffered bloody victories on behalf of his willpower to succeed. All he desired was a chance after losing to Holyfield to come back again and win the battle that he started. Late in Foreman's career, he suffered many setbacks in boxing. It seemed every time that he was drawing close to achieving his ultimate reward, he met an opponent that was much more physical and talented than he was. In the midst of fighting many opponents, his ever-burning desire to reclaim the heavyweight championship of the world would be put on hold because of being outboxed and defeated by other opponents.

Crossing many unchartered boundaries, Foreman would continue to be relentless in the pursuit of his quest to regain the title that once belonged to him. One year after losing to Holyfield, Foreman entered into the ring once more and fought another formidable opponent. The match left Foreman's face bloodied, swollen with cuts and gashes by which he was fortunate to win the tenth round by decision. Apparently, Foreman expended so much energy during the fight. It seemed that his aging body was getting the best of him.

At forty-two years of age, he would go on to fight another boxer, Tommy Morrison, who was much younger than he was, with incredible speed and punching power. Foreman fought Morrison, and the fight proved to be the greatest challenge to Foreman during his time of reemergence. The fight went twelve rounds, where Foreman lost by unanimous decision.

It seemed whatever hopes that Foreman had to regain his title from coming back a second time was all but slipping away. The window in his life was closing as he was no longer the young athlete who dominated other boxers and found a way to consistently win through his power and strength. The moment seemed to all belonged to someone else. Even though he tried to recapture the moment, there was nothing he could clearly do if it was not intended for him at the time he wanted it to reemerge. Foreman was left with a choice: to walk away from boxing forever or continue to fight until he gets what he wants. After much thought, Foreman decided he needed time away to regroup so that if and when he decides to return, he will put himself in the best possible position to win. After all, the excessive beating that he was taking from his opponents left him no other choice but to walk away and find the best possible means to recover.

The year would be now 1994, and Foreman reached the age of forty-five years old; so much has changed since his last fight in the ring. The new champion of the world at that time was Michael Moorer, who defeated Holyfield for the heavyweight boxing championship of the world. Foreman had not been in a boxing ring since his last defeat, but he demanded that because of his strong credentials and record as a fighter, he should be granted a match with Michael Moorer.

After the boxing league reviewed Foreman's profile, they believed he was a worthy candidate to get a shot at a title fight against Moorer. The fight would be Foreman's ultimate chance of redemption. He trained effortlessly for his fight against Moorer. Clearly, Moorer, who was nineteen years younger than Foreman, was the favorite to handedly defeat him. He prepared for the fight like any champion who wanted to defend his title. On the night of November 5, 1994, Foreman would get his chance to battle for recovery and claim the title that belonged to him. For ten rounds, during the match, Foreman trailed on every scorecard. He appeared to be losing all the battles of uppercut, body blows, and jabs.

The match looked as if he was going to come away yet with another heartbreaking loss. However, something gave him a surge of confidence that he needed to continue with the match. In the tenth round, he landed a long hard punch to Moorer's chin, which caused him to immediately fall to the canvas. Moorer was bleeding profusely with a gash that opened the bottom of his lip. The referee got on the ground and counted all the way to ten, which symbolized Moorer's defeat. When the referee signaled the match was over, Foreman won the match by knockout and became the oldest boxer at the age of forty-five to win the heavyweight championship of the world. Suddenly, the title that he lost twenty years ago to Muhammad Ali was all but a distant memory. People all across the world watched and stood in amazement as an unthinkable and lion-driven human being accomplished a remarkable feat in his life. He made history, and sometimes when you make history, you need to do historical things.

## The Last Stand

At the expense of his victory, he would be recognized again as the heavyweight champion of the world. All was not over for Foreman as he now had to find the means of defending his championship. One fighter would challenge him for his belt, but it was a challenge that he ultimately refused. After rejecting the fight, the league had no other choice but to strip Foreman of his heavyweight title. Foreman earned two titles as a heavyweight champion; each of them was taken away by the league after he decided not to defend his title against anyone. Soon enough, he would retire again. However, his strong affinity for the sport did not allow him to leave it for long as he intended. In the heart of redemption, Foreman wanted to prove himself again by fighting boxing champion Lennox Lewis.

At the age of forty-eight, he would go in the gym to practice and put himself in gear for the potential fight, one in which the league stated that he would need to prove himself by winning other matches before he could fight Lewis. Foreman would go on to fight Crawford Grimsley, through which he scored a decisive victory. In his next match, however, all his hopes came crashing to a halt when his eventual match with Shannon Briggs came up short. Foreman was left now to walk away from the sport, this time, for good. But in his emotion of surrender, one spark of fire still ignited a flame in his soul to never give in. That fire remained lit, and several years later at the age of fifty-five years old, he talked about yet another opportunity to come back to the sport. Though his intentions were strong, some people believed his wife strongly advised him not to return because of his age, and the fact that it could be dangerous to suffer any injuries that might be life threatening in the ring at his age. After much careful consideration, Foreman left the boxing world for good. He would be recognized as one of the most powerful black entrepreneurs who catapulted his way to success through the invention of the George Foreman Grill and other business venues that has his name on it (2011, January 19 Retrieved 17:48 *George Foreman, In Wikipedia, The Free Encyclopedia*).

Somehow, life, no matter how much a moment belongs to you, it can never be intended to last forever, because just as the moment is burning for you, it is also burning for someone else. As you keep fighting to keep it alive, the flame in every fight and every year that it is lit keeps getting dimmer and dimmer with time until it starts to suddenly fade away. While one flame is being taken out, another one is being lit for someone else. How vital it is in life for you to believe the impossible at times so the possible things in life can emerge. Foreman was an individual who didn't believe in surrender.

He didn't quit until he got what he wanted, and when it seemed like he was down, he constantly found a way to reemerge and will his way back to victory. Indeed, how evident life is when you don't have a relenting surge of passion to fight back, it will erupt every time without you having an answer for it. Thus, you must be always willing to attack because life has no sympathy for you when ultimately the true sympathy that you should have is what you can display to the rest of the world that will bring you self-satisfaction.

Foreman was an athlete who had consecutive comebacks in boxing and consecutive emergences from retirement. Whenever he found a means, he would make it possible at all costs to recover from all his losses. Just how many people have that passion in life where they can do what Foreman did? How many people have that will power that constantly and consistently find ways to win even at the expense of them losing what matters to them the most? Not everyone has that will power, and not all people know how to overcome the lessons that life teaches when failure and defeat comes knocking at their door. So many times a voice cries out from within to never quit and keep pressing on, but we at times shut the voices down, never to emerge with the same magnitude we once had that made us victorious. Every moment you experience a setback must be a setup for another comeback. No one said all the mountains in life are permanent. One day, all of them will move. One day, it will be your moment to overcome adversity, challenging legal obstacles, career endeavors, and broken marriages. That is why you may be down in life, but when it comes to emerging your dreams, it's never too late to make them rise again.

> *Your thoughts can be your greatest friend or your deadliest enemy, holding the chains of death or the keys to the power of life.*

## Exalted

American singer, performer, and songwriter Natalie Cole was known widely for her incredible voice and history made in music. Cole's passion for singing elevated her talents to achieve enormous success singles, such as "Unforgettable with Love" and "Inseparable." Her performances allowed her to win numerous Grammy Awards, where she also gained the attention of worldwide audiences, selling over seven million copies over time.

At a young age, Natalie Cole, daughter of Nat King Cole, was surrounded by great singers in her family. She began performing early in life by singing high and low notes in songs and discovering more about her voice and the gift that she had to give to the rest of the world. At the age of fifteen, she suffered a tragic loss when her father died of lung cancer. Natalie's father was the one inspiration who pulled her life together and gave her the ability to never stop trying until she succeeded at all her targeted ambitions.

In spite of the loss, she carried on with her dreams and her father's hope and vision to see them actualized. Cole had plenty of soul in her singing. She sang with intense emotion that separated her from many other singers in the industry. It was evident Cole had a voice that moved and mesmerized people. She consistently used her talents and exercised them by performing at clubs over the weekend. Through her performance, she impressed an audience of people who could never get enough of her. She later went on to release her first album *Inseparable* with a series of number one hits that earned her Grammy Award for the Best Female R&B Vocal Performance.

Two years later, she received other awards from American Music Awards and gathered two platinum albums. It seemed that each time she sang a song, an award was handed out to her for her performance. In no time, Cole sky rocketed to stardom in her career, but in the times of her success, she had to undergo rehabilitation for usage of heroin and cocaine addiction. Clearly, it seemed that memories of achieving success had somewhat started a steady and spiraling decline when she encountered this tragic obstacle. It would take a few years after her decline before she would find her way to rise back to the top by staging off a comeback with her album *Dangerous*, which also included hits as well as performing other songs.

During that time, she would win the Soul Train Music Award for Female Singer of the Year. She would later channel her success with other artists, such as Bruce Springsteen and Freddy Jackson. Despite her collaborations with those artists, none of them would hold the magnitude that her father had on her life. The music and the inspiration from her father's voice catapulted her to sing twenty-two songs from his collection of music. Throughout her music career, Cole's consistent efforts in singing continued to get her worldwide recognition. She played out in many musical performances, and even after twenty-five years of singing, she was unshakeable in claiming another Grammy at the Fifty-first Grammy Awards.

Life all seemed too surreal for Cole until one striking announcement on July 16, 2008, through which she would announce to the world that she was diagnosed with hepatitis C, a disease affecting the kidney. Surely, life would take on a different turn for Cole as she would now need to battle with kidney disease, all while receiving a medication that physically caused her dehydration, muscle aches, and fatigue. The result left her in need of receiving serious medical attention where she later needed to receive dialysis for a failing and almost impaired kidney.

The result and ongoing struggles caused her to be in need of a transplant. At the expense of her pain, Cole would not be the only one battling with complications in her family. Cole's sister, who was diagnosed with cancer, had died from her struggle with the disease. On the same day her sister died from cancer, a miracle would arrive in the form of encouraging news from a donor who was willing to surrender his or her kidney to Cole in hopes for her survival.

Much to the surprise of many, she grew stronger with the transplant of her kidney, and when she was healthy enough, she returned to the stage and continued to do what she was passionate in doing all throughout her career. The disease has stricken her to take a fall in life where it ultimately led to a life or death result. Overwhelmed by emotion, Cole would take on many trying circumstances of drug usage and the setbacks of losing her father. Through it all, there were obstacles that made many attempts in a series of moments to knock her down, but as many times as she was knocked down, she found ways to rise again and again.

Every time she emerged, she was either nominated for an award, or she ended up winning the award for her nomination. It is interesting how forces never stop attacking people in spite of all the falls they have taken. Yet those are the same people who fall, while others around them believe they stand no chance to ever rise again. Consequently, through your moments of downfall is another moment that is opening its eyes for you to succeed. How tragic it would have been for Cole to be submerged by defeat never to break through her problems and rise again in life. She could have immersed all the pain of losing her father, her sister, drug abuse, and kidney failure and be overwhelmed by it all, not knowing how to rise above any of the circumstances and challenges she faced (2011, June 4 Retrieved 21:11 *Natalie Cole, In Wikipedia, The Free Encyclopedia)*.

However, as strong and valiant as Cole was, she emerged with power and found a way to rise after every moment of disappointment to bring alive a new moment of magnitude and victory. How many times has tragedy happened to you where you were buried by its circumstances? When one shovel of dirt is tossed, it seems another one keeps coming until you are constantly overtaken by the dirt that keeps getting tossed at you until you are buried in life. Look at how many people are hit by old age, disease, job layoffs, failed dreams, debt, broken marriages, failed businesses, and hardship, not believing they can emerge from moments that have constantly disillusioned them to having a necessary breakthrough that will achieve their hopes and fulfill their passion. Look at the many times people were knocked down, bleeding, tired, and winded, while their opponent stands next to them, looking down at them, wondering if they have what it takes to get back up and fight to achieve the things they want to achieve in this world.

When you are down, do you lay there and stay defeated, or do you continue to get back up and fight until you find a way to prevail? Life seems to constantly hit you with a boxing glove when it stares you down in defeat, waiting to see if you have any fight left in you to get back up. How many of us have been there where other people around us paint the same picture for our lives, feeling they will make it, but you will never make it. Just how many of us have experienced being knocked down on the mat, watching in daze as our dreams and visions in life start fading away. We have all crossed that boundary, but you can't be the majority who lets it slip away; you have to be the minority who holds on and who constantly brushes off the dirt every time it is tossed on you to emerge and fight for your dreams and moments that you desire to experience in this world.

Surely, not everyone you come across can be liked, and not everyone will like you. You may encounter enemies along the way through their own strong determination to tear you down so that they themselves can be successful and watch you as you fail. However, your vision can overcome their violence. Your grace can overcome their greed, and your humility can overcome their pride; your rights can overcome their wrongs, and your victory can overtake their defeats. It takes a tactful but a wise person to lead and be an example to others. But when it is marked and sparked by consistency and a never-ending passion to cast his or her desires on making himself or herself a success, he or she will not be taken lightly by anyone when the efforts projected are enough to change people's minds as well as their hearts by what these individuals can bring to the table.

*If you are ever going to get respect from anyone, people are more impressed by the results from what you produce rather than you producing something without the results.*

## Emerge with Change

One of my best friends was someone I met a few years ago. He was an individual who joined my church, and we became very good friends over the years. He would oftentimes talk about how he wanted to change his life for the better because he was tired of making worldly and ungodly decisions. He felt trapped in a world and faced pressure from a host of friends that existed outside of the church that was not taking him anywhere. One day I met with him, and he said to me, "Lloyd, I am tired of living this life and not going anywhere with it. I have to do something with my life. Every day is just like yesterday. I just need today to be different and not have tomorrow be the same." "What do you mean you want this day to be different from any other day?" "I mean, think about it, Lloyd, I practically do the same things every day. I go to work, and after I get from work, I would go home eat and sleep and get ready for work the next day. It's beginning to feel like I am in a cycle with no way out. That is why I decided to come out to church because I wanted to make a change from what I was going through.

"From now on, I want to make decisions based on the standards of the Bible. I know without God in my life, I will keep living the life I am living. So with him, why not live it differently? Why not change it now? I know for sure up to this point in my life, I would be fooling myself into believing that at any point, it will change. I know from all that I have been through so far, my life will never change, and even if it does change, it won't make a difference in how I already feel toward it."

After two weeks of coming out to church services, studying God's word, and putting into practice many of the Bible's teachings, no one was more eager about being baptized than my friend Ronald. Immediately, after he got baptized, it all seemed as if a new moment in Ronald's life emerged. No longer would he would be a person who would take on the same mind-set of the world, but he would be an individual who would take on the same likeness and mind-set of Christ. It seemed he crossed over into a new light where he no longer can see himself living in darkness.

I remembered before Ronald became a Christian, he was an individual who was considered by his family and friends a difficult person to change. His mother would challenge him on changing bad habits in his character, which ranged from smoking to being disorganized to having negative attitudes.

He would come home with a bad temper, and he seemed to be negative in his outlook toward life, not believing it would get better. He was buried in debt, single, and living with his parents at thirty years old. For all obvious reasons, he was already set in his ways. He could not change himself into anyone else. Whenever he would get in late at night, his disorganized and uncaring ways would be evident in the way he would leave his dishes for others to wash and not partake in many of the household responsibilities assigned to him. It appeared Ronald was upset with his life. He was in a cycle that he put himself in which he could not find any means of breaking to find his way out.

It would take more than three months of coming out to the church before he made a decision to turn his life over to God. Though I congratulated him on his efforts and new life as a Christian, many people thought that Ronald would still face challenges of trying to grow as a new believer in Christ. Like many new followers of Christ, Ronald would take on the walk and emotional battle of obeying God's word wholeheartedly. As a result of Ronald's baptism, he had a tug of war dealing with prideful issues in his character that he was challenged to change by other believers. Even though he was baptized, Ronald would face numerous challenges in his walk with God that tested his true love and devotion to him. It was obvious from the start, Ronald had a fire in him that was burning in his heart for God, but he had another fire that was also burning with the temptations of the world. Clearly, it was a side of him that was unresolved with the world's temptations still battling to overtake his heart.

Being a Christian for Ronald was easier said than done. Ronald would be swayed to go out to late-night clubs where many of his friends would be engaged in drinking, smoking, and other wild behaviors. It was tempting to Ronald, but his mind and heart made him remember why he counted the cost to surrender his life over to God. Unequivocally, if Ronald wanted to see growth and change in his relationship as a new believer in Christ, he would need to overcome the unrelenting temptations of the world. Days after and weeks of fighting for consistent change, he would read his Bible, pray to God, and share his faith with others, Ronald had no other choice but to get the help of other people in the church to help him overcome the temptations of serving other idols that would take away his time and focus from his new life as a Christian.

Deep in my mind, I thought how Ronald had a long way to grow and mature in his walk with God. After all, he was a young Christian who was still drinking milk like a child who has not yet developed eating solid food like an adult. Personally, I could only hope he has the ability to overcome his struggles because there are tests in life that if one is not able to overcome, one will never be able to see one's dreams actualized.

After two years of being in the church, Ronald was at a different stage in his life where he found a new full-time job where he was paid three times the amount he made at his other job. Ultimately, his transition into a new job allowed him to save his money so that he can have a chance to one day get out of debt, move out of his parent's home, and find a place of his own. It would be his first year as a Christian in the church, and Ronald's struggles would be noticeable by the people closest to him. He had difficulties that ranged from receiving counseling because of his pride and finding a Christian girlfriend. Ronald's luck would all but run out the first year as he battled to overcome many challenges in the start of his Christian life. Time would now reach the second year in his life as a Christian, and the same struggles he had in the first year would be ones that he encountered in the second year.

Ronald prayed and made some changes in his character to be more humble and giving to others. Still, in spite of all his efforts to improve his character, get along with others, and find a Christian girlfriend, Ronald faced multiple rejections from other sisters he was building with in the church. I told him, "Ronald, it just might not be your time. I think you should continue to persevere and see what God has planned for you. Not every sister you come across will like you. Maybe God has a better plan in store for you where you will meet the right sister at a time he feels is best." At the expense of sharing some encouraging words with Ronald, he did not accept what I told him, out of emotion and frustration, he vented in words, "I just don't understand, Lloyd. I don't get it! What do these other guys have that I don't have that makes it so easy for them to date the women in the church and go steady with them? I even built a great friendship with one of the sisters in the church.

"I was really attracted to her, and I would call her almost every day to encourage and talk to her about each day in my life, and she would also call and encourage me with the victories in her day. We had a great connection. I would go on a group date with her along with a few other church members and would use that opportunity to take her to the beach, mall, and even some nice restaurants. I thought she liked me, but after five months, she stopped picking up her phone. She never called me back, and she no longer acknowledged me when I would see her at the service. Lloyd, what do you think the problem is?" he said. "I am not sure what it could be. Maybe it was not meant for you to be with her. Maybe it is meant for you to be with someone else. I don't understand the way God works sometimes, but he cuts things off for a reason. Maybe he did that to let you know that if you pursued the relationship any further you will only get hurt in the long run," I said.

"Really, do you think so? I just find that hard to believe because this sister at one time seemed spiritual. She spoke to me about how much she loves God and admired my friendship with her. I just don't know why she just changed like that toward me. I didn't do anything wrong for her to treat me the way she is treating me now. I mean the least that she could do is come up and talk to me and let me know what is going on. If she doesn't want to speak to me anymore, then she should just try to talk to me and be forthcoming about it." "Well, just wait and see what God has planned for you.

"You can't possibly build a relationship with someone by force. If that person does not want to deal with you, then you might as well just let it go and move on to someone else who really cares. After all, there obviously must be a reason she is not talking to you and returning any of your calls. Maybe she is going through a difficult situation in her own life that you don't understand and without knowing you end up putting your feelings and emotions above her own. You know sometimes when you deal with people like that, there has to be a reason behind their actions. Even though the world doesn't center around one person, nothing will happen before its time, Ronald. You may want things to happen fast, but God's timetable is different from our timetable," I said.

**Hanging in the Balance**

It would be five years later of consistently going to the church, where Ronald battled with the same issue and frustration of not finding a sister who would like him enough to go steady with him. All of these challenges would be a true testament to his faith. Through it all, Ronald's mother grew uncomfortable with her son staying home past the age of thirty-five. She figured he should be more responsible and should start renting out his own apartment to pay bills on his own.

Unfortunately for Ronald, he felt no pressure because he was staying with his mother. He figured his stay with his mother would enable him to save enough money so that he would have extra savings in his account in the event that he gets married. Added to that, he can also save his income to get out of debt. Ultimately, for Ronald, five years seemed like an eternity of not finding someone who would appreciate him for who he stood for as a person. The elapsed time of no change in his life made him take an inventory of himself and the things he needed to change so that he could see different results.

After searching his soul so long for the answers, he decided to ask one of the sisters in the church that he was acquaintances with how she viewed him as a person. "Tabitha, I want to ask you for your honest opinion. How do you view me as a person?" said Ronald. "Well, I think you are encouraging. You always greet people and talk to everyone in the church. You make people feel right at home."

"Really, is there anything else about me that stands out to you that I can change in my appearance that will make me look better?" "Why, Ronald, why are you so self-conscious? Don't you know that if someone is going to love you, that person is going to love you for the heart you have, regardless of what you look like on the outside."

"Tabitha, I know all those things, but sometimes someone's appearance can also be a factor in being liked or not liked by others. I am not asking you because I feel everything is right with me. I am asking because I just want to get your opinion on what do you feel I can change in my physical appearance that will help me stand out to people." "No, Ronald, I believe you must continue to trust in God. I don't want to give you advice for you to take it and self-destruct. I think you should just keep trying and don't stop believing in yourself until you find a way," said Tabitha.

With Ronald, it made me realize that if he was ever going to change the circumstances around him, he would have to make choices with himself to change the opinions of everyone else around him. It would illustrate the battle to him is not only physical but also mental. The one greatest weapon people have is not what they hold in their hands but is what they have in their minds. Once a person can gain control of his or her mental state, it is up to him or her to create a sense of awareness where he or she can change his or her perspective from negative to positive. It is the ideal inspiration that someone needs to give to himself or herself to feel anything can still be possible as long as he or she has the desire to believe he or she can conquer all the obstacles that have been mounted in his or her life. Obviously, the mind always receives messages, but a message is never effective if there is no delivery and no action applied from the delivery that was made.

Ronald knew that something needed to change with him. He needed to create new choices that would later bring on new results. One year later, he would go through changes in his appearance where he received corrective surgery on his retina, which enabled him to no longer wear glasses. He also became more physically fit by regularly going to the gym to exercise. Soon enough, his appearance would take on an entirely new transformation. It all but seemed a new image had emerged within him. Ronald began to feel more confident in the way he carried himself toward others. He started trusting God more through prayer and relying on his word for patience and guidance. It was clear that his transformation readily took effect in the minds of other people in the church as he looked like an entirely different person after his eye surgery and workouts in the gym. No longer would he feel terrible about his image in front of anyone. No longer would he also feel incapable and incompetent in carrying himself as a person. Through his decision, it would take another two years after his transformation to find a woman in the church he would finally connect with.

Life all but changed as he reemerged from a person who has been stagnant and overwhelmed by circumstances to an individual who was now in control and confident with his life. It just seems, just like Ronald, we as individuals are sending ourselves messages all the time. If there is no application in the message that was sent, it is just information that is sitting there with no hope or chance of it being utilized. Ultimately, messages are being sent all the time. We always hear a voice that we either accept or reject. However, it is how the messages are being received that will determine its ultimate impact.

God is always willing to work, but you have to give him something to work with. It is proven that in order for you to see yourself and where you need to be, you need to make the necessary changes that will bring different results to your life. Change, for the most part in everyone's life, is essential if improvement and growth is to be made. Without it, you have no idea of how to live and how life supposed to be lived. Creating the change your life needs gives you the quality of life that you have been missing. Life can't exist without change. Change can't exist without a purpose, and purpose can't exist without a quality of life. As long as you have a desire to make it a fitting purpose to see changes in your life, all the hopes and dreams that at one time have been buried will find a way to resurrect themselves and emerge back to its surface.

Until you make a decision that you will no longer live in futility, you can see the quality of life you deserve when you live the life you dreamed of living. It is incredible how time passes by so quickly without anyone at times being able to have an impact on it. It is a force in life that never stops moving.

Thus, if you ever challenge yourself to get anything done, you have to deal with the forces of time and the impact it has on everyone's life. People will oftentimes have a strong desire to seek change in their lives, but there is an ever growing battle to make those changes emerge when they have not utilized the time given to them in this world. Obviously, there is power in the ability to emerge in life by being buried by all the circumstances that one can take on. Only when that power is actualized can one emerge all the possibilities in the world that never seemed imaginable.

*Don't start thinking about what you don't have;*
*start thinking about what you will have.*

## Just the Beginning

I examined all of my past efforts and knew they could not possibly be in vain. After all, all the actions I would take on would be constantly based on my working hard. However, at the expense of working hard to become someone special, I oftentimes fell short of my reaching my desired destination. Despite my setbacks, I refused to quit. I had to continue to believe in myself. I made choices that made me feel each road was no different from the next. I would have to learn, however, that my journey in the beginning stages was a rough one. It was a journey that started, and I had no way of stopping. It was going to ride itself through till it came to an end. Maybe when it ended, all that would matter was the final outcome. The struggles of finding the right career, being in a satisfying relationship, and achieving my own personal goals and ambitions would all come to an end. I would then have something in life that I can look forward to.

Because it seemed every time the struggles started for me, it also began with everyone else in my family. It was a ride that I took my children and my wife on that I will never forget. I was sure one day that it will end, but I didn't know when and how to make it come to an end. All I could do was stay for the ride and see where it would take me. All I could hope for was something that was promising in the moment that would make me forget the ride I had yesterday but enjoy the one that I am on today.

I knew there would come a time when I will emerge from all of my hardships, but I could not pinpoint exactly what day and time it would happen. I had to reflect on the life I was living now and forget about the mistakes and failures I experienced in the past. After all, each challenging moment had to be regarded as special in my life. The first time that I would do something significant and fail to achieve its rewards, the experiences taken from it would be one that I would remember. On a ride as hard and long as the one I have been on, I could never forget the beginning and what it felt like. All I desired was to bring it to an end because in life, I believe no circumstance or condition can last forever. As long as it takes you for a ride, the ride must come to an end one day, no matter how bad it appears to be in the beginning. Everything that begins and gives birth in life has to get old and come to an end in its lifetime. It is just a matter of time before my dreams are actualized because in the moment a tragedy occurs, time stands still. But in a moment of glory, it is hard for me to imagine why it should come to an end.

*If you can't make your moment happen, then it will be someone else's moment. If you can't make your possibilities happen, then it will become possible for someone else.*

## Never Surrender

What does it actually take to live a possible life with miraculous results? What steps should an individual take and continue on a path where he or she feels that it will lead somewhere? Personally, in every step I took toward my dream, I wanted to achieve something special in life that not too many people achieved. I would be tested and challenged en route to each one of them. However, as tough and grueling as the trials were, I was constantly reminded by a voice inside of me that cried out "Don't surrender," "Keep going," "Don't quit" when I was overwhelmed by the obstacles before me. It would be then that I had the answers to all the questions that challenged my ambition and ability to make me never to surrender to the circumstances that challenged my dreams in this world.

Growing up was never easy because I saw many people fall to the hands of the word "surrender." Watching them didn't inspire me to follow their example because I wanted to be one that would change the direction of the path that they took. Through my experience as a youngster, I was a witness many times to people who surrendered when the passion in their hearts got tested and their dreams got broken by the challenges of life, not believing they had what it took to put it back together again.

I have seen people in the Olympics struggle to win a gold medal because the moment for them to prove themselves became a pressure for them that they were not able to handle. I have seen athletes in sports give up competing in a game when they realized the score to overcome was too much of an uphill climb for them to win the game. In addition, I have seen other people who would battle with studying for a class that they managed to do poorly in the beginning, never to give themselves a chance to see what their abilities and talents could do for them in the end. Examine also the disease-stricken individuals' battle in a moment to survive not knowing the next breath they take will be their last. If only in their minds and hearts they don't surrender, there is no telling what the outcome will be.

As much as I have seen people fail and have given up on life, there is the other side where some of them don't believe in the word "surrender." These are the ones who constantly have a comeback power within them that fights back until they find a way to win. Losing and defeat may hit them, but it will be only for the moment because to them, they have every ability to bounce back from all the setbacks that have derailed them in life.

Look at the ones who struggle to win a gold medal in the Olympics. They may lose in the moment; however, four years after their loss, they come back with incredible effort and power to outlast any of their competitors to claim the ultimate prize that has eluded them in the past. In addition, imagine the miracles in sports where teams come back not only to win a game where they have been dominated by an opponent, but their strong tenacity and desire are displayed when they can come back and win a series that no one expected them to win. Take notice of the situations that people go through when they have failed something over and over again, looking as if they would never find a way to break through their failures. At any moment, they can find a second wind to emerge from all their disasters. For some, it could be fighting cancer, overcoming an accident, divorce, declining sales in business, or taking a crucial exam. Whoever the individual is, this person who has the ability to never surrender will always find a way to emerge and attack the challenges in life until they overcome it and place it under their feet. That is why many people just can't stop believing in themselves because some of them who are one step away from failing are also moments away from being successful.

For the ones who have emerged in life where the moment calls for them to rise higher than any obstacle that is out there, there is no giving in to the word "surrender." These are the individuals that have turned down the word "surrender" to live a possible life with miraculous results.

Examine the people who have risked their lives for others and put their own lives on the line, not knowing if it could be taken from them in a blood transfer, organ transfer, and through acts of heroism. The beginning is always possible, but the end projects an outcome that many people may feel can bring an impossible result when the challenges in life emerge. Obviously, there is no telling what the outcome will be, but when one displays actions of no surrender, one can channel oneself into experiencing miracles that one was destined for in the moment it emerges.

Whether it is someone rescuing another person from a speeding bus or taking on the actions of being a hero in front of others, nothing matters more to preserving life and the purpose it has to achieve the dreams it wants to achieve in the time it has left to achieve them in this world. The mind is an incredible weapon, but it is the heart that is the instrument of how that weapon is used. Of all the organs in the human body that sustains life, there is not one that can take precedence over the heart when it comes to the meaning of surrender. There is no greater source and moment that calls any organ forward to respond better than the heart itself. Even in a life-threatening accident, the heart is one of the many organs that will be checked to see if he or she still has life. It can't be overlooked if one must measure the lifeline of a survivor.

It is amazing how some people put so much pressure on maintaining everything else in their surroundings without considering what is most important to sustain inside of them. When some people's hearts have been hardened by circumstances, they focus more on their pride without trying to sustain their relationship with others which can enable them to develop a sense of self-worth for themselves. That is why the heart is indeed an invaluable instrument. You are measured in life by the way you live, love, give, and fight for what you want by the desires of your heart. When you leave this world, what kind of heart are you going to die with? Will you die with a heart of love, a broken heart, a heart of courage? Or will you die with a heart of no surrender? Indeed, how you sustain your heart will determine how it is carried to the grave. If you want to impact the world, you must continue to emerge and impact it with what you have already built and what will also never surrender inside of you.

CPSIA information can be obtained
at www.ICGtesting.com
Printed in the USA
BVHW081745060522
636305BV00008BA/696